STREET DRUG INVESTIGATION

ABOUT THE AUTHORS

Darin Fredrickson has been with the Phoenix, Arizona, Police Department since 1991 and has served with the department's Drug Enforcement Bureau since 1996, currently assigned to the Clandestine Drug Laboratory Detail. He also serves as a provisional Drug Enforcement Administration (DEA) Clandestine Drug Laboratory task force member. Previously, he served on the Drug/Homicide Task Force. Detective Fredrickson is also a certified instructor with the Arizona Law Enforcement Academy in Homeland Security, Street Drugs, Cultural Awareness, and Crime Scene Photography. In addition to normal duties, Detective Fredrickson develops and presents seminars to various private sector and community groups on law enforcement issues as well as providing in-service training for law enforcement agencies, and Superior Court personnel. Detective Fredrickson coauthored the books *Racial Profiling*, *Terrorist Attacks* (2nd Edition), *Applied Police & Fire Photography* (2nd Edition), and *Fundamentals of Physical Surveillance* (2nd Edition). He is the foreword author of the book *Fundamentals of Civil and Private Investigation* (2nd Edition). He has also written several criminal justice articles for various publications. Detective Fredrickson holds a Master of Education degree in Educational Leadership from Northern Arizona University where he graduated "With Distinction," and a Baccalaureate Degree in Management from Ottawa University, Kansas.

Raymond Siljander's diversified occupational history includes a variety of manufacturing and service industries in addition to the insurance industry, industrial security supervision, licensed private investigator doing general and undercover investigations, licensed process server, and local law enforcement as a certified police officer having graduated first in his class in the police academy. He served three tours of duty in Viet Nam. Mr. Siljander is the author and coauthor of twelve previous books addressing cultural and technical aspects of issues such as racial and criminal profiling, terrorism, police and fire photography, physical surveillance, private investigation, private process serving, and security and loss control. He has also written several magazine articles. Mr. Siljander has appeared as a speaker for in-service training seminars for law enforcement and the insurance industry, and college photography classes. His most significant social contribution is the recent creation of an adult literacy program for the Roma culture translated for implementation in Eastern European countries. A not-for-profit international association has assumed responsibility for promotion, translations, production, and distribution. Mr. Siljander holds a Master of Education degree in Educational Leadership, having graduated "With Distinction"; an individualized Baccalaureate degree with a Human Services/Criminal Justice concentration; and Associate degrees in Law Enforcement and Fire Science. He has also graduated from several proprietary educational institutions. He holds the professional designation Associate in Loss Control Management (ACLM®).

STREET DRUG INVESTIGATION

A Practical Guide for Plainclothes and Uniformed Personnel

By

DARIN D. FREDRICKSON, M.ED.

and

RAYMOND P. SILJANDER, M.ED., ALCM

Foreword by

Sherrif Joe Arpaio

Maricopa County Sheriffs Office, Arizona

CHARLES C THOMAS • PUBLISHER, LTD.

Springfield • Illinois • U.S.A.

Published and Distributed Throughout the World by

CHARLES C THOMAS • PUBLISHER, LTD.
2600 South First Street
Springfield, Illinois 62704

ISBN 0-398-07531-X (hard)
ISBN 0-398-07532-8 (paper)

Library of Congress Catalog Card Number: 2004051647

With THOMAS BOOKS *careful attention is given to all details of manufacturing and design. It is the Publisher's desire to present books that are satisfactory as to their physical qualities and artistic possibilities and appropriate for their particular use.* THOMAS BOOKS *will be true to those laws of quality that assure a good name and good will.*

Printed in the United States of America
CR-R-3

Library of Congress Cataloging-in-Publication Data

Fredrickson, Darin D.
Street drug investigation : a practical guide for plainclothes and uniformed personnel / by Darin D. Fredrickson and Raymond P. Siljander.
p. cm.
Includes bibliographical references and index.
ISBN 0-398-07531-X -- ISBN 0-398-07532-8 (pbk.)
1. Drug traffic--Investigation--United States. 2. Narcotics, Control of--United States. 3. Drug abuse--United States. I. Siljander, Raymond P. II. Title.

HV8079.N3F74 2004
363.25'977'0973--dc22

2004051647

To my loving wife, Mary,
and children, Erica, Devon, Max, Katelyn, and Olivia.
D.D.F.

To Dr. Stephen M. Hennessy
More than he knows, he enhanced my academic growth
and expository skills.
R.P.S.

FOREWORD

Illegal drugs and the far-reaching social problems associated with them have become a serious problem in American society, a problem that demands attention. Illustrating the seriousness of the situation is the fact that reliable estimates suggest that illicit drugs are responsible for 48% of all homicides, 60% of all assaults, and 80% of all property crimes. I have been in the trenches fighting this "war on drugs" from the United States to Mexico to Turkey to the Middle East and to Central and South America. Originally joining the United States Bureau of Narcotics in 1957, I concluded my twenty-five year career with the Drug Enforcement Administration as head of the DEA in Arizona in 1982. Now, as Sheriff of Maricopa County, Arizona, the fourth largest sheriff's department in the United States, I am responsible for about 9000 inmates, of whom a high percentage test positive for drugs when they are admitted.

There are numerous circumstances that contribute to the illicit drug problem, and therefore strategies to correct the problem must occur on many fronts and include parents, schoolteachers, social workers, social scientists, the business community, the judicial system, the corrections system, the legislature, and of course law enforcment. Nonetheless, in spite of the number of people and agencies that can contribute to a solution, each with something unique to contribute, they all represent just three basic categories–prevention, rehabilitation, and enforcement.

In addition to the enforcement efforts of the Sheriffs Office, I have launched innovative rehabilitation programs like "Hard Knocks High," the only accredited high school in an American jail. My ALPHA program teaches inmates to turn away from drugs and is one of my proudest accomplishments–it has resulted in a high percentage of ALPHA graduates leaving my jail clean, sober, and rarely, if ever, returning to incarceration.

Because the illicit drug problem is a complex social problem, law enforcement, the courts, and those in the judicial system cannot solve the problem, but only contain the problem while others find workable solutions. Meantime, law enforcement remains our frontline of defense.

Featuring a clear and concise writing style, and tastefully illustrated, this book, Street Drug Investigation, provides valuable information for law officers who are responsible for the enforcement of anti-drug laws. This book will leave readers with practical knowledge they can immediately begin applying on the street.

Sheriff Joe Arpaio
"America's Toughest Sheriff"
Maricopa County Sheriffs Office, Arizona

PREFACE

This book, *Street Drug Investigation*, addresses a multifaceted social problem that has far-reaching and serious consequences. In fact, today, the problem of illicit drug use permeates so much of American society that it exists not only among adults in the blue-collar trades and in the professions, it has even extended into our grade schools. A 2002 study conducted by the Substance Abuse and Mental Health Services Administration (SAMHSA) found that 8.3 percent of the United States population age 12 and older use illicit drugs and 18.45 percent of people between the ages of 16-29 use illicit drugs.

Statistics attest to a high incidence of illicit drug use, but how detrimental are illicit drugs to society? "Illicit drug trafficking and abuse of cocaine, heroin, and marijuana pose a serious threat to New York City, according to a recent assessment compiled by the National Drug Intelligence Center (NDIC), a component agency of the U.S. Department of Justice" (National Drug Intelligence Center, 2003). Although this assessment pertains to New York City, the problem is not limited to that city. Indeed, this is a problem affecting all American cities and towns, large and small.

This book begins by examining the history of drugs and alcohol in the United States. That discussion acknowledges the fact that a meaningful discussion of *Street Drug Investigation* requires acknowledging the history of drugs, and discussing the history of drugs is difficult without acknowledging the history of illegal alcohol. An understanding of today's drug enforcement problems is enhanced by understanding what occurred relative to illegal alcohol before, during, and subsequent to the years of national prohibition. That is because in so many ways the history of illegal alcohol and illicit drugs share common underlying dynamics. Such an understanding will enable one to better see how the current drug situation is reminiscent of what has occurred through the course of American history relative to both illegal alcohol and drugs; an understanding of the past enables one to better understand the present, and in some cases make cautious predictions about the future.

Following an examination of the history of drugs and alcohol in the United States, which concludes with perspectives on what can be done to reduce the demand for illicit drugs, discussion proceeds to an examination of the various illicit drugs that today's police officer is most likely to encounter on the street. Discussion then proceeds to drug enforcement techniques and methods such as knock-and-talks; managing informants; plainclothes, undercover, and uniformed drug investigations; conspiracy investigations; investigation of clandestine drug laboratories; asset forfeiture; report writing and courtroom testimony; and physical surveillance and surveillance photography.

One tends to think of undercover and plainclothes detectives when contemplating drug investigations. However, uniformed police officers, the backbone of law enforcement, play an essential role in combating illicit drugs. Considerable discussion is devoted to this issue because in many small departments, which are the majority of police departments in the United States, uniformed officers do all investigations. In addition, uniformed officers are making a major contribution to the war on drugs when they engage in highway interdiction to suppress distribution.

Whether the reader works undercover, plainclothes, or uniformed, whether employed by a large or small police department, the information in this book will provide a foundation of knowledge that is practical and useful.

D.D.F.
R.P.S.

ACKNOWLEDGMENTS

The authors extend their heartfelt appreciation to the following individuals for generously finding time to read the manuscript, or portions of the manuscript, and providing essential feedback. However, although they reviewed the manuscript and provided counsel, the contents of this book do not necessarily represent their personal views. The authors are indebted to, and thank:

Dr. C. A. "Dee Dee" Nevelle, Principal, Mirage Elementary School, Glendale, Arizona, and Adjunct Professor, Northern Arizona University. She generously took time from her busy schedule to review Chapter 2.

Dr. Stephen M. Hennessy, Associate Professor of Criminal Justice, St. Cloud State University, Minnesota. He generously took time from his busy schedule to review the manuscript and provide valuable feedback.

Bob Cropper, Detective, Asset Forfeiture, Phoenix Police Department.

Eric Skoog, former high school history teacher, and former U.S. Diplomat. He generously took time from his busy work schedule to review Chapter 1.

Mike Torres, Sergeant, Phoenix Police Department. Sergeant Torres is currently assigned to the Drug Conspiracy Unit; former Sergeant of the SWAT Unit.

Roger A. Siljander, mathematician and physicist. He generously took time from his busy schedule to review Chapters 1 and 2.

CONTENTS

STREET DRUG INVESTIGATION

Chapter 1

HISTORY OF ILLICIT DRUGS AND ALCOHOL IN THE UNITED STATES

PREAMBLE

Today, the enforcement of anti-drug laws is difficult because of circumstances that are reminiscent of those that complicated the enforcement of anti-alcohol laws during the years of national prohibition and beyond. *Amendment 18 to the United States Constitution*, also known as the *National Prohibition Act* and the *Volstead Act*, made the sale of beverages containing more than 0.5 percent alcohol illegal in the United States between the years 1920-1933. The government, however, found it almost impossible to enforce the laws. Because of the government's inability to enforce anti-alcohol laws with an acceptable degree of success, and because of the abundance of social, political, and crime problems associated with prohibition, on December 5, 1933, *Amendment 21 to the United States Constitution* repealed *Amendment 18*, the only amendment to ever be repealed. The repealing of *Amendment 18* rescinded national anti-alcohol laws leaving prohibition the option of individual states, counties, and cities.

It must be emphasized that when discussing the similar dynamics of the illegal alcohol and drug trades, and how the current war on drugs is reminiscent of the frustrating anti-alcohol enforcement efforts during the years of national prohibition, it is not being suggested that today's anti-drug laws should be repealed or that drug use should be legalized. Although law enforcement was unable to enforce the anti-alcohol laws during prohibition and to a similar extent has been unable to enforce today's anti-drug laws with satisfactory success, the authors do not consider legalization of drugs to be a solution. The authors strongly believe the war on drugs must continue, but to be successful, properly conceived and implemented drug prevention programs and rehabilitation services must accompany enforcement efforts. Refer to the subheading "Reducing the Demand for Illicit Drugs" at the end of Chapter 2.

The authors also propose that illicit drugs are not just a crime problem, but are one facet of a complex set of social problems–drugs cause some and aggravate other social problems. Hence, the authors postulate that including a historical overview and social perspectives is necessary and will enhance understanding of today's drug problem, an understanding that will benefit policy makers, law officers working the street, and officers who are called upon to speak to community groups and at schools.

Accepting that law enforcement agencies are social agencies, their social status attested to by the familiar law enforcement slogan, "To Protect and Serve," then logic suggests that viewing and evaluating the law enforcement function must occur from a social perspective; how do law enforcement agencies serve and affect society? It is for these reasons that a review of historical issues and social dynamics precedes discussion of modern *Street Drug Investigation* techniques.

INTRODUCTION

It would be difficult to discuss the history of drugs in the United States without acknowledging the history of alcohol, more specifically illegal (bootleg) alcohol. That is because in so many ways the history of the two are entwined, especially insofar as the underlying dynamics of each is concerned.[1] Indeed, there has scarcely been a time in America's unorthodox history, when bootleg liquor was not in evidence, a phenomenon that predated the *War of Independence* (1775-1783). Drug use has also permeated much of America's history.

Public policy (laws), social attitudes, and the economy have been persistent and significant factors driving what is today a multi-billion dollar underground economy fraught with social problems.

Today, illicit drug use in America is endemic as attested to by the existence of such government agencies as the Drug Enforcement Administration (DEA), the Substance Abuse and Mental Health Services Administration (SAMHSA), and the National Drug Intelligence Center (NDIC). Moreover, every major police department has a drug enforcement division. Finally, also attesting to a serious substance abuse problem in America are the many clinics that provide treatment for chemical dependency.

Readers without a particular interest in history will find this overview sufficient, but readers with an interest in history and sociology will likely find themselves doing further research on this interesting and exciting topic. Those with an interest in drug and alcohol history and an interest in the many social implications will need to do further study because space limita-

1. A recent newspaper headline read, "Methamphetamine is the new moonshine in the rural Panhandle" (*Naples Daily News*, August 10, 2003).

tions allow only an overview here. This is, after all, a book presenting the techniques of street drug investigation, not an exhaustive examination of the social and historical aspects of drugs and alcohol in the United States. Nevertheless, those whose responsibility it is to investigate violations of anti-drug laws will benefit from a general understanding of how current problems are in many respects similar to earlier drug and alcohol enforcement problems. An understanding of the past enables one to better understand the present, and in some cases make cautious predictions about the future.

DRUG AND ALCOHOL USE PERMEATES WORLD HISTORY

And he drank of the wine, and was drunken; and he was uncovered within his tent. (Genesis 9:21)

And they shall say unto the elders of his city, This our son is stubborn and rebellious, he will not obey our voice; he is a glutton, and a drunkard. (Deuteronomy 21:20)

Drug and alcohol use has existed throughout all of American history, beginning with the thirteen British Colonies. That alcohol was prevalent in the Colonies is not surprising inasmuch as alcohol was prevalent in the countries from which the Colonists emigrated.

In the early 1800s, prohibitionists began trying to stop alcohol consumption, with the government later attempting to stop alcohol consumption via the 1920 *Eighteenth Amendment to the United States Constitution.* The Eighteenth Amendment is also referred to as the National *Prohibition Act* and the *Volstead Act.* When viewing those efforts in light of world history, however, it is not surprising that such efforts failed. Indeed, when examining the history of drug and alcohol use, one finds that it predates the history of the United States by several thousand years–drugs and alcohol were in use long before the existence of the United States as attested to by various historical records and documents.

Drug and alcohol use in various forms has existed throughout world history with the first opium use traced to the Sumerians of Mesopotamia. How early that occurred is uncertain, however, because sources offer conflicting dates–5000, 4000, 3500, and 3400 B.C. Early Mesopotamia was located between the Tigris and Euphrates rivers in what is now Iran and Iraq.

The early Egyptians used alcohol in the form of wine, and there are many Old Testament biblical references concerning the intoxicating qualities of wine, sometimes problematic, with such references appearing early in the scriptures; Genesis 9:21 appears on page 15 in the bible from which the verse was taken.

Moses, *circa* 1450-1220 B.C., who wrote the *Book of Genesis*, wrote about events that occurred long before he was born. Moses recorded histories originally written by Adam, Noah, Shem, Isaac, and Jacob, with the historical nature of his work evidenced by his beginning his writings with the creation, and his recurring use of the phrase, "these are the generations [records-genealogies] of. . . ." Hence, accepting the bible as a historical document, we see that alcohol use occurred very early in history with excessive consumption even then observed to cause social and familial problems.

Marijuana use by the Chinese, for medicinal purposes, occurred as early as 2737 B.C. (*The Columbia Encyclopedia*, Sixth Edition, 2003). The extraction of substances from plants to make other drugs such as cocaine, morphine, and heroin did not occur until the nineteenth century.

REGULATION OF DRUGS IN THE UNITED STATES

Early Government Response

For many years following the practice of extracting substances from plants to make derivatives such as cocaine, morphine, and heroin, there was no regulation as to use and for that reason, many medical doctors regularly prescribed derivatives as a treatment for a variety of medical disorders. Although physicians regularly prescribed such drugs, obtaining the same drugs did not require having them prescribed by a physician inasmuch as they were readily available via mail order, from local drug stores, grocery stores, and from traveling medicine vendors.

The unregulated dispensing of drugs and the flourishing opium den trade in many western communities left many people addicted to drugs. The opium den trade was a by-product of Chinese immigrants who came to the United States to participate in the building of the first transcontinental railroad, construction of the railroad occurring between the years 1863-1869. In fact, by the late 1800s, the United States, with a population just over seventy-six million, had an estimated 300,000 plus people addicted to opiates. Not surprisingly, many Civil War veterans were addicted to morphine because of its use as a painkiller during the *American Civil War* (1861-1865). Aside from addicted war veterans, however, most of the opiate addicts of the time were middle and upper class women who found the drugs appealing because they were more socially acceptable than alcohol; it was not socially acceptable for women to drink alcohol at that time in history. Many women embraced the euphoria provided by drugs to counter the boredom associated with the puritan lifestyle they endured.

Initially the problem of drug addiction was not recognized. Once recognized, however, the government imposed experimental strategies to reverse the dilemma. In 1875, political leaders in San Francisco, California, passed an ordinance to render the opium dens illegal[2] and that was followed by the January 1, 1907, *Pure Food and Drug Act* that was the first federal law requiring labels on containers to disclose the existence of opiates and other drugs in so-called *patent medicines.* The term *patent medicine* reverts to eighteenth century England where some manufacturers of medicines applied for and received "Royal Patents" to protect ownership of their product. Patent medicines were marketable because of their alleged ability to cure a variety of disorders that were, in many cases, difficult to cure even with today's medicines. Disorders referred to include the common cold, tuberculosis, diabetes, cancer, and arthritis. The Harrison Narcotic Act of 1914 limited the dispensing of opiates and cocaine to physicians and pharmacies with the sale of heroin being outlawed altogether.

Recent Government Response

In response to the persistent problems created by illicit drugs, in 1968 the Bureau of Narcotics and the Bureau of Drug Abuse Control merged to create the Bureau of Narcotics and Dangerous Drugs (BNDD). In 1973, merging the Bureau of Narcotics and Dangerous Drugs, the Office for Drug Abuse Law Enforcement, and the Office of National Narcotics Intelligence created today's Drug Enforcement Administration (DEA). In 1992, Congress created the Substance Abuse and Mental Health Services Administration (SAMHSA), which is an agency of the U.S. Department of Health and Human Services (HHS), and in 1993, the National Drug Intelligence Center (NDIC), was established. Moreover, today, virtually every major police department features a drug enforcement bureau staffed by officers whose responsibility it is to investigate violations of anti-drug laws.

> SAMHSA is the Federal agency charged with improving the quality and availability of prevention, treatment, and rehabilitative services in order to reduce illness, death, disability, and cost to society resulting from substance abuse and mental illnesses. (Substance Abuse and Mental Health Services Administration, 2003)

---

2. Some historical scholars feel the ordinance was rooted more in ethnocentrism and xenophobia than a genuine concern for substance abuse problems. Specifically, some felt that the ordinance was an attempt to marginalize the Chinese population in the United States when the completion of the first transcontinental railroad diminished the need for their labor.

REGULATION OF ALCOHOL IN THE UNITED STATES

The National Prohibition Act

On December 18, 1917, Congress passed the *National Prohibition Act*, ratified it January 16, 1919, and it became law January 16, 1920, as the *Eighteenth Amendment to the United States Constitution.* Andrew Volstead authored the *National Prohibition Act*; hence the term, *Volstead Act.* Andrew Volstead was a Republican and member of the U.S. House of Representatives. Passage of the Act made manufacturing and selling beverages containing more than 0.5 percent alcohol illegal. Although the people belonging to temperance societies favored the law, and were a driving force promoting such a law, there were many Americans who were adamantly opposed to the law; they wanted to drink and they felt prohibition violated their constitutional right to drink.

Because of the numerous social, political, and criminal problems associated with the period of national prohibition, *Amendment 21 to the United States Constitution* repealed the *Volstead Act* on December 5, 1933. From then, prohibition was the option of individual states, counties, and cities and many chose to remain "dry." States, counties, and cities that prohibit the sale of alcohol are referred to as being "dry," while those that permit the sale of alcohol are referred to as being "wet." There were states that remained dry until the mid 1960s, and there are still numerous dry counties today–some counties are completely dry, some are partially dry, some dry counties have wet cities and towns, and there are dry cities and towns in some wet counties.

The Problem of Enforcement

During the years of national prohibition, 1920-1933, crime became rampant as rival traffickers fought for market share and citizens' respect for law and order diminished. Those factors are strong indicators of the social and enforcement costs of prohibition. There is disagreement as to whether prohibition actually caused an increase or decrease in alcohol consumption, and while some social problems associated with alcohol consumption may have decreased in response to prohibition, other more serious social problems became apparent, i.e., organized crime became an empire of unprecedented proportions.

Did prohibition cause an increase in alcohol consumption or was there simply the "appearance" of an increase because of the highly visible nature of the social problems that resulted? An examination of liver cirrhosis cases prior to, during, and after the period of prohibition reveals insight relative to a possible reduction in alcohol consumption, but even that issue begs cautious analysis.

The incidence of liver cirrhosis generally is a good indicator of the extent of alcohol consumption in a society inasmuch as most cases result from heavy alcohol consumption. Moreover, liver cirrhosis is difficult to conceal and it is serious enough to cause the victim to seek medical help resulting in the availability of useful statistics (Goldstein, 2001).

If there were a decrease in the rate of liver cirrhosis diagnosed during the early period of national prohibition (1920-1933), the decreased incidence would suggest an overall decrease in the rate of alcohol consumption. However, a later decrease in the rate of diagnosed liver cirrhosis may be the result of severe and widespread poverty restricting access to medical treatment. Indeed, the poverty associated with the Great Depression (1929-1941) left large numbers of people indigent. The Depression came nine years after the beginning of prohibition, but it takes time to develop liver cirrhosis from excessive alcohol consumption, and the Depression did not end until eight years after prohibition ended, and the Depression did not end as abruptly as it began. This is an issue worthy of further research.

It is impossible to accurately determine the number of people consuming alcohol during prohibition but research in several countries has revealed that the levels of liver cirrhosis is a strong indicator of alcohol consumption by a population. Studies reveal that when everyone drinks more, there will be an increase of persons at the tail of a statistical curve that are heavy drinkers, just as when less people consume alcohol there will be fewer heavy drinkers in that class. Persons often assume that when an entire population decreases its alcohol consumption, a group of hard-core alcohol addicts will remain. Facts refute this assumption, and, in fact, the response to reduced availability is that all groups drink less (Goldstein, 2001).

Applying this theory of a reduced drug supply creating reduced consumption, an examination of the heroin epidemic amongst United States military personnel in Vietnam is in order. In Vietnam, heroin was inexpensive, pure, and in abundant supply. Many thousands of soldiers, who would most likely never experiment with heroin, became addicted to heroin. When these soldiers returned home, however, the vast majority of them never used heroin again, which suggests that the consumption of drugs correlates with the availability of the drugs, which legal status influences. Even though there are persons who choose to break the law, and obtain and use illicit drugs, the fact that illicit drugs are not advertised, are expensive, and not readily available without the risk of legal intervention results in a reduced number of persons choosing to use illicit drugs. During prohibition, it was not as convenient for a person to obtain alcohol even though there were those who frequented speakeasies or purchased bootleg liquor from other sources. The attitude towards alcohol today is evident by its conspicuous presence in sports and advertising, and its availability. Today's culture, as a whole, is no doubt more of a drinking culture than it was during prohibition.

Accompanying the hedonistic lifestyle of the infamous *Roaring Twenties* was a demand for illegal alcohol and vices such as prostitution and gambling. Because alcohol was illegal but in demand, moonshiners increased manufacturing output. The bootleggers purchased alcohol from the moonshiners, imported it from Canada and overseas, and obtained it by raids on government warehouses. Additionally, selling raw materials such as sugar, grain, yeast, and containers to moonshiners, the operators of illegal breweries called "stills," became big business. In fact, illegal alcohol and the activities associated with it became such big business that it reached a point where, in Detroit, Michigan, for example, in the late 1920s, it was allegedly second, only by auto manufacturing employing an estimated 50,000 people.

It has been estimated that during the second half of the 1920s, Alphonse (Al) Capone's Chicago-based enterprises of illegal alcohol, speakeasies (also called Blind Tigers and Blind Pigs), brothels, nightclubs, and gambling activities were earning $100,000,000 per year. In today's dollars, that would equate to earnings of about $2,600,000,000 per year. Although most crime syndicates were not as large and diversified as that of the infamous Alphonse Capone, they were large nonetheless as evidenced by an excerpt from *Olmstead v. United States*, the first wiretapping case in Supreme Court history.

> The evidence in the records discloses a conspiracy of amazing magnitude to import, possess, and sell liquor unlawfully. It involved the employment of not less than 50 persons, of two sea-going vessels for the transportation of liquor to British Columbia, of smaller vessels for coastwise transportation to the state of Washington, the purchase and use of a branch beyond the suburban limits of Seattle, with a large underground cache for storage and a number of smaller caches in that city, the maintenance of a central office manned with operators, and the employment of executives, salesmen, deliverymen, dispatchers, scouts, bookkeepers, collectors, and an attorney. In a bad month sales amounted to $176,000; the aggregate for a year must have exceeded $2,000,000." (Olmstead v. United States, 277 U.S. 438 [1928])

Huge profits resulted in proliferation of the clandestine stills of the moonshiners, the illegal importation of alcohol, raids on government warehouses to steal the alcohol contained therein, and in some instances, legal breweries yielded to temptation and diverted product to the illegal market. Money has a tendency to corrupt and the owners of legitimate breweries were not immune to temptation. A good example of that is found in *Various Items of*

Personal Property v. United States, 282 U.S. 577 (1931), a case wherein the government seized the assets of Waterloo Distilling Corporation following their conviction for diverting alcohol for beverage purposes, forfeiture including a distillery, warehouse, and denaturing plant. This case can be found at www.findlaw.com.

Huge profits also caused criminal enterprises to become highly organized and enabled them to exploit the benefits derived by corrupting politicians, judges, law enforcement officials, and street level police officers who ignored violations. Huge profits also caused deadly clashes between rival gangs as they fought for, and defended, operating territory. The most widely publicized and best remembered gangland killing was the Al Capone inspired *St. Valentine's Day Massacre* on February 14, 1929, in an automotive garage in Chicago, Illinois. Members of Capone's gang dressed as police officers who pretended to be conducting a police raid perpetrated the killings; rival gang members were machine gun and shot gunned to death after being ordered to line up and face a wall, presumably to be searched. One of the intended targets of the attack was George "Buggs" Moran, the leader of an Irish rival gang, the North Side Gang. Moran was not there, as hoped, but six members of his gang suffered execution and a seventh unfortunate soul who was not part of the gang was also murdered.

As stated, with prohibition came increased moonshining and selling of bootleg liquor, but predictably prostitution, gambling, and the speakeasies became ubiquitous byproducts. Although prohibition did rid the country of legal saloons, speakeasies sprang up to replace them. Speakeasies were private clubs that sold illegal alcoholic beverages. How prevalent were the speakeasies? Exact numbers are unknown because speakeasies were often clandestine–estimates vary widely. One estimate suggests that by the mid-1920s, there were 32,000 speakeasies in New York City, although another estimate alleges 100,000. Chicago, by 1930, allegedly had 10,000 speakeasies, while Detroit allegedly had 25,000, but those estimates are probably as wildly speculative as those pertaining to New York City.

Although prohibition laws made the manufacture, distribution, and sale of alcohol illegal, law enforcement found it almost impossible to enforce the laws as a continuous cat-and-mouse game played out between law enforcement and those involved in the illegal alcohol trade. That situation is reminiscent of the difficulty of enforcing today's anti-drug laws. In fact, in many respects, today's frustrating efforts to enforce anti-drug laws are a repeat of what occurred during prohibition; someone is manufacturing and/or importing an illegal substance, someone is distributing it, and someone is purchasing it. Moreover, like the period of prohibition, there is a great deal of criminal activity associated with the drug trade with a multitude of social problems existing as a result.

On December 5, 1933, prohibition ended. Prohibition ended, in part, because of the social and crime problems such as violence and graft that erupted in response to a demand that was not being satisfied via the legitimate market. Once prohibition ended, the enormous profits organized crime syndicates had been realizing from bootleg liquor diminished and they were again more dependent on moneymaking strategies such as gambling operations, prostitution, loan-sharking, extortion/protection, and drugs. Heroin was the predominant illicit drug at that time and was so lucrative that in 1936, for example, a $100,000 investment generated a return of approximately $5,000,000, a lot of money relative to the economy of the time. In addition, organized crime began to penetrate legitimate business, although not always done in a legal manner.

Although the ending of prohibition left alcohol no longer as lucrative for crime syndicates, that period had caused them to become much more organized and sophisticated than they otherwise would have been. Those qualities served them in their post-prohibition activities.

Syndicate, The. The era of the 1920s had taught organized crime leaders the value of strong political connections and the disadvantages of internecine warfare, but it was not until the 1930s that Lucky Luciano (with Mafia connections) and Louis Lepke Buchalter created a tight interstate criminal organization called the Syndicate. It included many crime figures from all over the country in an invisible government, apportioning territorial boundaries, allocating the profits from crime, and punishing those who violated their decrees. The notorious Murder, Inc. enforced Syndicate decisions. (*The Columbia Encyclopedia*, Sixth Edition. Copyright © 2003 Columbia University Press. Reprinted with permission)

Prohibition Era, The. The organized-crime syndicate in the United States is a product of the prohibition era of the early 20th century. The efforts of federal officials to enforce the unpopular Volstead Act of 1920 generated the growth of highly organized bootlegging rings with nationwide and international contacts. Although loose alliances were joined among such groups as the Al Capone mob of Chicago, the Detroit Purple gang, and the Owney Madden ring of New York City, gang wars and gangland killings were distinctive features of the 1920s. Powerful gangs corrupted local law-enforcement agencies, even gaining access to high-ranking judges and politicians, such as Mayors Frank Hague in Jersey City, N.J., and James J. (Jimmy) Walker in New York City. (The Columbia Encyclopedia, Sixth Edition. Copyright © 2003 Columbia University Press. Reprinted with permission).

Illegal Alcohol Is a Present-day Problem

As discussed, illegal alcohol existed in the United States even before it had become the United States. Before the United States gained its independence from England, alcohol was being smuggled into the colonies to avoid payment of alcohol taxes, and privately distilled alcohol was common. Although illegal alcohol has been a persistent part of American history, is illegal alcohol a present-day problem?

Dry jurisdictions still exist with legally brewed alcohol being smuggled into those jurisdictions, and moonshining still exists. Because, in dry jurisdictions, there is not a legal supply to satisfy the demand for alcohol, smuggling legally brewed alcohol into those jurisdictions from elsewhere is lucrative–where there is a demand there will be a supply whether legal or otherwise! As for illegally brewed alcohol, it persists today for the same reason it has existed throughout American history–to provide a product that is otherwise unavailable, and to avoid payment of alcohol taxes. Tax-free alcohol is comparatively inexpensive, in most instances. Because there are dry jurisdictions, and because the tax on alcohol is significant, the moonshiners continue distilling and the bootleggers continue selling.

Although individuals purchase much of the illegally brewed alcohol, it also finds its way into the unlicensed bars, commonly called "nip joints" and "shot houses," those bars being reminiscent of the prohibition era speakeasy. Nip joints and shot houses are most prevalent in areas inhabited disproportionately by low-income people.

The existence of illegal alcohol today is evident from, among other sources, recent newspaper headlines. The following is, indeed, a modest sampling:

"Man, 59, Charged With Moonshine Possession"
(The Associated Press, November 10, 2002)

"White Lightening Strikes Again: Age-Old Tradition of Moonshining Is Still a Problem"
(ABC News Internet Ventures, April 9, 2002)

"Seven moonshiners face charges"
(The Associated Press, September 8, 2001)

"U.S. Cracks Down on Rise in Appalachia Moonshine"
(The New York Times on the web, March 23, 2000)

If news headlines are not enough to verify the persistent existence of illegally distilled moonshine liquor, consider the press release issued on May 7, 1999, by the Department of the Treasury, Bureau of Alcohol, Tobacco and Firearms. The press release summarizes the results of what they called "Operation Lightening Strike," an operation that targeted moonshiners in two counties in Virginia. Federal, state, and local law enforcement agents, at the conclusion of a lengthy investigation, executed ten federal search warrants on multiple locations of a suspected moonshining operation that was believed to be illegally brewing alcohol and distributing it to "nip joints" and "shot houses" in Washington, D.C., Baltimore, and Philadelphia. The targets of the raids were the multiple locations of a large operation that agents estimated had generated almost $7,000,000 over the previous four-years. The press release reported that, "this organization is being investigated for alleged violations of Title 18, United States Code, Chapter 95, and Title 26, Section 5601 (a) (1), unregistered manufacturing and operation of a still, and other federal statutes" (*ATF News*, 1999).

Today, the moonshiners continue to operate their clandestine stills, legitimate retailers continue to provide essential ingredients to the moonshiners, bootleggers continue alcohol distribution, and law enforcement continues to investigate. When comparing the investigation of illegal alcohol with the investigation of illicit drugs, one finds striking similarities. Like a large-scale drug investigation, the investigation of illegal alcohol entails interviews and interrogations, examination of records such as bank records, telephone records, and the inventory and sales records of those suspected of selling product such as sugar, grain, yeast, and plastic jugs to the moonshiners, and technical and physical surveillance remains essential. Additionally, like the large drug supplier who launders money, so it is with the large moonshine operation–they too launder money. Naturally, failing to declare moonshine income is of interest to the Internal Revenue Service (IRS).

Today, federal money laundering statutes and income tax laws are a potent weapon in combating moonshining, bootlegging, and drug operations. Indeed, violators who historically suffered light penalties under state laws are now, under federal laws, risking lengthy prison sentences, heavy fines, and forfeiture of assets.

Is the tide changing? Will the dealers of illicit drugs also begin facing stiffer laws drafted with reference to terrorism and weapons of mass destruction, instead of the previously more lenient state laws addressing controlled substances? A September 14, 2003, Associated Press headline read, "New Terror Laws Used vs. Common Criminals." In the article, which discussed the

Patriot Act and new state laws addressing the issue of terrorism and weapons of mass destruction, it mentioned a North Carolina man charged under a new state law that prohibited manufacturing chemical weapons, the man charged under that statute for operating a methamphetamine laboratory. The methamphetamine laboratory satisfied the statute, according to the county prosecutor because it was capable of causing death or serious injury, and contained toxic chemicals. Under the new law, the offense that would have subjected the defendant to perhaps six-months in jail under state drug laws leaves him facing the prospect of twelve years to life (Caruso, D., 2003).

WITH THE 1960s CAME DRUGS

During the later 1960s and into the 1970s, illicit drug use in the United States became epidemic, and was just one of many symptoms of the social change that was occurring in part because of America's involvement in the highly controversial and divisive Viet Nam War. In fact, it was the sudden and prevalent use of illicit drugs among young people during that time that later gave rise to the axiom, "If you remember the '60s, you weren't there!" Certainly, not all young people were suddenly using illicit drugs and dulling their intellectual faculties, but the evolution of such a saying attests to the magnitude of the problem.

It was during the period of the Viet Nam War that young people began questioning, and overtly challenging, old values. It was not uncommon to see, for example, bumper sticker slogans that read, "Challenge Authority," and one began to hear terms such as, "Power to the people," "Do your own thing," and "If it feels good, do it!" The controversy of the war gave rise to an anti-war movement accompanied by the birth of a counterculture that abandoned principles in favor of a pleasure-seeking lifestyle, a lifestyle characterized in many cases by social disorder, indiscriminate sex, and the largest unrestrained experiment with illicit drugs this country had ever witnessed.

Exacerbating the problem of widespread illicit drug use was the fact that there evolved, to some degree, increased social acceptance of drugs, at least towards certain types of drugs such as marijuana, that in the 1970s was decriminalized in some states and municipalities. Although widespread drug use began within the counterculture referred to by some as the drug culture, increasingly it permeated mainstream society. In fact, even a large percentage of military personnel began using illicit drugs with that being especially true toward the latter stages of the Viet Nam War. America's involvement in the war ended in April 1975 when Saigon, the capital city of South Viet Nam, fell to communist troops. With the final pullout of American troops,

America's involvement in the war was over and as a result, the anti-war movement ended. However, the rampant use of illicit drugs did not leave the American scene.

THE 1960s VERSUS THE ROARING TWENTIES

In some respects, the counterculture movement of the 1960s and early 1970's was reminiscent of the 1920s, the infamous though romantic and glamorous *Roaring Twenties*, the years of prohibition.

The *Roaring Twenties* was a period wherein, not unlike the 1960s and early 1970s, social values were challenged with perhaps the most conspicuous participants being young women, the "Flappers," who departed from puritan values by adopting an attitude and way of life characterized by risk-taking and fast living, a lifestyle of rebelliousness and pleasure-seeking. They adopted a less conservative style of dress, bobbed their hair, wore makeup previously unique to women of questionable morals, began to smoke and drink, and they became sexually liberated and participated in what was referred to as "petting parties."

All things must end, however, and after a decade of frivolous self-indulgence came October 24, 1929, *Black Thursday*, the *Great Crash*! The collapse of the stock market plunged the country into the *Great Depression* (1929-1941) and economically the hedonistic lifestyle could no longer sustain. Hence, more abruptly than it began, the *Roaring Twenties* characterized by joie de vivre were gone. And, with the ending of prohibition just four years later, gone were much of the huge profits that criminal enterprises dominated by Irish, Jewish, and Italian immigrants, and the first born of immigrants, had been realizing from the bootleg liquor business and related activities.

Conversely, although the anti-war movement of the 1960s and first part of the 1970s ended when the Viet Nam War ended, there was not a sudden decline in drug use. Drugs remained illegal but the demand for them persisted.

Chapter 2

THE PROBLEM OF ILLICIT DRUGS TODAY (SOCIAL PERSPECTIVES)

> *The illicit drug market in the United States is one of the most profitable in the world. As such, it attracts the most ruthless, sophisticated, and aggressive drug traffickers.* (U.S. Drug Enforcement Administration, 2003)

INTRODUCTION

Today, illicit drug use in America remains a plague that permeates virtually all facets of society with illicit drugs being responsible for considerable associated damage in the form of, but not limited to, burglary, robbery, prostitution, homicide, suicide, enforcement costs, incarceration costs, health care costs, embezzlement, diminished worker performance, business bankruptcies, and destruction of the family unit. The Federal Bureau of Investigation (FBI) has reported that illicit drugs are responsible for 48 percent of all homicides, 60 percent of all assaults, and 80 percent of all property crimes in the United States, these figures obtained from material presented in an El Paso Intelligence Center (EPIC) criminal highway interdiction course presented to law enforcement in the year 2002.

Illicit drug use is no longer restricted to the so-called "street-junkie" but exists among workers in the blue-collar trades, in the professions, and among our schoolchildren. As in the blue-collar sector, in the white-collar arena, one will find illicit drug users among hourly employees and in supervision and management. A recent study found that "in 2002, an estimated 19.5 million Americans, or 8.3 percent of the population aged 12 or older, were current illicit drug users" (Substance Abuse and Mental Health Services Administration, 2003). The same study found that an alarming 18.45 percent of people between the ages of 16-29 use illicit drugs or are alcohol dependent. This should be of special concern to employers, especially considering a recent study that found an estimated 77 percent of those purchasing and using illicit drugs to be full- or part-time employees (Substance Abuse and Mental Health Services Administration, 2003) (see Graph 2-1).

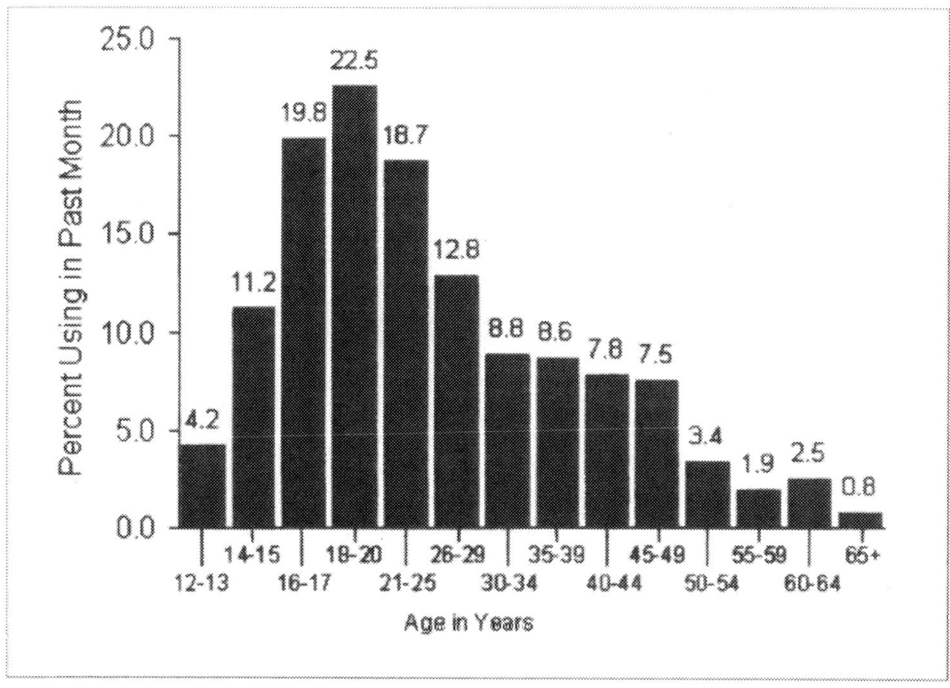

Graph 2-1. Illicit drug or alcohol dependence or abuse, by age: 2002. (Reprinted with permission. Substance Abuse and Mental Health Services Administration, 2003.)

Statistics such as these suggest a serious drug problem in the United States and illustrate the need for employers to require pre- and post-employment drug tests. One of the authors once told the human resource manager of a large well-known company that had no drug-testing program that if some Monday morning everyone arriving for work submitted to a surprise drug test, she would be shocked at how many, and who, would fail the test. Although that illustrated a point, following legal procedures would be necessary. He had periodically overheard even supervisors and managers discussing their illicit drug use. Moreover, he had observed the sometimes-erratic behavior among supervisors and managers that is often characteristic of illicit drug users. To this day, that company has no drug-testing program and top management appears to remain apathetic. In fact, that company retained an employee following a conviction for cocaine distribution but sentenced only to probation because "he was from a good family."

It is not surprising that the company eventually encountered profitability problems and devoted considerable effort to correcting the predicament, but quality drug testing was not part of the strategy. Although it would be difficult to say that their profitability problems were the direct result of employees using illicit drugs, and probably were not, drug use certainly affects quality decision making and that may have been a contributing factor. A high-level manager with a company that does test for drugs, but implemented the program only a few years ago, recently commented to one of the authors how surprised she had been when the initial test of all employees disclosed that her assistant was a user of illicit drugs.

The fact that so many drug users are employed full- or part-time should be sobering to any employer. However, add to that the fact that the American Management Association and the United States Chamber of Commerce report that that almost one-third of all business bankruptcies are the result of undetected employee theft, and also that "one out of four substance abusers in treatment admitted stealing from their employer" (Substance Abuse and Mental Health Services Administration, 2003). Employee dishonesty losses are particularly dangerous to a firm because it is impossible to make accurate advance estimates of the *maximum possible* or *maximum probable* loss. Clearly, employers must conduct efficient background investigations and test for drugs![3]

Employers who remain apathetic and decline to scrutinize the background of job candidates, and who decline to administer pre- and post-employment drug tests are literally gambling with the survival of the business. Not only do employers need to screen out the drug users, they also need to realize that many job candidates falsify their employment history. A recent study found that as many as 9 percent of today's job candidates claim an academic degree they do not have, with others materially misrepresenting employment history and experience, reason for discharge from previous jobs, and wage history. Failure to disclose a criminal history is also common.

DOES DRUG USE REPRESENT DEVIANT BEHAVIOR?

Why is it so difficult to enforce current drug laws? What factors are unique to drugs that continue to frustrate enforcement efforts? Perhaps there were and are too many members of society who did not and do not regard the use of an illegal substance as representing deviant behavior, even though illegal. Illustrating this point are the results of a survey conducted by the National Opinion Research Center (NORC). A survey they conducted in 2000, wherein they queried people age 18 and older, found that 32 percent of the

3. Although several times the author's emphasize the importance of conducting pre-employment background investigations and pre- and post-employment drug tests, it is important to apply those strategies within legal guidelines. Applicable laws vary from one state to another, and state laws sometimes differ from federal laws. Employers must be familiar with prevailing laws.

respondents favored legalizing marijuana. Although it is encouraging that 60.9 percent of the survey respondents reported worrying about the drug abuse problem, an alarming 39.1 percent of the respondents were not worried about the drug abuse problem. The 39.1 percent who report not worrying about drug abuse represents a larger segment of American society than the 32 percent who favor legalizing marijuana–the difference between the two figures, 7.1 percent, reflects people who do not favor the legalization of marijuana but simultaneously report lack of concern about illicit drugs. Considering the enormity of today's illicit drug problem, if almost 40 percent of the American people are unconcerned, then we have a problem of many people being either uninformed or apathetic, or both.

During national prohibition of alcohol, a sufficient number of people did not regard alcohol use as being deviant to affect social attitudes, and much the same situation exists today relative to illicit drugs. When the *National Prohibition Act* became law January 16, 1920, there had already been a long history of resistance to taxes, including alcohol taxes that many felt were unfair and oppressive, and for that reason the moonshiners and bootleggers were already well entrenched.

In 1787, *Shays Rebellion* occurred, an armed insurrection against high land taxes. The *Whisky Rebellion* occurred in 1794 in response to whisky taxes felt to be excessive. In an effort to finance the Union Army during the Civil War (1861-1865), high whisky taxes again were imposed, taxes that persisted during the period of reconstruction (1865-1877) following the Civil War and beyond. In 1894, Congress further increased the whisky tax and placed limits on alcohol production. All those taxes stimulated an underground economy rooted in alcohol that, in many respects, had become part of American culture and certainly was a significant part of the economy, at least in certain regions. Hence, when *National Prohibition* became law in 1920, resistance did not require writing a new script. The *National Prohibition Act* did not cause an underground economy rooted in illegal tax-free alcohol, but only served to increase the size and significance of that which already existed.

Another factor is the extent to which the period of *National Prohibition* and the *Great Depression* overlapped. Prohibition was in effect between the years 1920-1933, while the *Great Depression* occurred between the years 1929-1941. Hence, there were several years of overlap. People suffering economic hardship, especially when they believe their government is largely to blame for their misery, find it easy to rationalize participating in an underground economy, even though illegal. Indeed, there were several years during the *Great Depression* that the underground economy generated by illegal alcohol provided jobs for large numbers of people who otherwise would have been unemployed and living in absolute poverty.

If many people feeling that the government was treating them unfairly underscored the years of prohibition, certainly the feeling of disillusionment towards government reached a peak during the Great Depression. Such a feeling, naturally, would tend to neutralize any feeling that participating in an underground economy represented deviant behavior. During the 1960s and into the 1970s, when the Viet Nam War was so unpopular, there was a tremendous amount of dissention towards the government. Hence, members of the counterculture did not view their antisocial and often illegal conduct as representing deviant behavior.

Deviant behavior is any behavior that is inconsistent with the norms and values of the culture within which it occurs irrespective of whether the behavior is legal or illegal. Perhaps, today, too many people in mainstream society do not view drug use as being deviant even though it is illegal. Perhaps the difficulty of enforcement stems from the fact that illicit drug use does not offend the norms and values of a sufficiently large percentage of the American population, even though evidence abounds attesting to the deleterious and far-reaching consequences of drug use. In many respects, those who use illicit drugs, whether unemployed dregs or people employed in the blue- and white-collar sectors, are to varying degrees members of a subculture distinguished by drug use; they do not view drug use as being deviant, and frighteningly, they represent a large percentage of today's American population.

Of those who do not use illicit drugs, a high percentage appear to have become desensitized and are apathetic about the drug situation with the result being that many fail to view illicit drug use as representing *true* deviant behavior. We have a problem! In the final analysis, curtailing the rampant use of illicit drugs will require changing the values and attitudes of the culture within which the drug trade flourishes, but accomplishing that will not be easy.

SOCIAL COSTS OF ILLICIT DRUGS

According to United States government statistics, in the year 2000, Americans spent an estimated $64 billion dollars on illicit drugs, and the total cost of drug trafficking and drug-related crime to American society exceeded $160 billion dollars (NDIC). Estimates also suggest that American businesses lose $100 billion dollars a year because of drug-related lost productivity with that estimate being conservative inasmuch as it does not consider losses such as increased insurance costs and employee theft (embezzlement).

When thinking of illicit drug use in the United States, the image that most readily comes to mind is that of the so-called "street-junkie," the chronically unemployed whose place is with the supposed dregs of society, although that is an inaccurate perception. As previously stated, a recent study found that an estimated 77 percent of illicit drug users are employed full- or part-time. These drug users often appear respectable and are living what appears to be a normal mainstream lifestyle. Appearances aside, however, are they respectable? In spite of being employed and appearing to live a responsible life, like the stone tossed into a pond that causes outwardly expanding ripples, are they contributing to a multitude of far reaching social, economic, and crime problems? In short, are they contributing to the well-being of society, or defiling it?

If persons employed, even though respectable in appearance, are the buyers of illicit drugs, certainly, they are creating the bulk of the demand that sustains the illicit drug market. Hence, they are directly contributing to a multitude of social, economic, and crime problems. Are they not, therefore, just as responsible for the excess of drug-related crimes as the persons actually committing the offenses? Have they not, more than anyone else, contributed to the evolution of a culture that accepts illicit drug use as not representing deviant behavior even though not all members of society use illicit drugs or share their views?

Illicit drugs and the numerous collateral problems they create have become epidemic in American society. That is apparent when examining statistics relative to drug-related burglaries, robberies, assaults, homicides, prostitution to support a drug habit, sexually transmitted diseases from drug-related prostitution, the spread of diseases such as HIV and hepatitis from needle sharing, overdose deaths, and suicide deaths. Also included in the inventory of social problems caused by illicit drugs are the number of "crack babies" born, brain-damaged users, unemployment, and the detrimental effects illicit drugs are having on business and industry. Indeed, the social costs associated with illicit drugs are tremendous, and this list could continue.

A special education teacher in the public school system recently lamented to one of the authors about the number of pupils under her charge who were born "crack babies," babies born with crack cocaine (and/or other drugs) in their system. That begs the question, to what extent is the current problem of student underachievement as evidenced by poor test scores and dropout rates at least in part the result of women using drugs while pregnant with the underperforming child? It is a sad human tragedy and very costly to society when children are born damaged because their mother was consuming illicit drugs and/or alcohol during pregnancy (see Graph 2-2). One is also compelled to wonder how many under performing students are demonstrating substandard performance because of familial problems caused by parental substance abuse, or their own substance abuse and the detrimental lifestyle that often accompanies such behavior (see Graph 2-1).

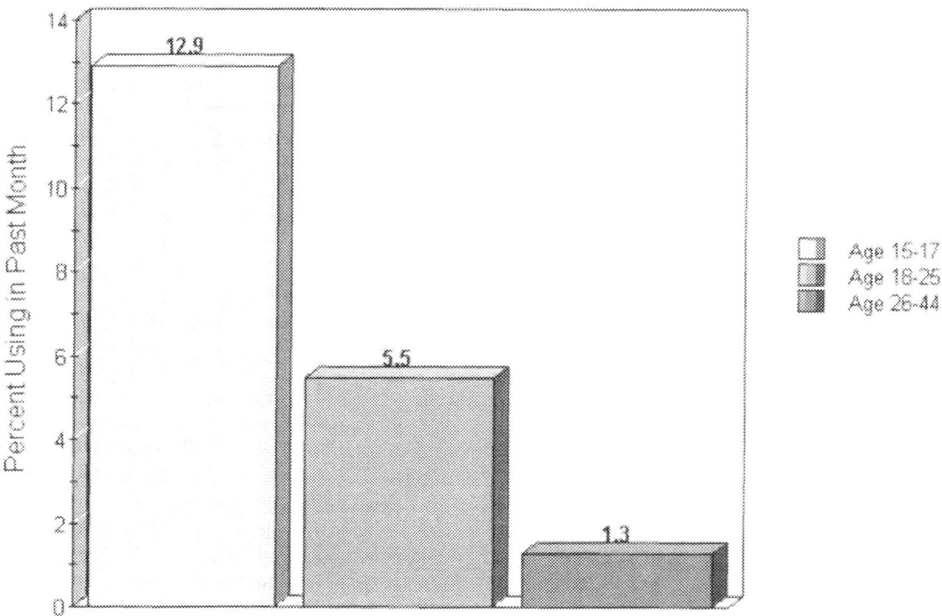

Graph 2-2. Percentage of pregnant women using drugs by age. (Reprinted with permission. Substance Abuse and Mental Health Services Administration, 2003.)

Today, in addition to being consumers of illegal street drugs, children as young as grade school age are "huffing." Huffing refers to breathing the fumes of products such as paint, solvents, glues, and fuels. "Youths who reported an average grade of 'D' or below were more than 3 times as likely to have used inhalants during the past year as youths with an average grade of 'A'" (Substance Abuse and Mental Health Services Administration, 2000). Refer to the subheading "Reducing the Demand for Illicit Drugs" that appears at the end of this chapter.

ILLICIT DRUGS AND TERRORISM– A CONTEMPORARY PROBLEM

There are numerous social costs associated with illicit drugs, as stated, but it does not end there. It is a sad fact that many terrorist organizations engage in criminal activity, including the trafficking of illicit drugs, to finance terrorist operations. A recent news article reported that three men agreed to extradition to the United States from Hong Kong to answer charges that they had arranged to provide drugs in exchange for anti-aircraft missiles that were allegedly destined for Osama bin Laden's al-Qaeda terrorist network. That article quoted United States Attorney General John Ashcroft as saying, relative to the relationship between illicit drugs and terrorism, the case served as a reminder of "the toxic combination of drugs and terrorism and the threats they can pose to national security" (The Associated Press, 2003). Since the September 11, 2001, terrorist attacks on the World Trade Center and Pentagon, it has become clear that it is important for police officers to be aware of the type of investigations that may result in the discovery of terrorist connections.

Just prior to the September 11, 2001, terrorist attacks mentioned above, a southwestern United States law enforcement agency was investigating a group of individuals who were ordering pseudoephedrine tablets from overseas and selling them to street-level methamphetamine manufacturers. Pseudoephedrine is the precursor chemical in making methamphetamine. The detectives involved in the investigation had reliable information that the proceeds from the tablet sales, which were in the millions of dollars, were being used to fund terrorist organizations originating in the Middle East. The detectives were not concerned with the terrorist connection, however, because terrorism on United States soil was not at that time regarded as being a substantial threat as far as they knew.

Unfortunately, just as terrorist organizations from the Middle East fund terrorist activities with proceeds from opium production,[4] other terrorist groups also utilize drug sales to finance terrorist activities. South American countries such as Columbia, Bolivia, and Peru have been victim to crimes committed by rebel groups (i.e., Columbia's FARC) funded by illicit drug operations. Domestic terrorist groups also often fund terrorist activities with illegal activities that are subject to discovery via often seemingly routine drug investigations and surveillance operations.

Although terrorist organizations are often involved in criminal activity just as traditional criminal organizations, the difference is their motive–to finance terrorist activities or to further a political cause. The September 11, 2001, attacks were a combination of both. The attacks that killed thousands of innocent people in the World Trade Center and Pentagon, and United Airlines Flight 93 that crashed in Pennsylvania killing thirty-three passengers and seven crewmembers before reaching the intended target, were violent

---

4. December 20, 2003, the news media reported that the U.S. Navy seized almost two tons of Hashish during its shipment through the Persian Gulf, the Hashish linked to Osama bin Laden's al-Qaeda terrorist network.

criminal acts designed to create fear in the community for political purposes, although economics may also have been a factor. It is believed those attacks netted the terrorists millions of dollars, for it was discovered afterwards that there was an unusual rise in the number of *put options* occurring in October. Many of these stocks were in two major airline companies that suffered major losses following the attacks. *Put options* will pay if the price of stocks decrease after a specified period. Refer to Chapter 10, subheading "Surveillance of Terrorist Organizations."

THE LAW ENFORCEMENT FUNCTION

Has Anything Changed with Time?

The illegal substance with which law enforcement is concerned will change with time and vary by location and culture, but, in spite of variables, the script remains surprisingly consistent. Someone is importing illicit drugs, diverting legal drugs to the illegal market, manufacturing illicit drugs, legitimate products are frequently used in the manufacture of illicit drugs, and someone is transporting and selling drugs to the consumer. Underscoring all that activity is a demand for illicit drugs, a demand that has resulted in a multi-billion dollar underground economy. That the dynamics remain consistent regardless of the substance in question becomes apparent when comparing today's illicit drug situation with what occurred relative to bootleg liquor before, during, and after the period of national prohibition.

Here is a bit of historical trivia. An elderly friend of one of the authors had transported moonshine whisky when he was young, the man having died several years ago. His occasional and brief reminiscing of those years was consistent with case law of the time relative to bootleg liquor. The man stated that he had not enjoyed transporting bootleg liquor in containers because, if stopped by police, he had a load of evidence. He preferred his 250-gallon tanker car because, he explained, it had a high-volume dump system that made disposal of the evidence possible if apprehension appeared imminent.

Although they existed, tanker cars do not appear to have been prevalent for transporting illegal alcohol and, likely, many did not feature a high-volume dump system. It is likely that he manufactured his own tanker as he would have had the foresight and requisite fabrication skills–he was never pressed for details.

REDUCING THE DEMAND FOR ILLICIT DRUGS (What Government, Employers, and Educators Can Do)

Introduction

Because of the confounding social complexities of the illicit drug problem, many facets of the problem defy examination in the limited space available here. Indeed, discussing the social implication of illicit drugs is a topic justifying a separate stand-alone book. For that reason, narrowing the topic was necessary. The following information facilitates illustrating the extent to which illicit drugs are just one facet of a complex set of interrelated social dynamics and why remediation strategies must feature a multi-pronged approach. Indeed, although the illicit drug problem can appear simple on its surface, it features many far-reaching though often subtle tentacles that permeate many facets of society.

Law enforcement agencies are, for the most part, social agencies. Moreover, although most people do not think of police officers as being sociologists or social workers, in many respects, they are. Police officers deal with troublesome social issues daily, under challenging circumstances, and therefore acquire sociological knowledge and insight from a perspective the classroom cannot provide. Nevertheless, supplementing experience based knowledge with formal academic study results in good understanding–one should respect and pursue what academia has to offer. The value of community college- and university-level psychology and sociology courses cannot be overemphasized.

Understanding today's problem of illicit drugs requires at least a rudimentary understanding of historical and social ramifications. Hence, that is the reason for concluding this chapter with the following information–to encourage readers to view illicit drugs from a social perspective, a perspective broader and deeper than just viewing illicit drugs as a crime problem.

The Importance of All-Embracing Abatement Strategies

The government continues to investigate and prosecute drug-law violations, even though law enforcement has only been successful in somewhat containing, although not eliminating, the problem. Meantime, prison populations often exceed intended capacity with a high percentage of inmates incarcerated for drug-law and related violations. Although enforcement efforts must continue, who is in a position to reduce the demand for illicit drugs?

Reducing the demand is a necessary ingredient of the war on drugs because until that is accomplished, law enforcement can, as stated, only hope to contain the problem. Government alone by means of legislation, law enforcement, and corrections has not been able to adequately suppress the drug trade because where there is a demand, there will be a supply.

Accepting that government alone cannot abate the drug problem, who is in a position to contribute to a solution by altering social values? Who is in a position to abate the underlying reasons for our drug epidemic? Who is in a position to reduce the demand for illicit drugs?

Government cannot effectively alter social values but to some extent, business and industry can, and parents and our schools can instill and nurture healthy values in our children. Successfully altering social values will require several forces working in concert, and although satisfactory change will not happen quickly, or occur without cost, we must get things moving in the right direction.

The illicit drug problem is part of a complex set of social problems and therefore the solution requires an all-embracing abatement strategy. For example, solving the crime problem, which includes the illicit drug problem, requires among other things solving the problem of illiteracy and that will take time and cost money. Fortunately, diluting the cost in many instances is the fact that addressing one problem often affects others. For example, solving the illiteracy problem will simultaneously improve the problem of unemployment, the number of people receiving public assistance, substance abuse, youth and adult crime, and prison overcrowding.

Drug Prevention Education

While those in law enforcement, the judicial system, and our penal institutions deal with those who violate anti-drug laws, America's children must benefit from well conceived and properly implemented drug prevention programs. This is important because values form at an early age, and many who begin experimenting with illicit drugs do so as early as grade school age. Additionally, studies reveal that illicit drug use is greater among youth who do not perceive drugs as a serious health risk, and the incidence of dependence is greater for those who began drug use at an early age.

> Adults who first used drugs at a younger age were more likely to be classified with dependence or abuse than adults who initiated use at a later age. For example, among adults aged 18 or older who first tried marijuana at age 14 or younger, 13.0 percent were classified with illicit drug dependence or abuse compared with only 2.8 percent of adults who had first used marijuana at age 18 or older. This pattern of higher rates of dependence or abuse among persons initiating their use of marijuana at younger ages was observed among demographic subgroups.

> A similar pattern was observed for age at first use of alcohol and dependence on or abuse of alcohol among adults. Among adults aged 18 or older who first tried alcohol at age 14 or younger, 17.9 percent were classified with alcohol dependence or abuse compared with only 3.7 percent of adults who had first used alcohol at age 18 or older. (Substance Abuse and Mental Health Services Administration, 2003)

Statistics provided by the Substance Abuse and Mental Health Services Administration (SAMHSA) suggest that drug education for our children is important and that it produces positive results. Children who report having seen or heard anti-drug messages also report a lower incidence of drug use–fewer such children had used drugs.

Research on drug abuse during the critical years of childhood and adolescence, when youth are curious and began trying drugs, with increasing use, has revealed that classroom education instructing children to resist drugs and say "no" is vital, but only goes so far in reducing youth drug use. This instruction must be part of a larger effort that involves the parents or caregivers, and the community. Without the multifaceted approach to reducing youth drug use, only marginal results will be evident. We must view drug prevention education for children as a fundamental part of bringing about an all-encompassing change in societal attitudes toward all addictive drugs.

If parents, schoolteachers, and government fail to provide compelling drug information, all that many children will have available to them is the information they receive from others who are often invalid sources.

Workplace Drug-testing

Accepting that 77 percent of drug users are employed full- or part-time, it is predictable that pre-employment, random post-employment, post-accident, and *reasonable suspicion* drug testing by employers will contribute significantly to suppressing the extent of the drug problem; it will tend to reduce the demand. For that to work, however, it will be necessary for the majority of employers to test for drugs. As it is, many employers ambitiously test for drugs while others do not. When and if there reaches a point where virtually all employers test for drugs, a large percentage of the drug-using population will probably (hopefully) discontinue drug use.

Will there come a time when most employers implement drug testing? There was a time when no employers were testing for drugs even though the drug problem was recognized and drug-testing technology existed. Shortly thereafter, many employers began talking about it, but almost no one was actually doing it, with many being hesitant out of fear that the issues of legal liability had not been adequately resolved by the courts. Then, there was an interim period where a few employers were testing for drugs, and today there are numerous employers who test for drugs, although some have a more proactive testing program than others do. Today, an estimated 87 percent of the major companies in the United States have drug-testing programs (DeMay et al., 1999).

Clearly, most major firms see the need for drug testing and are setting an example that small business owners should notice. For those employers who do not test for drugs, they need to consider the fact that as more employers implement drug-testing programs, increasingly those who use illicit drugs will gravitate to those employers who do not have a testing program. That realization should send a chilling signal to any employer who does not have a proactive drug-testing policy; they will suffer a disproportionate number of drug-using employees, and that can be very costly and even threaten the survival of the business.

Studies have shown, although it was predictable, that drug use increases the incidence of employee theft, on-the-job accidents and injuries, tardiness and absenteeism, and diminished work quality. Those are serious consequences for apathy and represent irregularities that can threaten the survival of a business. Additionally, "drug- and alcohol-related problems are one of the four top reasons for the rise in workplace violence" (Department of Labor, 1998).

One of the authors recalls speaking with the controller of a contracting company that had narrowly escaped bankruptcy because of the economic damage inflicted by employees who were using illicit drugs. The firm had suffered heavy theft losses of tools, equipment, and materials, and suffered heavy losses by way of the costs associated with callbacks for substandard fieldwork. Also included among the causes of economic hemorrhaging were the uninsured portion of losses, and insurance costs that had become disproportionate; excessive frequency and severity of claims resulted in abnormally high insurance premiums. Overall, operating costs had become excessive and to charge a billing rate sufficient to offset the losses would have meant no longer being competitive in the marketplace. The solution, an act of desperation, included terminating all employees except the controller and starting over with the new hiring criteria embracing an ambitious drug-testing program. That firm recovered and is again profitable, but they narrowly escaped bankruptcy. Moreover, there were the years they lost the profit they could have been realizing.

Clearly, employees who use illicit drugs have an incentive to steal and if not restricted from the workforce via quality hiring criteria, background investigations, and drug testing, they will be a large and dangerous part of the workforce. Employers cannot legitimately ignore a business risk of this nature, the reality of that confirmed by the *American Management Association* and the *United States Chamber of Commerce* who report that almost one-third of all business failures are the result of employee theft.

When examining the dynamics of the drug problem in the United States in light of the information provided in this section, it is apparent that the solution must include both government and the private sector. Although the government must continue to investigate and prosecute drug law violations, the private sector is in an ideal position to reduce the demand for illicit drugs.

In reality, this solution is deceptively simple–if employed people purchase and use most of the illicit drugs, forcing them to choose between their livelihoods and drugs will probably cause a high percentage of them to discontinue drug use. That would eliminate the largest portion of the demand for illicit drugs and economically emasculate the suppliers–where there is no demand there will be no supply!

Chapter 3

STREET DRUG IDENTIFICATION

INTRODUCTION

Drug pharmacology is a topic justifying an entire book, with this discussion being a summary of the topic provided for the benefit of those readers who do not have a background of training and experience relative to illicit drugs. For some readers, the information presented here will suffice and serve as an informative overview and as a convenient reference source, while other readers will find themselves compelled to research the topic further. Those desiring more information are encouraged to visit the website of the Drug Enforcement Administration (DEA) as it provides a great deal of valuable information with many of the street drugs discussed more comprehensively than space permits here. Valuable information also exists on the website of the Substance Abuse and Mental Health Services Administration (SAMHSA). In addition, a worthwhile investment is the book titled *Drug Identification Bible* by Tim Marnell.

DRUGS ENCOUNTERED ON THE STREET

On the street, the law enforcement officer will encounter drugs of many types, from many places, and in many forms. Typical scenarios include:

- Drugs manufactured legally in the United States but diverted to the illegal market.
- Drugs manufactured legally or illegally in another country but illegal in the United States and subsequently smuggled into the United States. Alternatively, if manufactured elsewhere but legal in the United States, they are diverted to the illegal market.
- Drugs such as marijuana smuggled into the United States after grown in another country.
- Drugs such as marijuana that is cultivated illegally in the United States.
- Illicit drugs smuggled into the United States in bulk and then packaged for illegal domestic distribution.

• Illicit drugs manufactured in the United States in clandestine illegal laboratories.

In the United States, marijuana is the most widely used illicit drug. Of the people who use illicit drugs, 59 percent use only marijuana, and 17 percent use marijuana in addition to other drugs. However, 24 percent of the people who use illicit drugs do not use marijuana at all. When combining those who use marijuana only, with those who use marijuana in addition to other drugs, we find that 76 percent of drug users use marijuana. The following graphs illustrate the extent to which marijuana only is used, or used in addition to other drugs or not at all, the graphs obtained from the website of the Substance Abuse and Mental Health Services Administration (SAMHSA), and reprinted with permission (see Graphs 3-1 and 3-2).

Drugs Used by Users Aged 12 and Older: 2000

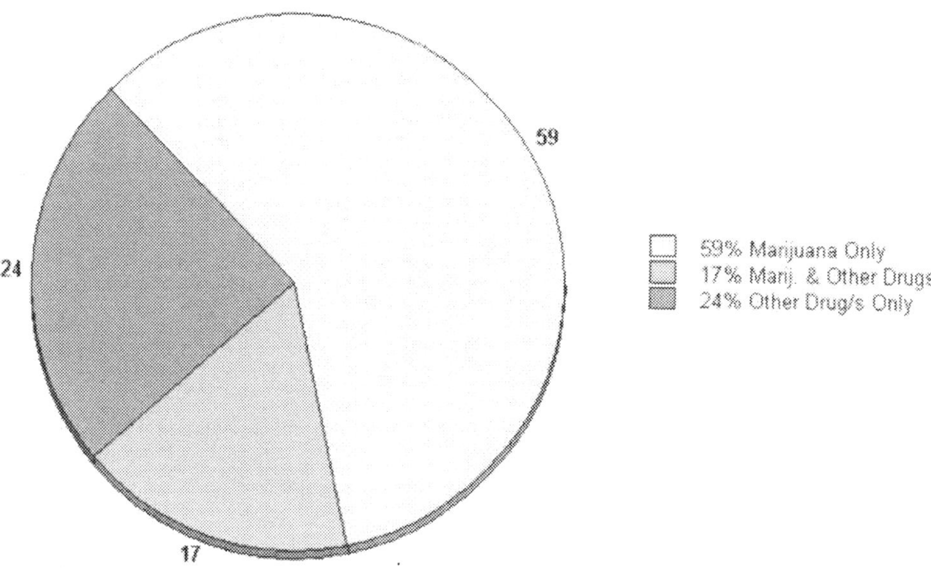

Graph 3-1. Drugs used (percentage) by drug users aged 12 or older: 2002. (Reprinted with permission. Substance Abuse and Mental Health Services Administration, 2003).

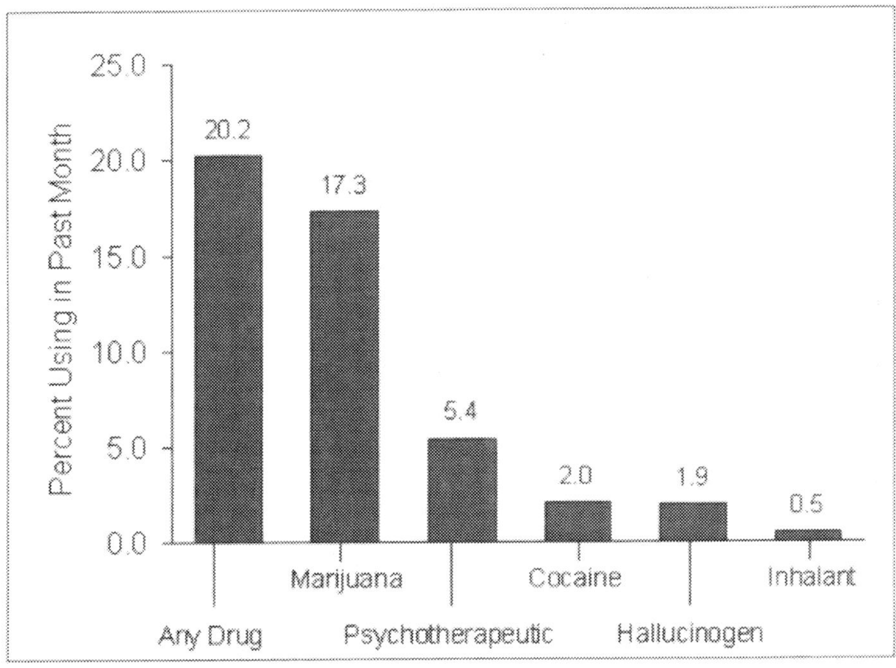

Graph 3-2. Use of selected illicit drugs among persons aged 18-25: 2002. (Reprinted with permission. Substance Abuse and Mental Health Services Administration, 2003.)

Drug users who inject drugs and share needles when so doing are at high risk of acquiring communicable diseases such as, but not limited to, HIV and hepatitis B and C. In spite of that, the following list of drugs does not mention that danger among "effects" because it is a well-known danger associated with needle sharing.

CONTROLLED SUBSTANCES ACT

The Controlled Substances Act (CSA), Title II of the Comprehensive Drug Abuse Prevention and Control Act of 1970, is the legal foundation of the government's fight against the abuse of drugs and other substances. This law is a consolidation of numerous laws regulating the manufacture and distribution of narcotics, stimulants, depressants, hallucinogens, anabolic steroids, and chemicals used in the illicit production of controlled substances. (U.S. Drug Enforcement Administration, 2003)

In this chapter, drugs from the categories identified above are presented and discussed in that order with *cannabis* (marijuana, hashish, and hash oil) added to the list.

NARCOTICS

Narcotics are a central nervous system (CNS) depressant, although the word "narcotic" is frequently used (misused) as a generic term referring to all classes of drugs. People, to describe various drugs that in reality do not have a narcotic effect when taken, use the word *narcotic* loosely. The true pharmacology of narcotics refers to natural, semi-synthetic, or synthetic substances that, when used in modest doses, dull the senses, relieve pain, and cause a feeling of euphoria. The same substances, however, when taken in excessive doses, can result in stupor, coma, convulsions, and death.

Natural or semi-synthetic narcotics, known as opiates, include heroin, morphine, codeine, hydromorphone, oxycodone, and oxymorphone. Morphine is the main ingredient of the opium poppy, and contains both analgesic (pain relief) and sedative qualities. Synthetic opiates, known as opioids, include meperidine, levorphanal, methadone, propoxyphene, fentanyl, and pentazocine. Many of these substances are more commonly known by their various pharmaceutical names, and are regularly prescribed as medicine for various ailments.

Narcotics should not be confused with other CNS depressants that are known as sedative-hypnotics or tranquilizers, but produce no pain relief (analgesia) effect.

The following list of narcotic drugs is limited to those most frequently encountered on the street by law enforcement officers.

• *Heroin*

DESCRIPTION: A highly addictive narcotic analgesic made from morphine that produces euphoria. Not used medically in the United States, it is very prevalent in the illicit drug trade.

EFFECTS: Most commonly include euphoria, confusion, drowsiness (referred to as "on the nod"), loss of coordination, slowed breathing and heart rates, nausea and vomiting, itching, and constipation. Chronic use can result in a number of physiological and psychological health problems. The user can develop a tolerance to the extent that the desired result requires a lethal or near lethal dose. Most deaths result from respiratory failure.

APPEARANCE: Street heroin is usually found in the form of a white to dark-brown powder, a sticky tar like quality (black tar heroin), and coal like rocks.

METHOD OF INGESTION: Injection, inhaling (snorting), and smoking (chasing the dragon).

SOURCE: Heroin is smuggled into the United States from countries such as South America, Mexico, Southeast Asia, and Southwest Asia.

STREET NAMES: Mexican tar is heroin and most often referred to as black, tar, or chiva (Spanish for goat). Powder heroin has dozens of names depending on location, but the more common names include dope, smack, thunder, hell dust, big H, nose drops, horse, and white stuff.

• *Oxycodone (OxyContin)*

DESCRIPTION: Oxycodone, commonly known by its brand name OxyContin, is a narcotic pain reliever and sedative made from codeine, and is more potent and addicting than codeine. Tablets and capsules are designed so that when ingested, the chemicals are slowly released over time, thus reducing the doses one has to take on a daily basis. If an OxyContin tablet is broken, chewed, or crushed, a large amount of oxycodone is quickly released, potentially resulting in a dangerous or fatal drug overdose. In recent years, the popularity of Oxycodone has increased dramatically, especially amongst youth.

EFFECTS: Same as heroin including euphoria, feelings of relaxation, respiratory depression, constipation, and analgesia.

APPEARANCE: Oral liquid, and capsule and tablet form. Also, found in several drug mixtures.

METHOD OF INGESTION: Although normally taken orally, addicts often crush or dissolve the tablets in water, strain it, and then inject it.

SOURCE: Pharmacies, drug dealers, as well as obtained by burglaries, thefts, and robberies of residences and pharmacies. Its abuse is concentrated in the eastern states, although the problem is expanding throughout the United States.

STREET NAMES: Oxy's, OCs, killers, poor man's heroin, and hillbilly heroin.

• *Methadone*

DESCRIPTION: Methadone, less addictive than morphine and heroin, is a synthetic narcotic used to treat chronic pain, and as a substitute narcotic for the treatment of heroin addicts.

EFFECTS: The effects of methadone are similar to morphine and heroin with tolerance and dependence being a risk accompanying chronic use. Methadone will block the euphoria from heroin in most addicts, and is the drug most often used in heroin maintenance and detoxification programs because cross-tolerance will prevent withdrawal symptoms (Liska, 1990).

APPEARANCE: Tablets, and injectable solutions.

METHOD OF INGESTION: Oral consumption by tablet or liquid. Users sometimes also inject.

PRINCIPAL USERS: Heroin addicts undergoing treatment, or street addicts that steal it from maintenance or detoxification programs, or buy it after it's diverted to the street market.

SOURCE: Manufactured legally but diverted to the illegal market.

STREET NAMES: Amidone, fizzies.

• *Fentanyl*

DESCRIPTION: Fentanyl, a morphine-like narcotic with a pain relieving strength about 100 times greater than that of morphine, is used medically for chronic pain management and in combination with other drugs before, during, and subsequent to surgery. Its product names include Sublimaze and Innovar.

EFFECTS: This drug can increase the effect of some narcotics. It depresses respiration, and excessive doses can stop breathing altogether. Fentanyl can cause blood pressure to drop to dangerous levels, and usually causes nausea, sweating, dizziness, and blurred vision.

APPEARANCE: Transdermal patch, tablets or pills, powder.

METHOD OF INGESTION: Smoke, inhaled (snort), and injection.

SOURCE: Manufactured legally but diverted to the illegal market, with similar drugs manufactured illegally in clandestine laboratories. Dozens of fentanyl analogs (designer drugs) have appeared on the street and can be much stronger.

STREET NAMES: China white, p-funk, p-dope, "P", goodfella, tango and cash, Apache, China girl, China town, dance fever, friend, great bear, he-man, jackpot, king ivory, murder 8, poison.

STIMULANTS

Stimulant drugs are central nervous system stimulants (CNS) that cause temporary arousal or acceleration of psychological and/or physiological activity. They are derived from both natural and synthetic sources. Natural stimulants include cocaine, nicotine, caffeine, and ephedrine, while synthetic stimulants include the amphetamines class, and analogs such as methylphenidate, more commonly known as Ritalin. Although the chemical structure and methods of action may differ among these substances, they all produce alertness, stimulation, elevated mood, euphoria, and intense feelings of well-being.

The following list of stimulants is limited to those most likely encountered on the street by law enforcement officers.

• *Cocaine*

DESCRIPTION: A stimulating narcotic extracted from coca leaves grown in the Andes region of South America, mainly in Bolivia and Peru, and representing the second most commonly used illicit drug in the United States. Legitimately used as a topical anesthetic to prevent pain, and as a local anesthetic for the eyes, nose, and throat. Crack cocaine and "freebasing" are identical refined products of cocaine known as base cocaine. This allows the cocaine to be smoked, thus producing a strong and intense high that often leads to physical and psychological problems.

EFFECTS: Cocaine produces a euphoric and stimulating effect. Excessive use may result in addiction in the form of a compulsive psychological need. Deaths often result from cardiac arrest.

APPEARANCE: Cocaine is in the form of white crystalline powder, with "crack" or "rock" cocaine being an off-white chunky material.

METHOD OF INGESTION: Powder cocaine is usually inhaled (snorted) or injected; "crack cocaine" is usually ingested by smoking.

SOURCE: Columbian organized crime groups control the majority of the world's supply of cocaine, smuggled into the United States, the primary point of entry being the United States-Mexico border.

STREET NAMES: Blow, coke, flake, crack, rock, nose candy, snowball, snow, snort, tornado, wicky stick, toot, white, and white thing.

• *Amphetamines*

DESCRIPTION: Amphetamines are chemically similar to adrenaline which is a hormone produced by the adrenal gland. Amphetamines are a central nervous system stimulant (CNS) that puts the body in a "fight or flight" condition. There are two forms of amphetamines, levo-amphetamine and dextro-amphetamine. Dextro-amphetamine forms are several times more powerful than its counterpart levo. An example of a dextro form is Dexedrine, which was marketed in 1945 as an appetite suppressant. Amphetamines are used legitimately as appetite suppressants, for the treatment of attention deficit and hyperactivity disorder (ADHD), mild depression, relief of fatigue and narcolepsy.

EFFECTS: Reminiscent of cocaine, effects include alertness and euphoria, increased heart rate and blood pressure, dilated pupils, decreased appetite, distorted thinking, and allows users to go without sleep for extended periods. In large doses the user can become irritable, aggressive, excited, and suffer from anxiety, hallucination, and paranoia. Users can engage in violent or risky behavior, and paranoia results in suspiciousness, hyperactive behavior, and dramatic mood swings.

APPEARANCE: Capsules, tablets, liquid, and powder. If obtained from a pharmaceutical source, they will be of various sizes, colors, and shapes. Powder and liquid forms are often methamphetamine and can be up to ten times more powerful.

METHOD OF INGESTION: Inhaled (snorted), smoked, oral, or injected.

SOURCE: Clandestine laboratories or diverted from legitimate sources.

STREET NAMES: Speed, uppers, cross-tops, bennies, pep pills, and dexies.

• *Methamphetamines*

DESCRIPTION: A methylated form of amphetamine that is able to produce intensified effects. A powerful stimulant of the central nervous system used medically for treating narcolepsy, attention deficit disorder (ADD), and attention deficit and hyperactive disorder (ADHD), and as an appetite suppressant for treating obesity.

EFFECTS: Methamphetamine causes the mind and body to become more active, and dangers include addiction, psychotic behavior, aggression, and brain damage. Because methamphetamine is an amphetamine, effects are the same. In fact, experienced users often cannot discern what form of amphetamine they ingest because of the similar effects. Binge use is common, resulting in days without sleep, minimal food intake, and continued use until the user "crashes" and sleeps for days before beginning a new cycle.

APPEARANCE: Forms vary depending on manufacturing process and finished product. Most forms are water-soluble and can be powders of various colors. In recent years, the most common form encountered is in the form of clear chunky crystals known as glass or ice. A tablet form of methamphetamine, known as "yaba" (Thai for "crazy medicine"), is popular throughout much of southeast and east Asia. Only recently have the pills found their way into the United States, predominately in the northern California area. "Yaba" tablets come in a variety of colors and often sport a "wy" logo. They are comprised of a blend of caffeine and methamphetamine.

METHOD OF INGESTION: Inhaling (snorting), smoking, orally, and injection.

SOURCE: Most illegal methamphetamine manufacturing occurs in clandestine laboratories in California and Mexico. Domestic laboratories exist primarily in the western, midwestern, and southwest United States. The laboratories, which are very portable, are often set-up in homes and motel rooms. Pseudoephedrine, the precursor chemical, is smuggled from Canada and Mexico, or domestically diverted from legitimate sources.

STREET NAMES: Speed, meth, crystal meth, ice, glass, crank, tweak, go-fast, Tina, "poor man's cocaine" and "G."

SPECIAL HAZARDS: The clandestine manufacturing laboratories present a serious toxicity/environmental, explosion, and fire hazard (see Chapter 8, "Clandestine Drug Laboratories").

• *Methcathinone (Cat)*

DESCRIPTION: Methcathinone is a drug that is chemically similar to methamphetamine and cathinone. Originally manufactured in Germany in the late 1920s, and used extensively in the former Soviet Union in the 1930s and 1940s for treating depression. Introduced in the United States in 1957 when an American pharmaceutical firm investigated possibilities for its use as an appetite suppressant. It is about one-and-a-half times as potent as methamphetamine.

EFFECTS: Methcathinone is similar to methamphetamine in effect and abuse potential.

APPEARANCE: Usually encountered as a water-soluble hydrochloride salt.

METHOD OF INGESTION: Inhaled (snorted) is the most common ingestion route followed by oral ingestion, and injection.

SOURCE: Made in illegal clandestine laboratories.

STREET NAMES: Cat, goob, sniff, crank, star, wonder star, bathtub speed, and wildcat.

• *Khat (Pronounced "cot")*

DESCRIPTION: Khat is a shrub-like plant (Catha edulis) used for centuries in parts of Africa and the Arabian Peninsula with social applications similar to westerners use of coffee.

EFFECTS: Causes euphoria and stimulation. Use can result in mild to moderate psychic dependence, with chronic use potentially leading to physical exhaustion, violence, suicidal depression, and hallucinations.

APPEARANCE: A shrub featuring dark green opposite leaves.

METHOD OF INGESTION: The three principal methods for consuming khat is to chew it, drink it as a tea, or smoke it.

PRINCIPAL USERS: Although khat use is most prevalent in the Middle East, use is not restricted only to that region. In the United States, users tend to be exclusively within Somali, Yemeni, and Ethiopian communities.

SOURCE: Today, it is cultivated in Africa and the Middle East and smuggled into the United States.

STREET NAMES: Abyssinian tea, African salad, qat, kat, chat, gat, catha, tohai, tschat, and miraa.

• *Methylphenidate (Ritalin)*

DESCRIPTION: A mild central nervous system stimulant used to treat narcolepsy in adults and hyperactivity and attention deficit disorders (ADD) in children.

EFFECTS: Methylphenidate is similar in its effects to cocaine and amphetamines, and has a high potential for abuse. Use can result in psychological addiction, psychotic episodes, and cardiovascular complications.

APPEARANCE: Found in tablet form.

METHOD OF INGESTION: Oral, or by injection after first dissolving the tablets in water. In addition, crushing the tablets and inhaling (snorting) the resultant powder is common.

PRINCIPAL USERS: There is increasing use of methylphenidate among adolescents and young adults.

SOURCE: Manufactured legally under the name Ritalin but diverted to the illegal market.

STREET NAMES: Ritalin, speed, and West Coast.

DEPRESSANTS

Depressants cause a decrease in bodily functions and suppress instinctive desires by dulling the senses. Depressants are sedatives, sometimes referred to as "downers." The following list of depressants is limited to those most likely encountered on the street by law enforcement officers.

• *Barbiturates*

DESCRIPTION: Barbiturates are a strong central nervous system depressant used as a sedative, hypnotic, anesthetic, and anticonvulsant. About a dozen are in medical use today. Because of the risks associated with barbiturates, medical use is diminishing in favor of other depressant drugs. Phenobarbital, amobarbital, pentobarbital, and secobarbital are all examples of barbiturates.

EFFECTS: Moderate doses produce symptoms similar to alcohol intoxication, but excessive doses can lead to coma and death. Physical and psychological dependence can result, and the user can develop a tolerance to the extent that the desired result requires a lethal or near lethal dose. Common effects include euphoria, decreased mental acuity, hypnotic, sedation, depressed respiratory function, anesthesia, anxiety suppression, decreased blood pressure, and hypotension.

APPEARANCE: Tablets or pills.

METHOD OF INGESTION: Oral.

SOURCE: Manufactured legally but diverted to the illegal market.

STREET NAMES: Downers, barbs, tranqs.

• *Benzodiazepines*

DESCRIPTION: Benzodiazepines are much like barbiturates although they produce less drowsiness and have a much greater safety margin. Benzodiazepines are among the top 50 prescriptions in the United States due to their perceived result in relieving anxiety and in promoting sedation. The most common benzodiazepines used for reducing anxiety are Librium, Valium, Xanax, Ativan, Serax, and Tranxene. Those used for a sedative-hypnotic effect include Dalmane, Restoril, and Halcion. Rohypnol is a powerful benzodiazepine.

EFFECTS: Depression, drowsiness, dizziness, nausea, dry mouth, fatigue, anxiety suppression, lightheadedness, poor coordination

APPEARANCE: Tablets or pills

METHOD OF INGESTION: Oral.

SOURCE: Manufactured legally but diverted to the illegal market. Flunitrazepam (Rohypnol), conversely, is manufactured worldwide, mainly in Europe and Latin America, where it is legally prescribed. It is, however, illegal to possess in the United States. Rohypnol is known as the "date-rape" drug, although according to law enforcement sources nationwide, GHB has surpassed Rohypnol as the substance of choice in drug facilitated sexual assaults.

STREET NAMES: Rophies, Rohypnol, roofies, rope, roach, forget-me pill, and Bennies.

• *Gamahydroxybutyrate (GHB)*

DESCRIPTION: A central nervous system (CNS) depressant that also creates a euphoric and hallucinatory effect. It gained popularity in the bodybuilding community where it was believed to stimulate the production of growth hormones, and aid in sleeping. Other associated chemicals include BD (1,4 Butanediol), and GBL (Gamma-butyrolactone) which is used in floor strippers, paint thinner, and other industrial products. GHB is produced illegally in clandestine laboratories mainly within the United States; the FDA banned it in 1990 because of the dangers associated with it. In 2002, the FDA approved its use only in treating a rare form of narcolepsy.

EFFECTS: The pharmacological and toxic effects of GHB and associated chemicals are similar. When used with other drugs such as alcohol or CNS depressants, the effects are often increased and are potentially deadly. In small doses users will often feel relaxed, while stronger doses usually cause feelings of euphoria, relaxed inhibitions, nausea, drowsiness, dizziness, confusion, and enhanced enjoyment of music, sensuality, and sexuality. Excessive doses can cause obvious difficulties with speech and motor coordination and may cause unresponsive sleep and overdose. Overdoses are more common with this substance as small increases of ingestion after reaching higher dosage levels can result in a coma-like state.

APPEARANCE: Most often, it appears as a colorless, odorless, and tasteless liquid, which makes it easy to add to a person's beverage by persons looking to intoxicate or sedate another. Often food coloring is added for marketing appeal. Also found in tablet, capsule, and powder form.

METHOD OF INGESTION: Orally.

PRINCIPAL USERS: Teenagers and young adults when attending raves or all-night parties. Some bodybuilders use it for its assumed anabolic effects.

SOURCE: Clandestine laboratories.

STREET NAMES: The more common include G, liquid E or X, scoop, water, GHB, easy lay, ever clear, fantasy, Georgia home boy, and grievous bodily harm.

HALLUCINOGENS

Drugs referred to as hallucinogenic are those that induce hallucinations, i.e. they cause people to see and/or hear things that do not actually exist. Although they cause altered states of consciousness, they are generally non-addictive. Other identifying terms for this class of substance is "psychedelics" and "entheogens." The following list of hallucinogens is limited to those most likely encountered on the street by law enforcement officers.

• *Peyote and Mescaline*

DESCRIPTION: Peyote is a cactus plant (Lophophora williamsii) whose active ingredient is mescaline. Mescaline is contained in the Peyote buttons harvested from the root. The plant grows in northern Mexico and the southwestern United States, mainly Texas, and harvested every two years. Some Native Americans use this drug in combination with religious ceremonies.

EFFECTS: Causes an altered state of awareness along with increased heart rate, salivation, respiration, perspiration, body temperature, and blood pressure. Muscle tension, nausea and vomiting, headache, dilated pupils, intoxicated gait, and lack of coordination are also common.

APPEARANCE: Small, spineless cactus that is only abut one to two inches in diameter and one-half inch tall. They are gray-green when harvested and after drying, they turn brownish.

METHOD OF INGESTION: Chewed either fresh or dry. Users often grind the button into a powder, put it into gel capsules, and swallow them to avoid the unpleasant bitter taste.

PRINCIPAL USERS: Historically, the natives of northern Mexico and southwestern United States used Peyote and Mescaline during religious rites. Today, non-natives use it as well, although it is rare because of its limited growing region and bitter taste.

SOURCE: Mescaline extracted from peyote button or produced synthetically.

STREET NAMES: Peyote is referred to as "mescal," while mescaline is also referred to as "peyote." Other street names include buttons, tops, cactus, chief, dry whiskey, and green whiskey.

• *Psilocybin and Psilocyn*

DESCRIPTION: Psilocybin is a hallucinogenic substance obtained from the mushroom Psilocybe mexicana. Psilocyn, related to psilocybin, is a potent hallucinogenic substance also obtained from a mushroom.

EFFECTS: Perception-altering, muscle relaxation, and emotional disturbances. Effects will vary depending on the variety of plant.

APPEARANCE: Dried mushrooms sometimes covered with chocolate.

METHOD OF INGESTION: The caps and stems are usually eaten either dried or fresh, or added as an ingredient in a recipe, or made into a tea. Because of the taste, users sometimes grind the dried mushroom into a powder and place it in gelatin capsules. Some users smoke it with marijuana.

SOURCE: Psilocybin and Psilocyn are drugs extracted from certain mushrooms found in tropical and subtropical regions of South America, Mexico, and the United States, and synthetically produced in laboratories. Mushroom spores can be purchased legally in many states, and can be cultivated into psilocybin or psilocyn. The spores can be obtained from internet sites as well as ads in counterculture magazines.

STREET NAMES: Magic mushrooms, shrooms, happy or funny mushrooms, mushrooms, sacred mushrooms, food of the gods, and blue halo.

• *Dimethyltryptamine (DMT)*

DESCRIPTION: A potent hallucinogenic substance occurring naturally in parts of South America and in the West Indies, derived from the apocynaceous plant Prestonia amazonica, and easily synthesized as well. It is chemically similar to psilocybin but shorter acting, 10-15 minutes, and similar to LSD but quicker acting.

EFFECTS: Perception-altering. On-set occurs within two minutes and effects last about thirty minutes.

APPEARANCE: Plants or seeds, Bufo toads.

METHOD OF INGESTION: Smoked, injected, or inhaled (snorted). When taken orally in combination with a monoamine oxidase inhibitor, it can be effective.

SOURCE: Found in certain mushrooms, seeds, and skin glands of Bufo toads.

STREET NAMES: Unknown.

• *LSD (lysergic acid diethylamide)*

DESCRIPTION: A potent organic hallucinogenic drug derived from lysergic acid that produces psychotic symptoms similar to schizophrenia. It is the most potent and highly hallucinogenic known to man.

EFFECTS: LSD causes hallucinations and pronounced perceptive impairment, and physiological changes. After use anxiety and depression is common, and flashbacks have occurred days and even months after use.

APPEARANCE: Tablets, liquid (sometimes colored), sugar cubes, blotter paper, stamps, gelatin.

METHOD OF INGESTION: Oral, dripped, or placed on the tongue. Drops placed in eyes.

PRINCIPAL USERS: Middle-class adolescents and young adults are the primary users of LSD, LSD use being most prevalent in the Midwest and on the West Coast.

SOURCE: Manufactured in clandestine laboratories, mainly in northern California. Mail order is a common method of distribution, with raves and rock concerts continuing to be a popular distribution point.

STREET NAMES: Acid, fry, blotter, blotter acid, dose, dot, L, microdot, paper acid, sid, spots, sunshine, ticket, and windowpane.

• *Ecstasy (MDA, MDMA)*

DESCRIPTION: MDMA and MDA contain both the properties of a hallucinogenic and stimulant-type drug, and have a high addiction potential. A substantial percentage of tablets are sold as Ecstasy but in fact contain little or no MDMA or MDA, and instead contain other drugs such as methamphetamine, or natural stimulants such as ephedrine or caffeine. An Ecstasy look-alike tablet known as PMA (paramethoxyamphetamine) contains a Mitsubishi® symbol and a potent and lethal synthetic hallucinogen. PMA is believed to be responsible for numerous deaths in the United States, Australia, and Canada, as users underestimated its strength or mistook it for ecstasy.

EFFECTS: Ecstasy suppresses the feeling of hunger, thirst, and the need for sleep. Hence, severe dehydration and heat stroke are common among users, especially when partying all night such as at raves. Other effects include muscle breakdown, seizures, stroke, kidney and cardiovascular system failure, and permanent damage to sections of the brain that are critical to thought and memory, with death being a persistent risk. Because Ecstasy often causes jaw muscle tension, users will often suck on pacifiers in an effort to relieve teeth grinding.

APPEARANCE: Tablets typically containing 100 mg of MDMA and featuring imprinted logos or designs.

METHOD OF INGESTION: Usually taken orally in pill form, with pills sometimes crushed and inhaled (snorted), injected, or inserted in the form of a suppository.

PRINCIPAL USERS: Ecstasy use is most common among middle-class adolescents and young adults, some being as young as twelve years of age, and most common among young people while partying at "raves." In fact, law enforcement estimates as many as 90 percent of youth attending raves are using ecstasy.

SOURCE: Most Ecstasy is smuggled into the United States after manufacture in Europe, mainly the Netherlands and Belgium. Illegal clandestine laboratories in the United States also produce Ecstasy. Ecstasy sales occur surreptitiously in legitimate nightclubs and bars, at underground nightclubs sometimes referred to as "acid houses," and at desert and warehouse parties called "raves."

STREET NAMES: XTC, go, X, Adam, hug drug, E, ecstasy, clarity, essence, doctor, ills, symbol on tablet.

• *Phencyclidine (PCP)*

DESCRIPTION: Phencyclidine is a drug originally used by veterinarians as an anesthetic but diverted to the illegal market; no longer manufactured legally.

EFFECTS: Phencyclidine, one of the most dangerous drugs of abuse, is a hallucinogen that can cause numbness, slurred speech, impaired coordination, rapid and involuntary eye movements, auditory hallucinations, image distortion, mood disorders, and amnesia. Some users develop psychoses indistinguishable from schizophrenia.

APPEARANCE: Phencyclidine is a white crystalline powder in its pure form. On the street, most phencyclidine is tan to brown because of contamination and feature a consistency varying from powder to a gummy mass. Phencyclidine also appears in the form of tablets, capsules, and liquid.

METHOD OF INGESTION: Inhaled (snorted), smoked, injected, or swallowed. Smoking is the preferred method of ingestion and is accomplished by dipping a commercial dark brown cigarette (brown paper) into PCP contained in liquid, usually ether. The cigarette is then dried and smoked.

PRINCIPAL USERS: Varies, although it is popular within the black community in some cities.

SOURCE: Phencyclidine, manufactured in illegal clandestine laboratories, is primarily a product of metropolitan Los Angeles.

STREET NAMES: Angel dust, ace, animal tranquilizer, crystal, dead on arrival, DOA, dust, elephant, formaldehyde, illy, hog, juice, supergrass, tac, tic, trank, wack, water, wet, PCP, killer weed or joints, embalming fluid, rocket or jet fuel, wack, ozone. PCP cigarettes are called sherm-sticks, sherms, wet-daddy, and wet-sticks.

STEROIDS

Participants in sports and related physical competitions commonly use steroids to increase physical strength. There are over 100 types of legally manufactured anabolic-androgenic steroids, each of which requires a prescription, but diversion to the illegal market is common. In addition to diverting legal steroids to the illegal market, they are also smuggled into the United States from Mexico and Europe, with Russian, Romanian, and Greek nationals being significant traffickers. Illegal clandestine laboratories are also a source of steroids. Commonly used steroids include Anadrol, Oxandrin, Dianobol, Winstrol, Durabolin, Depo-Testosterone, and Equipoise. Gyms, competitions, and mail order are common sources for illegal steroids. Method of ingestion is oral, injection, or applied to the skin in the form of gels or creams (Drug Enforcement Administration, 2003).

Steroids are not the subject of strong law enforcement effort, and therefore those who illegally manufacture and/or sell steroids suffer far less risk of arrest and prosecution than those who deal in other types of illicit drugs.

• *Steroids–A Class of Drug*

DESCRIPTION: Anabolic-androgenic steroids are synthetic substances related to male sex hormones (androgens) that stimulate muscle tissue and bone growth.

EFFECTS: Use can result in acne, breast development in men (breast reduction in females), shrinking of the testicles, enlarged prostate gland, irritability and aggression, liver cancer, heart attacks, and high cholesterol. Withdrawal includes mood swings, fatigue, restlessness, loss of appetite, insomnia, reduced sex drive, and depression that can lead to suicide. Depression can persist for a year or more after use if not properly treated.

APPEARANCE: Tablets, pills, gels and creams, and ampoules.

METHOD OF INGESTION: Oral, injection, or applied to the skin in the form of a gel or cream.

PRINCIPAL USERS: Young people or athletes who desire to increase their strength, such as sports players, commonly resort to steroids with use being more prevalent among males than females.

SOURCE: Commonly diverted to the illegal market from legitimate pharmacies. Steroids also arrive illegally from Mexico and European countries. Gyms, sports competitions, and mail order are common sources for the illegal purchase of these drugs.

STREET NAMES: Test, testo, decca, winstrol, juice, stack, and cycle.

CANNABIS

• *Marijuana*

DESCRIPTION: Marijuana is a drug obtained from the flowering tops and leaves of the cannabis (hemp) plant Cannabis sativa L. The active chemical in marijuana is delta-9-tetrahydrocannabinol (THC). THC levels have increased two to threefold since the 1960s. Law enforcement frequently encounters this popular drug because it is the most frequently used drug.

EFFECTS: Causes euphoria and relaxation. Marijuana use results in symptoms such as respiratory infections, increased heart rate, anxiety, panic attacks, tolerance, physical dependence, diminished memory, and impaired learning skills.

APPEARANCE: Marijuana, often ground like tobacco, has the appearance of dried leaves and is gray, brown, or green in color. The leaves on a plant are odd in number and have serrated edges. Sinsemilla (Spanish word meaning no seeds) is a popular form of marijuana whereby a female plant is cultivated prior to fertilization resulting in increased resin and THC levels.

METHOD OF INGESTION: Usually smoked as a cigarette or in a pipe or bong, and less frequently eaten.

PRINCIPAL USERS: A wide age range of people use marijuana and, in fact, no less than one-third of Americans report having used marijuana.

SOURCE: Marijuana, imported illegally into the United States from Mexico, Canada, and to a lesser extent Southeast Asia, is also cultivated illegally in the United States.

STREET NAMES: Weed, grass, pot, 420, chronic, blunt, ganja, sins, Jamaican gold, reefer, joint, bud, Mary Jane, dope, indo, and hydro.

• *Hashish*

DESCRIPTION: The concentrated resin produced by the Cannabis sativa L plant, which is on average 8-10 times more potent than cannabis. Hashish has not gained popularity in the United States due to marijuana's popularity, and a general unfamiliarity with the drug. Furthermore, domestic production has not proved economical to growers because of the labor-intensive process of extracting the resin.

EFFECTS: Causes euphoria and exaggerated sensations. The same effects as marijuana, although many users, because of a quicker and more intensive high, prefer it. Because of intensity, some individuals may experience hallucinations.

APPEARANCE: In the form of balls, cakes, and cookie-like sheets. Solid and chunky and ranges in color shades of light to dark brown, to almost black. Some forms have a yellowish tint.

METHOD OF INGESTION: Smoked in a pipe or water pipe but sometimes it is chewed or drunk in the form of a beverage.

SOURCE: Imported illegally, or grown illegally in the United States. Most imported hashish arrives from the Middle East, North Africa, Pakistan, and Afghanistan.

STREET NAMES: Shish, kif, charas, and nup. Names can also describe shape, color, and trademark symbols stamped onto the hashish.

• *Hash Oil*

DESCRIPTION: Hash oil is extracted from marijuana using solvents such as acetone or alcohol. After soaking for several hours, the plant material is removed and the solvent evaporated, thus leaving a thick oily substance. The substance smells strongly of hashish or marijuana.

EFFECTS: Euphoria and exaggerated sensations. Same effects as marijuana, although it is preferred by many users because of a quicker more intensive high. Because of intensity, some individuals may experience hallucinations.

APPEARANCE: Hash oil, a liquid, is amber to dark brown in color with a strong marijuana smell.

METHOD OF INGESTION: Applying a drop or two to a cigarette produces a result approximately equal to smoking a single marijuana cigarette.

SOURCE: Imported illegally, or grown illegally in the United States. Most imported hashish arrives from the Middle East, North Africa, Pakistan, and Afghanistan.

STREET NAMES: Oil, liquid hash, marijuana oil, cannabis oil, weed oil, and shish oil.

Chapter 4

KNOCK-AND-TALK INVESTIGATIONS (CONSENSUAL SEARCHES)

INTRODUCTION

The thought of going to a suspect's residence and overtly asking for their drugs and/or drug paraphernalia is sometimes difficult for officers to envision. Furthermore, many police officers, judges, prosecutors, and civilians find it difficult to believe that a criminal suspect would cooperate with the police under such circumstances. With practice, however, the art of conducting *consensual searches* can be productive and rewarding.

This chapter discusses the application of *knock-and-talks* at a residence relative to illicit drugs and drug paraphernalia, although the term knock-and-talk has been associated with officer contacts with individuals in various other settings and relative to various other types of criminal activity. Hence, the knock-and-talk application discussed in this book pertains to drug interdiction, even though the method is applicable for the investigation of almost any type of crime.

The knock-and-talk technique is a valuable tool for police officers in large and small communities. Although the per-capita incidence of illicit drug use is greater in densely populated areas, it is also prevalent in less populated areas. Furthermore, some of the people who deal in illicit drugs have moved to less populated areas, believing that the law enforcement threat is lower.

Accepting that most police departments in the United States are small, accepting that the incidence of illicit drug use exists even in our small and often-rural communities, all police officers find themselves challenged by the problem of illicit drugs. Police officers employed by small departments, where the number of officers and budgets are limited, will find the knock-and-talk technique a valuable tool, knock-and-talk being a method that is quick, easy, requires limited personnel, and is often effective.

WHAT IS A KNOCK-AND-TALK?

The term *knock-and-talk* refers to an investigative method whereby a police officer contacts an individual suspected of being involved in illegal activity, and requests permission to talk with that person. A knock-and-talk, properly done, can be one of the most effective street-level drug interdiction techniques utilized.

If it is reasonable to suspect that an individual is involved in illegal activity, the officer can ask for consent to speak with the person and to search their person and/or property. Be aware, however, that some jurisdictions are an exception–some jurisdictions do not permit this. Because of recent issues surrounding the alleged practice of so-called "racial profiling," some agencies such as the New Jersey State Police cannot conduct consensual searches unless there is *reasonable suspicion* of a crime. In other words, employing the knock-and-talk technique must be more than simply a so-called fishing expedition. Hence, before attempting any type of consensual search, whether it pertains to a person, vehicle, or residence, it must first be determined if it is legal in one's jurisdiction. It is unfortunate that some jurisdictions have prohibited use of this effective and valuable investigative technique because of a few officers who have abused the practice. Hence, it is important for police officers to remember that this practice, if abused, can be proscribed, thus depriving all officers its use.

WHEN SHOULD A KNOCK-AND-TALK BE CONDUCTED?

Except in jurisdictions that prohibit it, an officer may conduct a knock-and-talk whenever he or she believes it to be appropriate, with the decision governed by the objectives of the law enforcement agency or individual officer, with knock-and-talks best utilized in cases not otherwise subject to traditional investigative methods. For example, in instances where an officer receives a citizen complaint suggesting that drug sales are occurring at a certain motel room, apartment, or private dwelling, experience suggests that the information must be acted on quickly because drug suspects tend to be transient and are often evicted or move away before the complaint can be investigated. If the officer conducts a short-term surveillance and observes no suspicious activity, a knock-and-talk may be an excellent means under the circumstances to resolve the complaint. A knock-and-talk is useful under such circumstances because of the difficulty of remaining discrete when doing surveillance in an apartment and motel environment. If a reasonably long-term surveillance is necessary, the manager of the motel or apartment may permit the use of a vacant room from which to make long-term observations. Making such a request assumes, of course, there is no indication that the manager is an associate of the suspect.

The apartment or motel manager who is not in collusion with the suspect may provide valuable information. Useful information includes if the suspect still resides on site, his or her daily routine, the existence of roommates, the existence of associates, and what the suspect drives. The rental application may reflect valuable information including the names, addresses, and telephone numbers of references.

The knock-and-talk investigative method is a good option when:

- Suspect activity occurs at a location that makes physical surveillance difficult.
- The location and/or circumstances are too dangerous to consider use of undercover officers or informants.
- When traditional methods of investigation have been tried but failed.
- The suspect may not be at the location long enough to apply traditional investigative methods.
- Suspicion of illicit drug activity, or drug complaints, can be investigated via the knock-and-talk before the probable cause necessary for a search warrant exists. In fact, the knock-and-talk may result in the probable cause required for a search warrant.

Relative to physical surveillance, surveillance of the suspect location should precede the knock-and-talk when possible. Surveillance will often disclose subject routine and therefore the most appropriate time to conduct a knock-and-talk, and surveillance may result in other information with which the knock-and-talk officer should be aware. If a reasonably long-term surveillance is not an option, a short-term surveillance is a better alternative to no surveillance. Surveillance offers several benefits ranging from public relations to officer safety. At the very least, a cursory drive-by examination of the suspect premises should precede the knock-and-talk

Public relations is very important to law enforcement and if surveillance discloses no evidence of illicit drug activity, so advising the complainant will leave them satisfied that their complaint was at least taken seriously, that they were not trivialized. Officer safety is also important and surveillance will often provide valuable safety related information such as what kind of a situation the officer can anticipate. There are situations that present danger sufficient to preclude attempting a knock-and-talk.

WHO SHOULD CONDUCT KNOCK-AND-TALKS?

Plainclothes and uniformed officers can conduct knock-and-talks. Many large law enforcement agencies have entire squads devoted to conducting knock-and-talks, while other agencies have officers among undercover squads who conduct knock-and-talks. However, anyone whether plain-clothes or uniform can conduct a knock-and-talk, with effectiveness being the result of adhering to certain procedural steps. Naturally, when doing a knock-and-talk it is important to honor *search and seizure* laws, and all officers must understand them well; most do!

THE KNOCK-AND-TALK MINDSET

Perhaps the most important consideration when preparing for, and conducting, a knock-and-talk is mindset; a positive outlook is important. Officers must overcome the natural fear of rejection, rejection identified as one of the most common fears regardless of occupation. A suspect may deny access to a residence, and fearing that is natural. Similarly, a suspect who allows the officer to enter the home may refuse a request for permission to search, but that does not always mean the knock-and-talk attempt failed. At the very least, the fact that the police are at the suspect's residence requesting to speak with him or her is sometimes enough to cause the drug dealer to move, stop selling, or take precautions that disrupt their drug distribution. The mindset one should have is that a suspect will most likely allow entry into his or her home as long as the initial contact is positive and polite in nature.

A word of caution is in order! Knock-and-talks can be dangerous because of the limited ability to control the occupants. Thus, it is important that officers involved in the knock-and-talk be alert to their surroundings even though exhibiting a relaxed demeanor. If the suspect is guilty not only of the suspected offense, but perhaps other offenses or having outstanding warrants, he or she may perceive the officer as threatening his or her continued freedom and become desperate. Consider, for example, the suspect with two prior felony convictions who is operating in a state with a "three-strike" law. If he or she has incriminating evidence on site or on his or her person, he or she may see the knock-and-talk officer as being all that stands between him or her and a lifetime of incarceration. He or she may become very desperate.

PREPARING FOR THE KNOCK-AND-TALK

Introduction

A worthwhile truism says, "People do not plan to fail, they just fail to plan." That axiom is pertinent relative to preparing for a knock-and-talk investigation. Without proper planning, the likelihood of success diminishes, perhaps significantly. As for officer safety, proper planning or lack thereof can determine if an officer will be injured or killed while conducting a knock-and-talk investigation.

Adequate Human Resources

An important consideration when determining how many officers should participate in a knock-and-talk is what the court will consider as being coercive or intimidating in the eyes of the subject or subjects. The court will determine whether the apparent showing of force was excessive and likely to intimidate the suspect. The circumstances of the knock-and-talk must not leave the court feeling there was a showing of force sufficient to create a feeling of duress on the part of the suspect, a showing of force that likely left the suspects believing they did not have the option of refusing the officer's request to search their person or premises.

Because of the danger involved, a lone officer should never attempt a knock-and-talk. Two officers can efficiently conduct most knock-and-talks and, in fact, the knock-and-talk technique anticipates two officers. If intelligence reveals that there are numerous subjects at the property, or that violence is a likely response, assigning three officers is acceptable. If because of on-site danger more than three officers are determined to be necessary, perhaps a knock-and-talk is not appropriate under the circumstances. Assigning more than three officers to a knock-and-talk may give the appearance of using an overwhelming show of force to cause duress; a strategy calculated to obtain consent the subject would otherwise refuse. If a court finds evidence of duress, it will probably suppress all evidence obtained. Furthermore, any evidence subsequently acquired will also be subject to suppression under the "fruit of poisonous tree doctrine" if rooted in the improperly conducted knock-and-talk.

Scouting the Location (Preliminary Survey)

Prior to conducting a knock-and-talk, the officer should conduct surveillance or at least do a drive-by of the subject's location. This will often provide the officer with information that can be followed-up on such as vehicle license plate numbers. Officers have experienced a great deal of success by just contacting locations of drug complaints with nothing more than the complaint and a little follow-up information. They are, however, at a disadvantage because of limited information about the occupants or events at the location.

When doing a drive-by of a suspected drug location, it is beneficial to utilize a mini voice recorder to eliminate having to attempt memorizing license plate numbers, or trying to write while driving. A mini recorder is especially useful when documenting vehicle descriptions and license plate numbers of vehicles at the subject's location. Conducting a drive-by at different times is often beneficial because if activity reveals a pattern, that knowledge eases the task of determining the best time to conduct a knock-and-talk.

Determine if the Suspect Has a Criminal History

When the officer makes contact with a suspect at his or her place of residence, the officer is usually contacting the suspect for a specific reason, such as having received a drug complaint. What the suspect usually does not know, however, is why the officer has appeared at the door, and what the officer may ask.

It is important to know as much as possible about the subject before making contact. It has happened where a suspect had just committed an armed robbery of a convenience store, and an unsuspecting officer knocked on his apartment door to talk about drug activity. Not all dangerous situations are subject to discovery and avoidance, but by conducting a records check on all known people at the subject's location, the officer has a better chance of not going into a situation entirely unaware. Checking criminal history usually enables the officer to anticipate the type of people that will be encountered, and predict any violence potential.

Technical Equipment

Other than the weapons in the officer's possession, the most important piece of equipment for a knock-and-talk is a mini tape or digital voice recorder. Most prosecuting agencies hesitate to file consensual encounter cases where a voice recording is not available because of the difficulty convincing a jury that an encounter was in fact consensual; they cannot hear the conversation that took place between the officer and suspect. In addition to words, such things as a person's tone of voice and voice fluctuation can indicate if the officer is engaged in coercion or otherwise threatening conduct to obtain the subject's consent.

A digital voice recorder is an excellent choice for recording a knock-and-talk because they are compact and easily carried in a shirt pocket, or in the front pocket of a concealable bullet resistant vest. Digital recorders offer better clarity than a tape recorder, and it is easy to transfer the digital recording to a computer or compact disk for permanent storage. Most units will record at least five hours, which is usually more than adequate for a knock-and-talk investigation. Recorders feature a built in microphone, but attaching an external microphone to the recorder can sometimes enhance voice quality. It is important to test the equipment prior to executing a knock-and-talk.

The laws of most states permit surreptitious use of voice recorders if at least one party to the conversation is aware of the recording, and that party may be the officer or an officer's informant. Before using a voice recorder, however, it is important to check one's own state and local laws to ensure that surreptitious recording is legal. If surreptitious recording is not legal in one's jurisdiction without first obtaining a warrant, proceeding without a warrant is a serious violation.

When doing a knock-and-talk, it is important that police radios, voice recorders, and any other electronic equipment be equipped with new or freshly charged batteries. Actually, it is advisable to replace or recharge batteries daily unless it can be determined with reliable accuracy how long the batteries will last. Daily replacement or recharging of batteries may seem excessive, but the application is too important to justify relying on chance. Battery failure can result in losing a case if the lack of a recording causes the prosecutor to refuse the case, or lack of a recording leaves a jury unconvinced that the search was consensual. If it is the agencies policy to record all knock-and-talks, failure to produce a voice recording that proves consent may leave doubt in the mind of jurors.

Personal Protective Equipment (PPE)

Many times, when doing a knock-and-talk, the officer is entering an unknown environment. If the officer is at the location with the intent to discover if drug crimes are being committed, the possibility of drugs, drug paraphernalia, and drug manufacturing chemicals being on the premises is high.

Drug chemicals present a health risk, and also presenting a health risk is the fact that disease and often an unsanitary lifestyle accompany illicit drug use. Because of the diseases, filth, and drug-related chemicals that an officer will frequently encounter, it is important to carry at least one pair of latex or nitrol gloves. In addition to the gloves, it is advisable to carry a folded gallon sized plastic bag for evidence collection, evidence discovered during the search. It is not advisable that gloves be displayed or used in the initial search, as suspects will often become concerned that an extensive search will be conducted and withdraw consent. It is important that the suspect be at ease and feel no intimidation. Latex gloves produced prior to a search will very likely cause the suspect to refuse consent.

Notifying Other Law Enforcement Agencies

When a drug investigation takes officers into another jurisdiction and surveillance and perhaps a knock-and-talk is anticipated, it is important to contact the appropriate person in the drug unit of that jurisdiction and let him or her know what is occurring and why. It would be unfortunate to spend hours investigating a location only to have officers in that jurisdiction unexpectedly show up to execute their own knock-and-talk or search warrant. Many large metropolitan areas have a system whereby officers at all levels, from patrol to multi-jurisdictional task forces, can call and ascertain the status of a location. This is beneficial when various agencies may have occasion to investigate a single location.

There are also other reasons to notify local authorities when a drug investigation takes one into another jurisdiction. When surveillance will occur, having provided proper notice can prevent a patrol car arriving to investigate a suspicious vehicle complaint–the untimely arrival of a marked patrol car can compromise surveillance. Having provided proper notification will also facilitate having a marked patrol unit stand-by in close proximity to a knock-and-talk location for quick response should a situation become volatile and require backup, or to assist if a suspect must be secured following arrest or detention.

Coordinate with the Local Prosecutor

Depending on the locality, it is often mutually beneficial to contact the prosecutors who will receive knock-and-talk cases. The meeting can provide the officer with the necessary requirements for submitting cases for prosecution, and some prosecutors, if they have not had experience with consent cases, will need indoctrination; explain to them what constitutes consent. A law degree does not mean the attorney knows more about *search and seizure*, and *consensual encounters*, than the officer who has had specialized legal training relative to those issues and is involved with them on a daily basis.

Canine Use

Generally, a drug detection dog can be used anywhere that an officer has a legal basis to be. A dog utilizes its incredibly keen sense of smell to locate drugs, just as an officer can use his or her sense of smell to locate and identify drugs, such as fresh or burnt marijuana. Nevertheless, before attempting to use a drug detection dog during a knock-and-talk, it is important to obtain consent from the suspect. Although a drug detection dog can contribute to a knock-and-talk, the dog is often unnecessary during the initial stages, and besides, the dog's mere presence during the initial stages may cause a suspect to refuse a consensual search. Hence, it is best that the dog not be present during the initial contact with the suspect.

CONDUCTING THE KNOCK-AND-TALK

Uniformed or Plainclothes?

When doing a knock-and-talk, appropriate clothing is important. It is best to wear clothing that is casual, such as a polo style shirt and jeans or casual slacks, and the clothing should bear some type of insignia identifying one as a police officer. A large southwestern United States police agency that utilizes knock-and-talks as an important element in their drug suppression efforts has a policy on what is worn and grooming standards for the officers who conduct knock-and-talk investigations. The officers wear a blue polo style shirt that has the name of the agency, the unit, and the officer's name embroidered on the front. Because of the danger of chemical contamination when investigating illicit drug activity, the department's policy recommends jeans over shorts. Full-length jeans present the desired professional appearance, but in the event of contamination, the shorts underneath permit their prompt removal. The service weapon, handcuffs, and chemical defense spray are concealed but readily accessible.

If casual clothing is not an option, a uniform is acceptable. When doing a knock-and-talk while in uniform, however, the officer must do whatever he or she can to avoid giving the appearance of intimidating the suspect. There must be actual consent, not consent given because the suspect believes refusal is not an option. Remember, the uniform itself is intimidating to some people, especially those with a guilty conscience. A defense attorney will use whatever means necessary to find a consensual search invalid, and will generally focus on whether the consent to search was actually voluntary. Therefore, while a uniformed officer can conduct a knock-and-talk, and do so very effectively, the uniform is an issue that may require explanation. This should not discourage the uniformed officer from conducting a knock-and-talk search, but the officer must proceed with an understanding of the drawback the uniform represents.

In the final analysis, uniformed officers can effectively perform knock-and-talks, but it is important to ensure that the suspect is not intimidated and therefore provides consent freely, not consent given because of a feeling of duress, a feeling that refusing is not an option.

Often, in conspiracy investigations, officers execute multiple search warrants at a series of locations simultaneously, but there are often locations suspected of being involved for which sufficient probable cause for search warrants do not exist. Many times those locations are in close proximity to the search warrant locations, and the timing of the execution of the warrants is an excellent time for officers to conduct knock-and-talks at those locations. Often, when doing knock-and-talks under these circumstances, the attire will be raid clothing and it is not possible to change to casual clothing. In spite of that, a knock-and-talk remains a good option. In some cases, when it is foreseen that there are locations that merit knock-and-talks, officers who specialize in knock-and-talks can be contacted in advance and assigned to do knock-and-talks at the various locations, with that activity to occur simultaneous with the search warrant raids.

Preparing for the Contact

Before attempting a knock-and-talk, it is advisable to do a drive-by to see what vehicles may be at the suspect's location, and if one has done the necessary research the drive-by will facilitate determining if the primary suspect(s) are likely at home. If it is determined that the time is appropriate to conduct a knock-and-talk, the officer should notify the dispatcher of the location where they (officer and partner) will be, and what type of activity they are involved with. Example: "V316 . . . I'll be at 410 E. Apple Street on a drug complaint follow-up." If it is possible that the suspects have police scanners, telephoning the dispatcher with the information is advisable.

When using a voice recorder, tape or digital, a leader statement will ensure that the recording accurately identifies the officers, date, time, and location of the knock-and-talk. Example: "This is Detective Hawkins, serial number 546, with the Metropolis Police Department's Drug Enforcement Bureau. Today's date is December 10, 2004, and the time is 1433 hours. Detective Thomas, serial number 371, and myself are going to 410 E. Apple Street reference a drug complaint." The voice recorder should be left running until completion of the investigation, or until the residence is secured pending the obtaining of a search warrant. It is often beneficial to leave the recorder running even after the residence is secure, although if the officers consult with their supervisor or other detectives about administrative issues relative to the search warrant, little evidence is to be expected. If the recorder is left running, leave it with an officer close to the suspects if leaving the vicinity is necessary. This will be beneficial should the suspects make incriminating statements.

Approaching the Location

When approaching the location of a knock-and-talk, it is important to be alert to activity occurring in the area with special attention given to the home of the suspect. Being alert to door, window, or curtain movement can indicate whether occupants are in the residence and if they are aware of one's presence. Important–be sure contact is made at the correct location. An officer once conducted a knock-and-talk, and after a search of the entire home, discovered it was the complainant's home. There were two homes on the property and both featured the same address except the number of the rear home included a "1/2" indicating a rear property.

When approaching the site of a knock-and-talk, officers should be alert for "friendlies" in the neighborhood, those who are sympathetic to the suspects. Friendlies can include neighbors, family members living nearby, or even lookouts for the drug dealers.

When doing knock-and-talk investigations, always practice good officer safety. Never become so focused on the suspect's location that any peripheral threats may escape notice, threats in the neighborhood that may be unrelated to the suspect.

At the Door

Upon reaching the suspect's door, pause briefly before knocking to look and listen, collect one's thoughts, ensure that the other officer is in position and prepared, and protected from threats that may originate from the door or windows. While pausing, listen closely to any sounds inside the residence. It is important to identify sounds because once contact is initiated by knocking or ringing the bell, any change in sounds will indicate whether anyone is home. Occupants will sometimes extinguish all sounds in an effort to make it appear no one is home, that done immediately upon realizing someone is at the door. Commonly, too, if housedogs begin barking in response to the knock or doorbell, the occupant will hush them with the foolish belief that if all is quiet, it will appear no one is home, although the act of hushing the dogs leaves it obvious that someone is home but avoiding contact.

The Contact

If the suspect opens the door, that is the sign of a good beginning, a sign suggesting that success of the knock-and-talk may be forthcoming. Frequently, however, the door remains closed with the occupant speaking through the door requesting to know who is calling and what is wanted. When that occurs, identify one's self as a police officer and identify the agency one works for, and display a badge and commission card at the door's security peeper. The officer should explain that he or she is following up on complaints received relative to the location, and request to speak with the occupant to resolve the issue. Many times this will satisfy the occupant and he or she will open the door. Few persons involved in drug activity have not had problems with neighbors, and they may think this involves such petty matters as barking dogs, weeds, or the junk that has accumulated in their yard.

Once the door is open and conversation occurs face-to-face, the officers should display their badges and commission cards and ask for permission to enter to discuss the complaint. Officers should be cordial and polite to the suspect as that is not the time to be stern, short, insensitive, or authoritative. If weather conditions are appropriate, use the weather as an excuse to enter the residence, weather such as heat, rain, wind, or cold. Another good reason to talk in the home, explained as a benefit for the suspect, is that neighbors do not need to see or overhear the conversation. The suspect must freely consent to the officer's entry. The suspect who has something to hide will often be hesitant at this point and inquire about the complaint. When asked about the complaint, the officer should disclose the official reason for the visit while using phrases such as, "would it be all right to come in and talk to you?"

Whether or not a suspect permits entry into the home, the officer should request consent to search. On one occasion, although a suspect denied consent to search, he admitted to possessing a marijuana pipe located in his bedroom. When asked to surrender the pipe, the suspect refused stating, "What do you think I am, stupid?" Nevertheless, because the suspect admitted to having the pipe, the officers succeeded in obtaining a search warrant for the pipe, and associated drugs. The probable cause supporting issuance of the search warrant was the suspect having admitted to possession of the pipe. The search revealed drugs for sale including ecstasy, mushrooms, marijuana, methamphetamine, and a large quantity of drug paraphernalia.

Obtaining Consent to Search

After the officer determines a person's standing at the location, specifically that he or she is legally a resident and therefore authorized to grant consent to search, the officer must obtain permission to search. Some states honor a third-party grant to search if the police had reason to believe the person had authority, even if in fact he or she did not. Officers should check the laws in their jurisdiction pertaining to third-party consents.

In order for a search to be legally valid, consent must be clear, specific, and unmistakable. Consent must also be voluntary and provided in the absence of duress. In other words, the suspect must not provide consent because the officer's authority and demeanor leaves him or her afraid to refuse, or incorrectly believing refusal is not an option. For example, considering a parallel situation, when a police officer stops a motorist for a traffic violation, he or she commonly says, "Good evening, may I see your driver's license?" In that circumstance, the officer is not making a request in hopes that the motorist will comply, but is demanding to see the license and will take action if the person refuses–the officer is simply being diplomatic. In that circumstance, the motorist knows he or she has no choice, that refusal to produce the license is not an option. A situation of this nature is not acceptable when requesting permission to conduct a search during a knock-and-talk. The suspect must understand that refusal is an option even though it is not necessary to advise him or her of that right overtly!

Miranda warnings are not required prior to requesting consent to search, because the suspect is not in custody or otherwise deprived of his or her freedom. In fact, the officer may request permission to search even after a person has asserted Fifth Amendment rights to remain silent, and/or requested an attorney. Moreover, contrary to many opinions, a defendant may give valid consent to search while in custody. Once taken into custody, however, the officer should read the Miranda warning, the Miranda warning advising the suspect of his or her legal rights.

This may seem to contradict earlier discussion, but it is not required that the officer explicitly advise a suspect that he or she has the right to refuse a request to enter the premises or to conduct a search. Even so, unambiguously advising the suspect of the right to refuse, and documenting that notification using a voice recorder, the case is stronger because the recording will disprove any subsequent allegations by the defense that consent was not voluntary, that consent was the result of not knowing refusal was an option.

Capacity is important. The condition of the person granting consent is important and will influence whether a court will accept the consent as having been valid. In other words, what was the person's capacity to provide consent? Circumstances that may invalidate consent, based on lack of capacity, is the age of the consenter (a juvenile), whether the consenter was intoxicated or under the influence of drugs at the time consent was given, or suffering an adverse mental condition such as diminished intelligence or diagnosable mental illness.

Equally important, as it pertains to voluntary consent is the person's conduct. That is important because certain types of conduct tend to demonstrate that consent is voluntary. For example, if the suspect assists in the search, that behavior suggests a voluntary state of mind. Similarly, statements a suspect makes can substantiate voluntary consent. Conversely, the court will likely rule that consent was not voluntary if the suspect impedes the officer's search. Indications that consent was not voluntary, or that consent was at some point withdrawn, include blocking access to certain areas of the residence, or in the case of a vehicle search, throwing one's keys away from the vehicle.

Voice recorders are useful for documenting a suspect's verbal consent to enter the premises, and to conduct a search. If consent is non-verbal, such as may be the case with a suspect who is hearing impaired and cannot speak, obtain written consent when possible. Although consent may not be verbal or written, a suspect can imply consent by gestures. Silence, such as a suspect ignoring an officer's request to enter or to search does not constitute consent because every person has the right to remain silent.

Inside the Residence

When the officer receives permission to enter the residence, and there are others in the residence, it is best that the officer speak with suspects separately, and confirm that each person spoken with lives at the residence. If a person has no standing, or in other words is not the legal resident, his or her consent to enter is not valid. Moreover, anyone residing at the residence may grant consent to search the common areas and his or her own bedroom (private spaces), but he or she cannot grant consent to search the bedroom of a roommate–only the roommate has standing to consent to a search of his or her bedroom.

If an occupant of the residence grants consent to search and in a common area such as the living room, the officer observes a suitcase belonging to a roommate, the officer may open it to examine the contents. If the owner of the suitcase is present and objects to the opening of the suitcase, the officer may not open it. If the owner of the suitcase is not home and therefore unable to grant or deny consent to examine the contents of the suitcase, the officer may open it. The occupant who granted consent to search, however, may instruct the officer not to open the suitcase even though it does not belong to him or her, but rather, the roommate.

People often deny living at the location even though previous surveillance and other indicators suggest they do. Indicators suggesting place of residence include the suspect's mailing address, utilities in his or her name, DMV records (driver's license and vehicle registration), etc. Standing can also be determined by questioning the individual about personal property in the home–what belongs to them, and how long they have resided at the location.

If there are children present, the officer should request that they go elsewhere in the residence so as not to embarrass the suspect. If it has been determined that children reside at the location that a knock-and-talk will be conducted, it is best to knock early in the day, preferably when the children are at school, or early enough in the afternoon to avoid the children being in bed. Children in bed is a common reason for suspects refusing consent to search their residence.

If the suspect asks the officer to sit down, the officer should strongly consider accepting the suspect's hospitality, provided it is safe to do so. The more rapport that can be established with a suspect, the greater the likelihood that consent to search will be granted. A relaxed attitude will generally put the suspect at ease, but never compromise officer safety to accomplish that.

The officers conducting the knock-and-talk should be alert for weapons that may be visible, be cognizant of where their own weapons are, and stand with their weapons away from the suspect. Officers should maintain a safe distance from the suspect and ask if there are others at the residence. If additional subjects are on site, it is advisable that they remain unaware of the officer's presence to avoid their destroying or hiding evidence. Chances are others will know the officers are in the residence, will attempt to leave or hide their drugs or contraband, with this situation being difficult to avoid. It can also be dangerous if numerous subjects in the residence are free to move about as they please, but this cannot be avoided if consent to search is to be requested. Officers can request that suspects sit in designated areas, but too much control will destroy a voluntary or consensual contact. If there are distractions such as a stereo or television, cordially request that the volume be turned down. If there are dogs at the residence, the officer should request that they be placed into the backyard–specifying where to put them is important because, otherwise the suspect will most likely put the dogs in the room containing the drugs or drug paraphernalia.

Inform the suspect of the nature of the complaint, explaining that information received suggests that drug sales are occurring at the residence, and that the contact is in reference to that complaint. Explain to the suspect that the agency receives numerous drug complaints each year, and that enforcement emphasizes drug dealers and manufacturers. The officer should explain that the residence was under surveillance, if that is true, and explain that the activity observed is or is not consistent with drug sales. If physical surveillance determined a high volume of traffic to and from the residence, ask the suspect to explain the nature of it. The officer should also ask the suspect if he or she is selling drugs from the residence and if so, what types of drugs are sold and how long that has been occurring. Chances are the suspect will not admit to sales at this time. Ask the suspect if there is casual drug use occurring on the premises, or possibly a little partying on the weekends with perhaps just a little weed. At that point, anything can happen such as the suspect admitting to casual drug use, blaming their friends for using drugs, or denying the drug allegations altogether. When this line of questioning begins, expect one of three scenarios to occur.

• SCENARIO 1. The suspect admits to drug use. If the suspect admits to using illicit drugs, the officer should request to know the type of drugs used, and when the suspect last used drugs. When making this inquiry, downplay the suspect's drug use to put him or her at ease. For example, ask the suspect, "Are you using a little weed or what?" Ask the question in an unexcited noninterested tone. Often the suspect will admit to using a drug and if making such an admission, ask how they administer the drug into the body such as injection, smoking, or snorting. After they respond, ask them where the items of drug paraphernalia are. They most likely will tell the officer where the items are, and, if they do, probable cause exists. If they refuse to produce the items, and possession of drug paraphernalia is a crime in the jurisdiction where the knock-and-talk is occurring, obtain a search warrant for that and other items associated with the paraphernalia. On the other hand, if the suspect is willing, the officer can ask the suspect to show the item and ask if he or she can come along to retrieve it. After the item of drug paraphernalia is in the officer's possession, ask the suspect if he or she has any drugs left. This may seem blunt, but it is very effective in obtaining the drugs; the suspect may or may not provide the drugs. If the suspect denies possession of drugs, request permission to search his or her room. If the suspect refuses to give consent, it is up to the officer whether he or she believes a search warrant is necessary based on drug paraphernalia being a crime. If the suspect gives up his or her drugs, the officer should still ask permission to search for additional drugs and paraphernalia. If the suspect refuses to give consent, probable cause for a search warrant exists. Secure the premises pending obtaining a search warrant.

• SCENARIO 2. The suspect begins blaming drug-using friends for his or her problems. When that occurs, the officer should ask if the friends reside in the home, or just frequent the location, and ask the suspect if he or she has knowledge of any drugs or paraphernalia that friends have left at the location. Chances are the suspect will admit to nothing and is just looking for a way to get out of the situation. The suspect may also be attempting to establish an alibi for any drugs and/or drug paraphernalia the officer may find when conducting a search.

• SCENARIO 3. The suspect denies drug use. The officer should act somewhat relieved and tell the suspect that is great, and that resolving the complaint should be no problem. The officer can then ask for permission to search the house to confirm that there are no indications of drug use, to make the report complete. The officer should display an attitude of believing the suspect even if his or her behavior, along with other indicators in the residence appear to conflict. The officer can say something to the effect, "That is great Mr. Smith that there is no drug use going on, that makes things easier for me . . . can you show me around your house so I can tell my boss there doesn't appear to be any drug activity?"

Scope of Search

Consent can be very broad, or limited, depending on circumstances such as the temperament of the suspect, and the investigative style of the officer. For example, one officer may obtain general consent and begin searching everywhere and everything without obtaining additional consent as the focus of the search narrows. Conversely, another officer may request consent to do a limited search and then request consent to search specific locations as the search progresses. Circumstances such as the temperament of the suspect and investigative style of the officer will determine which method is most appropriate. Experience has shown, however, that it usually works best if the officer first requests permission to perform a general search such as by asking, "May I take a look around?" The officer can then expand the search by subsequently requesting permission to look in a specific drawer or cabinet, or some other area of the premises such as garage or storage room.

Whichever method the officer chooses, relative to circumstances, it is important to keep the search valid in terms of legalities, and as non-intrusive as possible. That is important to prevent the suspect withdrawing consent, or having a court fail to honor the consent. The officer who receives consent and then embarks on a broad and blind search, obtrusively opening drawers, cabinets, containers, etc., may find the scope of his or her search disapproved of by the court. Such a search increases the risk that a court will rule that the scope of the search exceeded what the suspect actually consented to. On the other hand, when a suspect has provided general consent, they will usually honor requests for permission to look in specific areas during the search, especially if the officer has established an appropriate rapport with them.

By taking the time to establish a rapport with the suspect, and getting them into the habit of saying "yes," and by obtaining many affirmative responses, the fact that they were agreeable and consented to the search will be more apparent should the case go to court. It is important to remember that consent may be revoked, limited or expanded at the whim of the suspect. For that reason, a reasonable rapport sustained by diplomacy is important. Furthermore, because it is the prerogative of the suspect to revoke, limit, or expand the scope of his or her consent, at any time, he or she must either be at the scene of the search or with an officer who can immediately relay information to the officer conducting the search.

To illustrate the importance of following consensual search guidelines, consider the recent case wherein a police officer obtained consent to search a suspect's property, but before the search was performed the suspect was booked into jail. Once in jail, the suspect was unable to revoke, limit, or expand his consent to search. To complicate matters, the officer did not search the suspect's premises until the following day, at which time the suspect was, as stated, in jail. The manner in which the situation evolved was not consistent with the original agreement between the officer and the suspect. Subsequently, the court ruled that the search was illegal and suppressed all evidence obtained during the search. In addition, under the "fruit of poisonous tree doctrine," all subsequent evidence, if traced to what was acquired or learned during the initial (illegal) search, if shown to be a fruit of that search, would be subject to suppression. Had the officer conducted the search immediately upon receiving consent and kept the suspect at the scene, or had the suspect been in constant contact with another officer who could have immediately relayed instructions to the searching officer relative to revoking, limiting, or expanding the search, the search would have been valid and the resulting evidence admissible in court.

The courts, when considering the scope of consent, will generally apply the standard of "objective reasonableness." When an officer receives unrestricted consent to search, whether it be to search a vehicle or premises, or both, causing damage to the property or otherwise employing unreasonable search tactics will usually result in the search ruled unreasonable. Within reasonable guidelines, an officer requesting unqualified consent to search a location for such things as weapons, drugs, or large sums of currency is justified in searching any area and opening anything that he or she reasonably believes may contain such items. Hence, when making a request to search, it is important to be reasonably specific as to the purpose of the search, and when consent to search features no limitations, the scope of the search may be broad even though it must remain reasonable.

The Search

Suspect Provides Consent to Search

When the suspect has provided consent to conduct a search, officers can affably request that he or she "show them around the house." During the tour of the premises, the officers must be alert for any drugs or contraband that is in *plain view*, and watch the suspect's hands, as he or she will conceal evidence, or wield the weapon should an assault occur. When discovering undisclosed contraband, be especially vigilant and watch the suspect closely, his or her response may be unpredictable. It is also important for one or both of the officers to continually converse with the suspect. This will cause the suspect to think more about the conversation and less about the search–it is difficult for the suspect to concentrate on the search and think about revoking consent while engaged in conversation and being bombarded with questions, even if the questions are unrelated to the search. Conversation also serves to enhance any rapport that may exist.

Talking, in other words "patter," has value, "patter" being a term used by magicians in reference to the entertaining storylines used during a performance. When performing magic, magicians talk (patter) constantly, and there is a reason for it that extends far beyond their desire to entertain the audience. When properly done, patter dulls the senses and serves as misdirection so that the audience mentally focuses on what the magician is saying while rendered somewhat oblivious to what he or she is actually doing. The value of patter lies in the fact that the human mind can concentrate fully on only one thing at a time and will tend to focus on that which represents the strongest stimuli. In the case of the magician, the talking (patter) captures the person's attention and concentration, thus greatly diminishing the ability to concentrate fully what he or she is doing; officers can use this phenomenon to great advantage, as mentioned above.

When finding an item of drugs or paraphernalia during the tour of the premises, the officer should pause and mention the item to the suspect, but when so doing minimize the apparent importance of the item. Minimizing its importance will reduce the likelihood of the suspect becoming alarmed at the officer's discovery and withdrawing consent. At the time of discovery, it is important for the officer to attempt to obtain a verbal statement from the suspect acknowledging ownership, and an explanation relative to the item's significance and purpose in the residence. If there is no danger that the suspect or others in the residence will remove or destroy the item, leaving it in place for later seizure is acceptable, leaving it in place pending completion of the tour. Leaving the item in place helps to keep the suspect pacified, as that act supports the effort to minimize the seriousness of the situation, thus minimizing the likelihood of consent withdrawal. If the discovery of drugs or paraphernalia results in withdrawal of consent, the officer has accomplished his or her mission, that is to say, probable cause sufficient for a search warrant exists based on the contraband found.

If no illicit drugs or paraphernalia are located in the public areas of the dwelling, chances are the search will end in the suspect's bedroom. That occurs because the bedroom is generally the room the suspect does not want a police officer scrutinizing–avoidance causes them to save the bedroom for last. Once in the bedroom, the officer should continue looking for anything illegal that might be in plain view and if nothing apparently exists, the officer should approach the most likely location that could contain drugs and/or paraphernalia. In most residences, that is the top right dresser drawer. The drawer will most likely contain legitimate belongings, or the suspect's drugs, money, scales, or paraphernalia in addition to normal belongings. Before taking the liberty of walking over and opening the dresser drawer, the officer should ask, "Is it all right if I look in a couple drawers?" If consent is given, the officer should quickly open the drawer and visually look at the contents. If nothing is observed the officer can ask, "Can I look through it real quick?" Depending on circumstances, the officer may feel that he or she has obtained adequate consent by the first request and not make subsequent requests for consent. Each officer must make that determination him- or herself depending on circumstances.

If nothing is located in the drawer, the officer should request permission to search additional items. Generally, however, with diplomacy the officer can obtain consent to search entire units such as rooms, dressers, and containers rather than requesting permission to search each specific item such as drawers or cabinets. If, as the search progresses, nothing of value is located, the officer should consider the merits of continuing to search.

When making an initial knock-and-talk contact, and during the search, the officer should watch the demeanor of the suspect. Reading people is as important as obtaining consent to search someone's vehicle and/or residence. Furthermore, when conducting a search, in some instances when entering a room containing contraband the suspect will fleetingly glance at the location of contraband concealment thus betraying their existence and location. In almost all cases when the subject agrees to provide a tour of the premises, he or she will avoid escorting the officer to the room containing contraband, and that avoidance is a clue that contraband is in fact on the premises, and its location.

Sometimes an officer can resolve a complaint just by speaking with the subject of the complaint, and not conducting a search of the premises or vehicle. Apply good judgment in those situations where the complainant's information about possible drug activity is inconsistent with what the officer observes and hears when making contact with the subject of the complaint. This is not to suggest that searches are never necessary if the officer's initial perception suggests innocence. Initial perceptions can be incorrect, and circumstances can change as the interview progresses, with change in demeanor also being possible as a subsequent search progresses. For example, is the suspect becoming increasingly nervous during conversation, or during a search? What types of statements is the subject making, and are statements consistent or laden with inconsistencies and contradictions? Is the suspect's demeanor one of consistent cooperation and candor, or during a search is demeanor becoming more guarded as the officer approaches certain rooms or areas within a room?

The familiar axiom, "trust your instincts," does not always apply. A drug officer in Arizona, who has conducted hundreds of knock-and-talk investigations, has had occasion to search homes and find contraband even though his initial impression of the subject suggested he was innocent and the victim of a false complaint. In one such instance, his search of a premises produced drugs, weapons, currency, and drug paraphernalia. On yet another occasion, while speaking with the subjects of a drug complaint received from a neighborhood resident, the officer concluded that the subjects were not drug dealers. Then, for reasons the officer will never understand, without having requested permission to search the premises, the subjects invited him to conduct a search, and he discovered contraband. In that instance, rather than decline the offer and leave, but in an effort to limit time spent on site, he went immediately to the suspect's bedroom and opened the top right dresser drawer finding a sizeable quantity of drugs, drug paraphernalia, a scale, and packaging material. Based on experience, he knew that location offered the greatest likelihood of finding a stash of drugs and related contraband. Hence, he went there first.

Officers should use discretion when deciding whether to request consent to do a search, but often a quick cursory search will rule out a suspect's involvement in drug activity, or confirm the validity of a complaint. Because knock-and-talk searches are cursory, officers will sometimes overlook drugs and paraphernalia, or other evidence of illegal activity. Logic and experience both suggest that will occur, but a successful average will result. In spite of its shortcomings, the knock-and-talk allows for a quick cursory search that is generally non-intrusive, and it enables the officer to conduct a search when the probable cause necessary for a search warrant is lacking. During a knock-and-talk, officers are looking for the obvious–drugs and drug-related items. If a cursory search of the premises produces no drugs or other contraband, that is the end of it, at least for the present. However, the discovery of drugs or other contraband will leave the officer proceeding accordingly such as securing the premises and obtaining a search warrant.

The following are options that an officer can apply depending on the circumstances of a search, and the preference of the officer doing the knock-and-talk.

Suspect Revokes Consent

If during a consensual search, the suspect tells the officer that he or she has decided that they do not want the search to continue, then the consent search is over. Nevertheless, if prior to the suspect withdrawing consent to search, the officer found drugs or drug paraphernalia sufficient to create the *probable cause* necessary to obtain a search warrant, the officer then has the option of securing the premises while a search warrant is obtained.

If under the circumstances, the officer believes obtaining a search warrant represents the best decision, he or she should advise the suspect that the search will cease as requested, but that it will resume upon issuance of a search warrant. A search warrant may not be productive, however, if the officer has reason to believe that a continued search will produce little more evidence, or that the suspect(s) are just users not dealers. Many officers choose to obtain a search warrant anytime they have obtained probable cause, and consent to search is subsequently revoked by the suspect, and that is not necessarily incorrect. Indeed, there is no right or wrong strategy when it comes to deciding whether a search warrant is justified; it depends on circumstances and the objectives of the officer.

When a suspect initially grants consent to search, but subsequently changes his or her mind and revokes consent, the change of mind can occur for a number of reasons, but generally they are afraid of what the officer will find if the search continues. Many times, after a suspect revokes his or her consent to search, consent to resume searching is granted once informed of the officer's intent to obtain a search warrant. When that occurs, no search warrant is necessary.

When, after revoking consent to search, the suspect changes his or her mind and permits the search to resume, reversal of the decision is often rooted in a reluctance to endure the time-consuming process of search warrant procurement, a period during which the premises is secured by police. When a suspect indicates a desire to permit the officer to continue searching after having revoking consent, it is legal to continue searching. Prior to continuing the search under those circumstances, however, it is advisable to obtain written consent from the suspect while carefully explaining that he or she is not required to submit to a search, and he or she can require a search warrant. It is important to explain in detail the suspect's options because, if the case goes to court, the suspect will often claim coercion and argue that he or she believed there was no choice but to submit to a search.

When Drugs and/or Drug Paraphernalia Are Observed

If the officer observes drugs and/or drug paraphernalia prior to entering a residence or anytime while legally in a residence, *probable cause* for a search warrant probably exists. In that circumstance, it is the officer's discretion whether a search warrant is necessary, but when making that decision, remember that a consent search is the weakest type of search while a search supported by a search warrant is the strongest.

If during a consent search, an officer begins locating significant quantities of drugs or other items such as currency or weapons, obtaining a search warrant is encouraged. Seizing significant items of evidence may lead to more severe charges, and thus an increased likelihood that the suspect will contest the charges in court.

Obtaining a Search Warrant

If at some point during a knock-and-talk the officer determines that the best course of action is to discontinue the consensual search in favor of obtaining a search warrant, the suspect should be required to accompany the officer to the living room or some other area suited for securing the suspect and any other occupants in the residence. The officer should thank the suspect for his or her cooperation, and explain that it is in his or her and the officer's best interest to seek the issuance of a search warrant. Regardless of what the suspect says, such as encouraging the officer to continue searching, a search warrant is always the safest and most stable legal remedy.

After advising the suspect of the intention to obtain a search warrant, the suspect should be required to remain in the living room pending issuance of the warrant, and completion of the subsequent search. When that occurs, a search for weapons in the room must precede the suspect's confinement to that area, with the bathroom also checked for weapons. At this point, the subject and anyone else subject to detention are not free to leave if the officer chooses to keep them at the residence, as all occupants are under *investigative detention.*

As soon as circumstances permit, the officer should make a *protective sweep* of the residence and any other pertinent structures on the property, although the protective sweep will not include other structures occupied by persons not suspected of being involved in the activity that is the subject of the investigation. The purpose of the protective sweep is to look for other occupants who could destroy evidence prior to issuance of a search warrant, or who could harm the officers. Hence, the protective sweep is a search for people, not evidence, and therefore it is limited to areas that logically could contain or otherwise conceal a person.

Evidence that is observed during a protective sweep can be included in a search warrant, but the *initial* probable cause should be the predominate basis for the search warrant. The *elephant in the matchbox* theory is applicable in this situation, that is to say, if an officer is searching for an elephant, he or she will not look for it in a matchbox. Officers are encouraged to check with their agency's policy regarding the obtaining of search warrants.

Any officer can author the application for the search warrant, but the investigating officer is the most appropriate person to do so. It is the investigating officer who spoke with the suspect, and who most likely discovered the evidence that serves as probable cause for the warrant. The investigating officer is most familiar with the case and therefore in the best position to complete a search warrant application.

To Arrest or Not to Arrest

At the completion of a knock-and-talk, and the successful seizure of drugs and/or drug paraphernalia, what becomes of the investigation? This is a matter of discretion on the part of the investigating officer. For example, if a seizure involves drug paraphernalia but no drugs, the officer must decide if prosecution is really an option. Many prosecuting agencies refuse to accept such cases because the large caseload they maintain requires prioritizing. When that is the situation, they tend to select only the more serious cases and those that represent a strong likelihood of resulting in a conviction.

In instances where no charges are likely, it is not necessary that the suspect be aware of that fact. It is better to inform them that the incident will be documented (even if only on a work log) and that the information will be available should a similar situation arise in the future. The officer should leave the suspect believing that the incident will always be on record. In fact, circumstances such as that represent an excellent opportunity to gather intelligence on individuals the suspect knows is manufacturing drugs, dealing drugs, or involved in other criminal activity. The suspect may even be cultivated as an informant to "work-off" the possible drug paraphernalia charges whether or not charges are actually filed; check department policy.

An important part of drug investigations is cultivating informants, and simplifying the cultivation process is the fact that many drug suspects will cooperate with police when that is necessary to avoid arrest and prosecution. The likelihood of cooperation naturally depends on how much evidence the officer has on the suspect–how strong the case will be if it goes to trial. Also affecting the likelihood of cooperation is whether the suspect has prior convictions or is on parole, both of those conditions possibly resulting in a harsher sentence. Although drug suspects often cooperate by providing police with information about others, they tend to provide cautiously measured information, revealing no more than necessary, and usually they provide information only about those with whom they have a vendetta.

People who deal in illicit drugs tend to feel little loyalty one to another and if compromising someone else is necessary to extricate themselves from a compromising situation, most will do so, if only to the extent necessary. Many people have heard the age-old saying, "honor among thieves," a code of honor that once existed but today has largely been lost to history. Perhaps the best-known example of honor among thieves was the Mafia's code of silence, the code of "Omertá." In recent years, even that code has deteriorated as young members fail to honor old traditions and changing times and values have even affected some older members.

The first failure to honor the long-standing code of Omertá occurred in 1962 when American gangster Joseph Valachi, a member of the Lucky Luciano crime family, testified against the Mafia (La Cosa Nostra). More recently, the gangster Salvatore "Sammy the Bull" Gravano defiled Omertá by providing testimony that resulted in the 1992 conviction of the now deceased Mafia boss John Gotti. Gravano, being the underboss to John Gotti, was significant in the sense that betrayal by someone of his ranking signified a deterioration of the Mafia infrastructure; loyalty and discipline were breaking down. His betrayal also echoed the deterioration of social values generally; sense of community and loyalty is not as strong as it once was with that being true for society in general, and for criminal enterprises. Indeed, there is no longer honor among thieves, with that being especially true of those involved with illicit drugs.

In the event drugs are located during the consensual search, that is to say during the knock-and-talk investigation, the officer can exercise one of three options:

- Issue the suspect a citation.
- Arrest the suspect and book him or her into jail.
- Permit the suspect to remain free, but advise him or her of the intent to submit a report for prosecution.

In many cases, if the suspect was cooperative with the officer and it appears the suspect is genuinely concerned about the situation, not booking the suspect into jail can save the officer time. In view of generally lenient drug laws, however, if the suspect is not booked into jail, he or she most likely will not serve any jail time, but instead receive probation or diversion into a drug treatment program. Usually the tone of the situation will determine the officer's decision regarding disposition of the suspect.

Departure

When leaving the residence following a knock-and-talk, whether or not there was a seizure of contraband, the officers should be courteous and respectful. They should thank the suspect and any other occupants or associates that may be present, and ask if it is all right to return in the future to speak with the suspect.

If the suspect has refused consent to search, the officer should advise the suspect that the investigation will remain open until the officer is satisfied that illegal activity is not occurring at the residence. This will most likely cause the suspect to be concerned about the possibility of surveillance and cause a change in behavior–illegal activity probably will not cease, but modus operandi (MO) likely will change to some degree, even if limited. This is one reason why knock-and-talks can be a success even if consent to search is denied. The suspect will become paranoid and always be vigilant in an effort to detect the police, and never knowing for sure whom to trust.

When a suspect refuses to grant consent to search, the officer must treat him or her with respect, and in no way threaten or otherwise intimidate, although he or she may make statements such as those discussed above. The officers must not take the refusal personally, and must remember that he or she is not usually responsible for a suspect's actions or behavior. Failing to receive consent to search does not indicate that the officer has in any way failed.

To verify the fact that officers do not conduct consensual searches in the absence of consent, officers should document all refusals. The results of documentation are valuable when the officer is required to testify in court as to the number of knock-and-talks conducted, and the results, with documentation serving as rebuttal if a defendant claims a search was done in the absence of consent.

The officer who continually encounters rejection and is refused consent to search should review the circumstances of the refusals to determine if the style of the approach needs modification. Sales people, during training, learn to analyze themselves after each sales attempt to determine why a sales effort was successful, or why it failed, so that professional skills will improve. Just as self-analysis is important for sales people, self-analysis is important for the knock-and-talk officer. Self-analyses helps to ensure that the officer will keep doing what is working, and change what is not working. A college professor, who taught a sales course, issued a list of reasons for a lost sale that he called, "Autopsy of a Lost Sale." He instructed students to review the list every time a sales effort failed. Whether a suspect grants or denies consent to search is very much dependent on the *sales job* done by the officer.

Knock-and-Talk in Court

Issues debated in court regarding knock-and-talk investigations usually focus on the extent to which consent to search was voluntary, with the nature of the statements made at the time of the search materially affecting how the court will rule. The officer requesting consent to search can control many factors that a court will consider when determining whether consent was voluntary, but the person granting or refusing consent can also control deciding factors. Although many factors will affect a court's ruling relative to whether consent was actually voluntary, in the final analysis, the courts generally consider the totality of the circumstances.

Chapter 5

PLAINCLOTHES, UNDERCOVER, AND UNIFORMED DRUG INVESTIGATIONS

PLAINCLOTHES DRUG INVESTIGATIONS

Plainclothes investigations generally refer to assignments where police officers are dressed in civilian clothing but do not conduct undercover operations by assuming an identity and role other than that of a police officer. Plainclothes officers usually must adhere to dress and grooming standards established by their agency.

Plainclothes officers generally participate in knock-and-talk details, surveillance operations, drug interdiction, conspiracy investigations, and asset forfeiture and crime suppressions units. The officers typically drive unmarked vehicles, which provide the means to conduct surveillance of suspects and target locations. The plainclothes officer will find most of the investigative techniques discussed in this book useful.

AIRPORT DRUG INTERDICTION

What does a drug or money courier look like? Is there a profile that fits a traditional pattern of drug couriers? Investigators assigned to drug enforcement details utilize profiles to identify individuals and organizations involved in the use and/or distribution of illicit drugs. The various drugs have different but perceptible physical and psychological affects on a person, and the methods of distribution feature many indicators unique to the type of drug distributed.

Drug courier profiles will differ in that some profiles are relevant to dealers from drug source cities, and some are relevant when considering money source cities. In the southwestern United States, for example, drug investigators assigned to an airport are alert for profiles or indicators of persons arriving with money to purchase drugs, and persons flying out of the area with drugs.

Most often, the investigator receives a tip (information) from an informant or investigator from a city that is the importer of illicit drugs. An investigator in Arizona, for example, may receive a tip that a person or persons in New York City purchased a two-day round-trip airline ticket to Arizona with a money order on a holiday normally associated with heavy airline traffic. The ticket buyer appeared to be with a female who also purchased a ticket, but appeared to be trying to distance herself from the other passenger. Both purchased tickets at the airport, and neither purchaser checked baggage. Both purchasers appeared to be nervous.

On the surface, the information may appear insignificant, but significance can become apparent when analyzing the information against other factors. For example, the Arizona investigator will determine such things as whether the individuals have a driver's license under the names used to purchase their airline ticket, and if either person has a criminal history. The race or national origin of the passengers may or may not be relevant depending upon circumstances.

Law enforcement officers investigating drug or money smuggling to or from New York should familiarize themselves with Jamaican Posse organized crime methods of smuggling because they are a major participant, but not the only participant, in drugs (predominately marijuana) transported to New York.

The Jamaican Posse is a criminal gang that originated from the ghetto areas of Kingston, Jamaica. From the late 1970s to a violent election in 1980, civil unrest forced many rebels to leave the country and flee to the United States with many settling in New York City. In the United States, the gang members employed old gang alliances to form posses and began muscling their way into the cocaine trade. The gangs began to draw new members from those that had also fled Jamaica due to economic hardship. The posses used illegal immigrants, and continue to use them, to provide security for stash houses, with loyalty maintained by threatening the immigrant's family. Many in Jamaica revere the Jamaican Posse members, viewing them as role models, because they often return to Jamaica wearing expensive jewelry and driving expensive cars (DEA).

Jamaican drug trafficking organizations operate in most areas of the United States and purchase marijuana from Mexican sources along the southwest border. Arizona, popular due to its close proximity to Mexico, is a location frequented by Jamaican drug smugglers for the purpose of procuring drugs for exportation to the East Coast, and to the Midwest. Because of close proximity, lower price, abundant supply, and ease, a high percentage of the drugs in the United States are smuggled into this country through Mexico. The proceeds from drug sales are then smuggled back to the source area and the profits transported to Jamaica and possibly Europe.

Jamaican Posse groups use various methods and tactics when smuggling in an effort to avoid detection by police. One Jamaican Posse group utilizes

Jamaican women along with a white female to transport money and/or drugs. Typically, they use single mothers, often with children, and utilize threats of violence to maintain control of the women. The women are generally dressed in business attire, and purchase airline tickets with a check or money order. They often purchase the tickets from different travel agencies and airlines, and travel on busy holidays and weekends.

As can be seen, drug couriers often make an effort to avoid conforming to a profile known to law enforcement, but in that effort, they often unwittingly create a new and unique profile. It is a bit reminiscent of the infamous United States criminal John Dillinger (1903-1934) who used sandpaper to remove his fingerprints in an effort to thwart identification via the science of fingerprints, but in the process made his own fingerprints highly distinctive.

The Investigator who incorrectly or disproportionately bases his or her courier profile on race or national origin, a Jamaican from New York City, for example, could be practicing what has come to be termed racial profiling. Although the investigator may be effective at intercepting drugs and money because of a profile that works for him or her, the case may not hold up in court if race or national origin is the dominant factor in the profile. More importantly, the investigator is probably missing good seizure opportunities because he or she is too narrowly defining who may be a suspect. Case in point. An investigator learned during an interview of a black suspect that he generally functioned as a decoy. Because he believed he would be the target of a drug courier profile stop, he would caravan with a white female who would drive a load vehicle (vehicle containing contraband) while he drove a second vehicle, a van. The hope was that law enforcement would target him while the load vehicle proceeded without scrutiny to its destination.

Drug distributors often use drug courier profiles to their benefit. Take, for example, a large Ecstasy distribution ring that was using the John F. Kennedy Airport as a main receiving point for Ecstasy pills sent to the United States from Europe. The organization employed the use of decoy drug couriers to capture the attention of law enforcement while authentic drug couriers slipped by without scrutiny. That organization was fond of using single mothers with children, handicapped persons, and Hasidic Jews. The Hasidic Jews were paid approximately $1,500 to transport Ecstasy from Europe to New York City, but they were told they were smuggling diamonds and therefore did not know that they were trafficking Ecstasy. Additionally, they received an additional $200 finder's fee for recruiting other Hasidic Jews to transport the supposed "diamonds."

Because law enforcement began placing a greater emphasis on the seizure of Ecstasy entering the United States via airports on the East Coast, Ecstasy distributors have begun utilizing traditional distribution networks established by Mexican organized crime syndicates. That has resulted in large Ecstasy seizures in Mexico and in the United States along the American-Mexican border.

A southwest United States investigator will utilize different profiling techniques to identify a drug or money courier. Taking the example of the ticket purchaser attempting to distance himself from the female ticket purchaser, one must look at the totality of the circumstances. If investigators are experienced in airport drug investigations and aware of the methods of smuggling money and drugs through airports, they will recognize indicators that fit the profile of a drug or money courier. Keep in mind, however, that the indicators (profile) of a drug or money courier do not give the investigator probable cause, but often provide reasonable suspicion.

COMMERCIAL DRUG INTERDICTION (PARCELS)

Introduction

Drug dealers commonly use commercial and private shipping companies for the interstate shipment of drugs and currency, shipments made using the United States Postal Service, FedEx, UPS, and so-called "mom and pop" mailbox stores that have a contract with UPS and FedEx.

Shipping companies offer drug traffickers a rapid and reliable means of transporting drugs and currency virtually anywhere in the world while cloaked in anonymity and rarely having their illicit activities discovered.

When one considers the high volume of packages shipped each day, it is understandable why it is easy to ship drugs, or ship currency to purchase drugs, with little fear of detection. Considering that the multitude of legitimate packages obscures the comparatively few illegitimate packages, how does a police officer or shipping company employee identify illegal packages? Fortunately, there are indicators.

When drug traffickers ship drugs or currency, they usually make an effort to (1) conceal their identity, (2) disguise or mask the contents of the package, (3) choose the quickest shipping option, and (4) track the status of the package.

Drug Shipments

In "source states," drug traffickers receive money for drugs, and it is from source states that traffickers ship drugs. Source states generally include Arizona, California, New Mexico, and Texas because these states border Mexico. Mexico is the source for much of the drugs transported into the United States.

Indicators that a package contains illicit drugs often include, but are not limited to, the following:

- Package reflects a fictitious return address.
- The shipper's name is absent, or consists of a first initial and last name.
- The shipping label is handwritten.
- The package is generally large and may be a retail box that originally contained a legitimate product.
- The package is heavier than normal for its size and alleged contents. When shipping illicit drugs, the shipper often glues one box inside another in a manner that will reveal if someone opened the box between the point of shipment and its destination.
- Packages containing illicit drugs commonly weigh between 15-25 pounds.
- Customer specifies "overnight shipping" to the destination city.
- The shipping fee is inconsistent with what a normal person would pay to ship the alleged contents, i.e., paying $140 for overnight shipping of "books and clothes," or to ship a computer monitor box allegedly containing such a product.
- Payment made in cash.
- The package exudes the aroma of coffee, clothes freshener, or other product intended to mask the odor of the contents. Smell is inconsistent with alleged contents.
- Customer brings the package to the shipping location just prior to the scheduled pickup by FedEx or UPS.

Officers interested in interdicting illicit drug or currency parcels should become acquainted with U.S. Postal Service, UPS, and FedEx employees who work in their city or town. These employees are often very perceptive to what is a normal shipping practice, and can often detect illicit shipments by the appearance of the package and the method in which the customer presents it for shipment.

A popular practice of drug traffickers is using so-called "mom and pop" mailbox stores to ship their packages. Most of these stores have a contract with UPS and FedEx. Employees at these locations can often provide information and tips on packages that are for any number of reasons suspect.

It is important to handle the investigation in a manner that reduces the likelihood that the employee will become "material" in the case should drugs or currency be seized. However, this is difficult to do, and is the main reason most employees do not want to get involved. Fortunately, there are employees willing to assist law enforcement, and confidentiality is possible to some degree. As for a drug shipper retaliating against someone, when the suspect questions why the packaged did not reach its destination, the employee can state that drug-detection dogs in a warehouse somewhere en route detected it and police confiscated it.

A recent case in Phoenix, Arizona, is worth relating because it is consistent with a popular method of shipping drugs from Arizona to a destination (demand) state. The case involved a discount shipping supply company that also contracted with a major shipping company to ship packages from the store. In the late afternoon,two black male subjects arrived at the store, one carrying a 3x1x1 foot box. The male carrying the box approached the counter and requested to have the package shipped overnight to Jamaica Queens, New York. The clerk asked what was in the box and the male replied, "Books and clothes." The package weighed twenty pounds and the shipping fee was $140. The subject paid in cash. Both suspects reportedly had heavy Jamaican accents and wore clothing consistent with dress styles of Jamaican citizens. The clerk had many years of experience in the shipping business and immediately suspected the package contained drugs based on established patterns (modus operandi–MO) consistent with drug traffickers utilizing commercial and private shipping companies.

In this case, the clerk took it upon herself to open the package, which was a courageous act in light of the situation. She discovered an outer cardboard box glued inside another, that being consistent with the packaging practices for drugs shipped from source states. The clerk also discovered a large oval shaped object wrapped tightly in black plastic wrap. Upon making such discoveries, she called the police.

When detectives arrived, it was apparent, based on the indicators, that the package contained an illicit drug, although its type was unknown and they detected no odor. This would be an opportune time to utilize a drug-detection dog to establish probable cause, although most likely, probable cause already exists in such a circumstance. At this point, it is debatable whether officers should obtain a search warrant before further opening the package. If in doubt, erring on the side of caution and obtaining a warrant is advisable. However, in this case, the customer had provided no return address, and the telephone number he provided was for someone other than himself; detectives learned that when calling the number.

In a circumstance such as this, the option exists to conduct a controlled delivery to the receiver if law enforcement in the jurisdiction of the package destination cooperates. In this case, that was not an option.

The detectives decided to open the package, and began cutting the wrap with a knife. Immediately upon puncturing the plastic wrap, a white liquid they recognized as latex paint began oozing from within. Drug dealers commonly use latex paint as a masking agent as well as a warning to the receiver that someone opened the package. Drug dealers instruct receivers to refuse any package that has paint on it, or otherwise reflect signs of tampering. Continuing past the paint layer, detectives discovered an eighteen-pound bale of marijuana. The smell of marijuana was very pronounced at this point.

The issue now was what to do if the suspect called back after realizing the package failed to reach its destination. Detectives asked the clerk if she provided the suspect with a tracking number–she had not. Tracking numbers enable drug traffickers to monitor the progress of their currency or drugs as it travels across the country, passing through shipping stations. Moreover, shipping a package "overnight" makes it significantly more difficult for law enforcement to prepare for and conduct a controlled delivery, as time is working perilously against them. If a controlled delivery is the selected option, generally police obtain a search warrant to identify the contents. This takes time and can impede the normal transportation of the package. Most drug traffickers are very aware of this and that is one of the reasons they specify overnight delivery. By monitoring the progress of their shipment, drug traffickers will usually know immediately when there is an interruption in shipping.

The clerk advised the detectives that she scanned the package into the store, and that would reveal to the suspect that it was in the major shipping company's possession. This seemed adequate to distance the clerk from the discovery of the drugs because she could claim the shipping company had the package, and advise them to direct questions about the package's status to the major shipping company. The detectives did not anticipate that the suspects would call in the event the package was diverted and not delivered because drug traffickers tend to consider seizures a part of doing business, and accept seizures an acceptable loss. Dealers accept such losses as long as they are confident that employees of the shipping store or major shipping company did not rip them off (steal the drugs).

The following morning, the suspect did call back and angrily demanded to know why the package had not left the store. Apparently, the suspect called the shipping company immediately after leaving and obtained from them the tracking number of the package. When he checked the status of the package the following morning, he discovered the package was still at the store. This created a potentially dangerous situation if he suspected that employees had stolen the drugs. In fact, the police had confiscated the package and it was sitting in a storage locker at the police station. When the suspect called, the store clerk alleged the package had left the store and offered to call the shipping company to determine the status of the package, and asked for a phone number. The suspect refused to provide a phone number stating he would call back in a little while. The clerk immediately called the detective. The detective advised the clerk that if the suspect called back, she was to tell them that she learned the package was in police custody and they should call the detective with any questions.

The suspect did call back and the clerk was able to get a valid cell phone number from him before advising him the status of the package. He expressed surprise in hearing the police had the package, but nothing further was heard from the suspect.

Currency Shipments

Currency usually comes to a drug source city from destination (demand) cities on the East Coast and the Midwest–currency arriving from any city or town that is a destination for drugs. It is common for currency to arrive from New York, New Jersey, and Baltimore, and more specifically from cities in those areas dominated by Jamaican Posse gangs, such as Jamaica Queens. These gangs are notorious for shipping and couriering money (via airports) into source states, such as Arizona, to purchase illicit drugs. Officers should identify what types of drug traffickers or dealers are prevalent in their localities, to realize the greatest success in drug interdiction efforts. Some traffickers are independent operators, while the majority are affiliated, or part of, large sophisticated criminal organizations that may or may not be race or ethnically based.

Indicators that a package contains money for the purchase of illicit drugs include, but are not limited to, the following:

- Package reflects a fictitious return address.
- The shippers name is absent, or consists of a first initial and last name.
- The package is generally small, and its weight is consistent with paper currency.
- The customer specifies "overnight" delivery.
- The shipping fee is inconsistent with what a normal person would pay to ship the alleged contents.
- The shipping label is handwritten.
- Payment made in cash.
- Customer brings the package to the shipping location just prior to the scheduled pickup by FedEx or UPS.
- Box construction is heavier than normal, i.e., one box glued into another box.

As can be seen, the indicators of currency shipments are similar to drug shipments. Although currency shipments usually do not feature the clandestine security efforts characteristic of drug shipments, the sender does practice precautions because losing currency to law enforcement represents a loss much more difficult to recover in the normal course of business. Replacing lost drugs is easier, and the wholesale rate is the cost of replacing lost drugs. Conversely, money is difficult to replace, and its face value represents the amount of loss.

Conclusion

Drug and currency parcel interdiction can be very rewarding and effective if officers take the time to learn the processes and workings of commercial and private shipping companies, and identify methods of trafficking within their jurisdiction. Valuable contacts and relationships can be cultivated with personnel within shipping companies, people who can provide timely and helpful information regarding those involved in drug trafficking. However, the officer must make diligent effort to protect employee's identity and keep their involvement secret. This is important because employees are reluctant to get involved because of the potential danger these situations represent.

When considering initiating this type of interdiction, it is important that officers do not disrupt the normal flow of a parcel company's business. Disrupting the business operation will put a chilling effect on cooperation, and interdiction efforts will suffer as a result. Establishing relationships that are mutually beneficial is most effective. Most people do not condone drug trafficking and will cooperate with police interdiction efforts, but when law enforcement officers exercise poor judgment and cause the shipping company to suffer dissatisfied customers because of disrupted service, everyone loses.

These types of investigations are not fishing expeditions. It is important to select packages for interdiction based on strict criteria that has a reliable record of success, a selectiveness that results in the seizure of drugs or money and minimal disruption to the business. When an interdiction is successful, the shipper tends to be more tolerant of a slight business disruption than when an interdiction results in no drugs or money discovered and seized.

UNDERCOVER DRUG INVESTIGATIONS

Introduction

Exciting novels, movies, and television shows have captured the imagination of many who sometimes live vicariously through a character who has infiltrated the crime underworld. Although undercover work can be exciting and dangerous, rarely does it occur in the manner so commonly portrayed by Hollywood. Instead, undercover operations are calculated operations governed by policies and procedures that allow little spontaneous action.

Undercover operations are fraught with unexpected twists and turns, and each new and often unexpected development requires patience and critical thought. When undercover operations suffer compromise, it often occurs because emotion impaired good judgment, and indicators of pending failure went unseen. *There is no amount of drugs or money worth jeopardizing the life or liberty of a police officer; it is best to err on the side of caution.*

Private sector individuals or government agents, depending on the objectives of the operation, conduct undercover operations. Although not generally thought of as being undercover, surveillance is the most common form of undercover work. Undercover operations can include both civil and criminal offenses, often comprising both. This section will discuss undercover investigations as it pertains to illicit street drugs, although the strategies are applicable to other types of investigations.

Why Go Undercover?

The illicit drug market is largely underground with offenses perpetrated by individuals using drugs recreationally, individuals supporting an addiction, and individuals profiting from the proceeds of drug sales and/or trafficking. Due to the secretive nature of the drug business, it is often necessary for officers to assume a role other than that of a police officer. Going undercover is necessary to obtain information and intelligence that is beyond the reach of conventional investigative techniques and methods. Undercover officers, amongst other things, gather evidence for prosecution, identify drug dealers and associates, and confirm the reliability of Confidential Information sources (CIs).

Qualities of an Undercover Officer

Not everyone is suited for undercover work because it requires a variety of qualities that determine an officer's success. An undercover officer must be enthusiastic about the work, and have a high level of courage and confidence if he or she is to be successful. A high level of confidence is required because undercover work requires assuming a role that is often very different from the lifestyle of most police officers. If an officer lacks confidence, he or she will find it difficult to play the role well. An alert suspect will detect even subtle discrepancies that can result in a failed operation and even a violent encounter.

Undercover officers must be able to adapt swiftly in changing situations and make quick decisions, sometimes referred to as "thinking on your feet." The nature of undercover work requires officers to make decisions without supervision, decisions for which they are responsible. Demonstrating good judgment is certainly one of the most important qualities of a good undercover officer.

Officers working undercover must have the ability to remain calm when faced with difficult situations. At times, situations develop that test an officer's ability to resist taking action, such as when witnessing an assault or crime. This is difficult and takes practice.

There are also situations that may require the officer to compromise his or her undercover role and assume a police officer status to prevent a serious crime, injury, or death. Prior to responding in a manner that may betray their cover, undercover officers must consider the safety of themselves, the informant, and any other personnel involved in the operation. Normally, disclosure of one's identity as a police officer will end the undercover assignment.

Other qualities essential for the undercover officer include having good observation and memory skills, technical skills, and physical stamina. Officers must also have a good understanding of the criminal element, be able to display appropriate knowledge and slang terminology relative to the subjects of the operation, and in general have "street smarts."

Some officers are better suited for certain investigations because of physical appearance, race, gender, or cultural understandings of the suspect(s). Correctly matching an undercover officer with the requirements of an investigation will enhance the likelihood of a successful investigation. The members of some races tend to trust "their own" more than they trust someone of another ethnicity, and that tendency can be exploited; an undercover officer of the same ethnicity will tend to be more successful because the subject will tend to be less suspicious when partaking in a criminal act such as selling drugs. Exploit this advantage whenever possible.

Male vs. Female Drug Enforcement Investigators

Who makes a better drug enforcement investigator, men or women? It is impossible to say because it is more a question of qualification than gender. However, it would be accurate to say that generally anything a man can do, a woman can also do. However, in certain instances, women enjoy an advantage. One private detective agency, whenever it was necessary to interview a subject's neighbors using a pretext such as updating the subject's credit, always assigned an attractive female.

The following list of advantages enjoyed by female investigators is not drug investigation specific; the items listed are relevant to female investigators generally regardless of the bureau in which they work. Some of the advantages enjoyed by female investigators include:

- People have a tendency to be disarmed by a female, and less likely to suspect that she is a police officer much less an undercover officer.
- People will often more readily provide information to a female.
- Women are less apprehensive about opening their door for an unknown female than an unknown male.
- Men, usually, will open the door for a female, especially if she is attractive.
- Females, during surveillance, can inconspicuously follow another female into areas in which a man cannot go. That can be very advantageous when the subject of surveillance is a female.
- A female sitting in a parked vehicle for an extended period, such as during surveillance, does not arouse suspicion and anxiety to the extent that often results when a male is sitting in a vehicle under the same circumstances.
- Females find it easy to disguise themselves (see Figures 5-1 and 5-2).

Figure 5-1. Female investigator without a disguise.

Figure 5-2. Same investigator with a disguise.

Establishing an Assumed Identity

Undercover officers usually assume a false identity for an investigation. This identity can remain static throughout the officer's undercover career, or change depending on the investigation. Often it will be a little of both. In short investigations, usually in cases of a drug location requiring quick buys, officers only need to blend with the cliental frequenting the location for the purpose of making drug buys. These types of buys are generally user quantity purchases. For a long-term investigation, or when a specific target is the focus of an investigation, an officer will often obtain official identification to back up a false name.

The cover for long-term undercover operations, as stated, requires suitable identification to support a fictitious identity. A state driver's license is usually obtainable by contacting the Motor Vehicle Department's (MVD) investigative unit. The Motor Vehicle Department can authorize the creation of a state issued "false" identification card and/or driver's license. The authoritative department may vary with locality, so it is necessary to determine which department can assist. The Social Security Administration will issue a Social Security card under the fictitious name with a fictitious number. When the undercover investigation is complete, the Department of Motor Vehicles and the Social Security Administration delete the false identities from their records.

As stated, the identity selected will largely depend on the requirements of the investigation. A background story (cover) is essential, and the officer's partner and confidential informant, if involved, must know the story. Avoid an entirely fictitious background story because such stories are harder to remember, and less likely to withstand scrutiny. An assumed identity should also be somewhat benign in that it should not draw attention to the undercover officer. If an officer chooses a so-called "bad ass" role, there is increased likelihood of confrontation or the possibility the suspect will choose not to deal with the officer because of his or her attitude. Conversely, an officer does not want to assume a nerdy role because a subject may perceive him or her as an easy target to rip off or exploit in other ways. It is best to be friendly, and portray a businessperson image, the image of one who will not hesitate to call off a deal if it is unfavorable.

In the preceding paragraph, creating a background story that is fictitious in every respect was discouraged. It is preferable, when creating a background story, to remain as close to the officer's real-life circumstance as possible, and keep the story as simple as possible. The story should fit with the officer's personality and past. If the officer has children, the background story should include children. This enables the officer to be less concerned about trying to remember his or her background story, and better able to gather intelligence and evidence against suspects. Conversations, and suspect inquiries, will go much smoother if the officer is intimately familiar with the background story, a story that approximates his or her real-life situation as closely as circumstances permit.

A good background story exploits mutual points of interest when possible, and enables the officer to make frequent innocent appearing contacts with the suspect. The background story should not limit the officer's freedom, but provide for wide latitude of movement.

A good background story also features provision for communicating with other officers, as well as a reason for leaving a location if necessary. Assuming an intermediary role is best for drug operations because it provides an excuse to delay drug transactions and/or meetings, thus allowing time for planning. Assuming an intermediary role also defers the cash to a "money man" who will fund the purchase. This can minimize the likelihood that a suspect will plan a rip-off during the money flash.

Officers are discouraged from creating background stories portraying themselves as ex-cons (former prison inmate). Such a background story is acceptable only if the investigation will benefit by it, and the officer can successfully assume the role, i.e., the officer is very familiar with the prison facility in which he or she claims to have served time. It would be unfortunate for an officer to announce he or she is an ex-con only to find out the suspect realized incarceration in the same prison. This mutual "point of interest" could become difficult for the officer to perpetuate considering the suspect's past and intimate dealings with the prison.

The fictitious name chosen by the undercover officer should be easy to remember and be one to which the officer will respond. Middle names may serve as a false first name. There is also merit to selecting a false name that results in initials consistent with those of the officer's real name. For example, if an officer's initials are D.D.F., a fictitious name should feature the same initials. This can eliminate situations where an officer has personal items bearing his or her initials and the suspect consequently questioning ownership of the items, or questioning the officer's real identity.

The Undercover Assignment

Having identified a target, whether it is an individual, group, or location, the officer conducts an assessment to determine the best method for resolving the situation. If an undercover officer will participate, the officer will receive a false identity, or an officer selected who has an established false identity that is appropriate for the selected role.

Having selected an undercover officer and established a cover story, consider the best method for the undercover officer to approach the subject. Study of the subject will facilitate this decision. Officers should attempt to identify the subject's name, aliases (AKAs), street names, associates, interests, dislikes, prejudices, occupation, criminal history, and propensity for violence. It is also important to know the type and quantities of drugs the suspect deals with, as well as the extent of the suspect's participation in drug use and sales. If the suspect has an arrest history, the officer can learn a great deal from the circumstances surrounding the arrests by interviewing officers who participated in the arrests. Also, review the reports generated from prior incidents.

The undercover officer should anticipate questions the suspect may ask him or her, and the sequence of events that may occur. The officer should attempt to think like the suspect and perceive the situation from the suspect's perspective. Because the suspect will probably be very knowledgeable in this area, the undercover officer needs knowledge sufficient to execute the role he or she has assumed. It is imperative that the officer be very familiar with the drug he or she will purchase, be familiar with slang terms, know current street prices, know how the drug is packaged, and know how the drug is used.

Establish an efficient means for the suspect to contact the officer. The affordability of cellular phones provides officers with an economical means of communicating with suspects, but the cellular phone selected for that purpose is for that purpose only. Use a personal phone for other calls.

When purchasing personal use quantities of drugs in an undercover capacity, dealers will often attempt to have officers use some of the drugs they are buying to prove they are not a police officer. This generally does not happen in larger drug purchases, although a suspect may want an officer to sample the drug to demonstrate he is selling a superior product. Undercover officers must establish an excuse for not using or sampling a drug. Excuses successfully used in the past have included medical reasons such as high blood pressure, heart conditions, or allergic reactions. Alternatively, the officer can state that to avoid being robbed he or she does not want to get high. The most common excuses officers provide is that they are on probation or parole and believe they are going to be drug tested soon or that they are getting drugs for a female in hopes of getting her high in return for sex. If the officer uses the parole excuse, as stated, the officer must be familiar with the prison he or she allegedly attended.

Drinking alcoholic beverages may be necessary to gain the confidence of the suspect. The consumption of alcoholic beverages, nonetheless, must be limited to only those drinks necessary to gain the suspect's acceptance. This is important because alcohol will affect an officer's judgment.

When dealing with suspects of the opposite sex, undercover officers must avoid situations that can lead to an intimate relationship, or accusations of intimacy. Female undercover officers may encounter sexual advances more frequently than male officers may so they should have a background story that permits them to oppose advances without creating suspicion. Whether undercover officers are male or female, close surveillance and documentation is essential to refute claims of inappropriate relations.

Undercover officers are encouraged to carry a gun during all operations because suspects commonly carry guns. Anticipate a suitable explanation to justify the gun should the suspect become aware of it.

When carrying a firearm, it must be readily accessible. Many undercover officers have found themselves at a great disadvantage when required to access their gun in a time of crisis. During firearm range practice, officers are encouraged to practice exercises wherein they fire after taking the gun from its location of concealment.

Operational Planning

Introduction

This phase of an undercover operation is fundamental to realizing success in obtaining evidence, affecting arrests, and maintaining officer safety. When a meet or purchase has been arranged between an undercover officer and a suspect, an operational plan should be developed that outlines the objectives and parameters of the operation. A detailed operational plan should include every aspect of the case and involve all officers involved in the investigation. A thorough background report should be obtained on all suspects and associates involved. The background report should include such things as prior arrests, outstanding warrants, and if suspects have used weapons or other forms of violence in the past. Provide current photographs of suspects, associates, locations, and vehicles to all officers involved in the operation. Emergency information such as the closest trauma center, and phone numbers of local fire and law enforcement departments should also be included in the operational plan.

Develop optional plans based on possible and desired outcomes of the operation. If a suspect responds in a certain manner, the response may require a change of plans, or executing a different response. Discuss every option prior to taking action. This is not to say that officers should change plans in order to appease the suspect's demands or wishes, but be as flexible as necessary and reasonable to accomplish operational objectives. Yet, even with the best of intentions, the suspect's actions will often determine the results of an operation. However, calculate actions to lead the suspect according to the operational plan.

The Briefing

A briefing is important and must include all personnel involved in the operation. Brief all personnel at the same time, even though a large operation may require briefing individual groups after the main briefing relative to individual functions within the smaller groups. A main briefing, nonetheless, is essential to ensure that during the operation all personnel know who is doing what, when, and where.

It is important to identify undercover officers and informants to all personnel involved in the operation, especially patrol units that may assist with arrests. This will reduce the chance that a suspect will be mistaken for an officer, or vice versa. If officers from other agencies assist with the operation, they should also be identified and provided raid jackets if necessary.

Communication between officers is essential during the entire operation. If personnel from other agencies do not have the capability to communicate on their systems with other operational personnel, provide them with radios, or team them up with officers who are in contact. Instruct personnel to avoid using the name of suspect, streets, locations, or the undercover officer's name over the air. This is important because the news media, citizens, and suspects often monitor police frequencies. Use encrypted or secure frequencies when possible.

During the briefing, assign personnel their respective tasks. Large operations may require assigning a task to a group, with sub-briefings conducted with individual teams to ensure they understand their task. Also discuss the undercover officer's role, and the role of the informant and moneyman, if either is used.

Use of Electronic Listening Devices (Wires)

When using an electronic listening device (wire) during the operation, an officer familiar with the undercover officer's manners and voice should monitor his or her conversation with the suspect when making the transaction. This is advantageous because the monitoring officer will detect changes in the undercover officer's voice and behavior that may indicate problems are developing. The monitoring officer should also have visual observation of the undercover officer, and be as close as to the location of the "deal" as circumstances permit. The monitoring officer's assistant should relay the "bust sign" when it is heard or observed. Do not assign the task of relaying information to the monitoring officer because that will distract him or her from the important listening responsibility. A second officer can monitor the conversation and relay information to the troops.

Prior to using a wire, test it for operational efficiency in the environment its use will occur, if circumstances permit. Furthermore, install new batteries, or fully charge batteries prior to use.

Audio and visual signals should always accompany the use of a wire. For safety purposes, assume that the wire will fail at the worst possible time during the operation, and have other signals upon which to rely. Expect the best, plan for the worst.

Undercover officers should not dominate the conversation; avoid talking when the suspect is talking because that makes it difficult to monitor and later transcribe what the suspect says. Officers should get in the habit of listening well, and limit their talking to only that which is necessary for the operations success.

Audio and Visual Signals

Investigative teams should develop audio and visual signals for use during undercover operations. Devise signals to indicate such things as, the subject completed the offense sufficiently to justify arresting him or her, the observing of drugs and/or currency, or that there is trouble.

Audible signals should remain consistent to facilitate ready recognition during monitoring. When referring to arrest signals, or to advise that drugs or currency are observed, terms such as "awesome," "super," or "tight" are effective. The undercover officer can incorporate any current slang term into a statement indicating a signal. An example would be "this weed looks *tight*." Audible trouble cues should include the type of threat such as "Come on dude, put the *gun* away," or "Why do you have a *knife*?" The undercover should provide sufficient details, if possible, to allow a cover team to react in the most appropriate manner.

Visual signals will generally accompany verbal signals. Visual signals should remain consistent with consideration given to weather conditions or the time of day. Signals that can be displayed regardless of environmental conditions are generally best. A common visual signal for an undercover officer to perform is to take off a hat or sunglasses. The latter would not be a visual signal that would likely remain consistent because weather and limited light conditions restrict the use of sunglasses. Prescription glasses may be suitable as a visual signal but consideration should be given to signals that are easily observed in substandard conditions. A common visual trouble signal is to raise one's hands in the air in a surrender posture. Other signals can include throwing a chair or item out a window or honking a vehicle horn.

Covering Officers

Personnel assigned to cover the undercover officer during a meeting or drug purchase must ensure they can maintain visual contact with the undercover officer at all times. If visual or electronic surveillance is broken at any time, send a code to the undercover officer's pager or cellular phone alerting them to that fact. Covering officers must blend with the environment, and, depending on circumstances, be in position to respond quickly to assist the undercover in the event of a threat.

Undercover and Patrol Vehicles

When selecting a vehicle for undercover operations, choose an inconspicuous vehicle. Vehicles will blend with the environment if the make, model, and colors are consistent with most vehicles in the area.

Drug dealers often employ countersurveillance strategies to avoid being ripped off, and these associates may spot personnel involved in the surveillance. An increase of government looking vehicles may also tip off a drug dealer or his or her associates.

To avoid detection by an arriving or departing suspect, patrol vehicles must be far enough away or concealed in some other suitable fashion. If a patrol vehicle is present to assist in an officer rescue or suspect apprehension, it may be necessary for the patrol vehicle to be uncomfortably close to the deal, although concealing its presence is important.

During the briefing, identify and describe all undercover and suspect vehicles in the operation. This will increase the likelihood that an officer will identify a suspect vehicle should one arrive prior to or during the operation.

The undercover officer meeting the suspect should be very familiar with the operation of the vehicle, especially if it is new to him or her. It would not look convincing if the undercover officer is portraying the role of an affluent drug dealer and cannot open the trunk or windows of his or her luxury automobile. The image and role established by the undercover officer must remain consistent with his or her behavior and lifestyle.

Undercover officers must ensure that all police equipment is properly secured and all radios are off. Two-way cellular phones should be put on silent or vibrate to avoid receiving an audible transmission during an operation. During one drug enforcement operation where street dealers where targeted, an undercover officer in Arizona, while in his vehicle, contacted a street dealer to attempt a drug purchase. The police radio, concealed under the driver seat, had slid into view. During the negotiations, the female drug dealer asked why there was a police radio on the floorboards. The undercover officer stated he had just stolen it and was looking to sell it asking if the female knew of anyone interested in buying it. The female suspect believed the story and sold the officer crack cocaine. After her arrest, she admitted she was skeptical but was hard up for sales. Drug dealers at this level are usually willing to take greater risks because they are supporting their own addiction with the proceeds from minor street sales. Often they are referred to as "chippers" because they will "middle" a deal and chip a portion off the rock for their own use before providing the drug to the customer, or, in this case, the undercover officer.

Initial Contact with a Target

Once selecting a target or suspect for enforcement, the undercover officer must approach the suspect. An approach can include an informant introduction, a cold hit, or a planned "accidental encounter" whereby the officer befriends the suspect. The initial contact with a suspect is the most important point in the investigation because the suspect will make a judgment of the undercover officer in the first few seconds of the encounter. That contact will usually set the tone for the remainder of the investigation. Whatever approach is used, the suspect must accept the undercover officer if progress is to be realized. If the suspect does not accept the officer, for whatever reason, a different approach or new officer may be necessary.

An informant often provides the quickest and most reliable means of making contact with a suspect because there is the increased likelihood the suspect will accept the officer. A greater chance of acceptance is the result of the informant vouching for the officer. It is like a referral in the business world, whereby a person receives greater consideration after a known or trusted source refers them. Usually, trust results more quickly in these situations.

When dealing with informants, know the informant's motives. In these circumstances, it is the informant's objective to introduce the undercover officer, but the officer still must make the case. The informant and undercover officer should have a good understanding of the officer's background story in the event the suspect questions the informant about the officer. If the informant has identified the subject or target location for possible investigation, the informant should be completely debriefed about the subject or target location. If learning that the subject or other persons at a target location are overly paranoid, or have a history of violence, using only the informant may be a better option. Many informants are better prepared by virtue of being accustomed to dealing with people in the drug culture. Refer to Chapter 6, "Managing Informants," for further considerations when using informants in undercover operations.

During an Operation

Introduction

Drug enforcement operations may last minutes or continue for weeks, months, or years, depending on the needs and therefore the objectives of the operation. If a large sophisticated drug organization is the target of dismantling, tremendous time, effort, and resources are usually required to accomplish the objective. The operation may require long-term infiltration by undercover officers or informants. On the other hand, operations can be quick, targeting individuals or areas known for drug sales. Regardless of the length of the operation, there are operational methods that will ensure the objective is not lost and progress continues to a successful conclusion of the operation.

Constant assessment to ensure the operation stays focused and continues in the chosen direction is essential. Assessment may also reveal that the target is more or less significant than first believed to be. If the target is less significant than first believed, consider alternatives to a lengthy and expensive investigation. This may result in lesser charges but permits the allocation of resources to higher priority targets.

When countless hours, resources, and effort will result in charges that could be obtained much earlier, at lower cost, and that result in essentially the same consequences for a suspect, it is pointless to permit an investigation to continue unless the costs result in achieving other worthwhile objectives. Alternative objectives can include identifying significant co-conspirators, or learning the locations of contraband and/or currency.

Maintaining Suspect Confidence

After the suspect has accepted the undercover officer and a level of trust evolves, even though the trust is minimal, the officer will continually face the dilemma of avoiding suspicion. Drug dealers are usually cautious and suspicious in their dealings with others in the drug world. They know they are a potential target for robbery and that they are forever at risk of compromise by an informant working off charges or informing for money. The undercover officer should try to maintain a friendship with the suspect, although this may force the officer to join in some of the suspect's activities. The suspect may on occasion challenge the officer's trust by accusing him or her of being a police officer or informant. The undercover officer should respond to such accusations with counteraccusations against the suspect, and express anger that the suspect questions his or her loyalty. The suspect may on occasion ask to search the undercover officer. The officer should use the same degree of caution as the suspect, and reciprocate with similar actions such as searching the suspect on occasion. The officer should appear as if he or she does not trust the suspect anymore than the suspect trusts the officer.

Electronics

When using electronics during an undercover operation, continually check them to ensure they are working properly. Check body wires continually and if a unit fails, immediately notify the undercover officer of the failure. The undercover officer should talk over the wire at every opportunity so the monitoring officer knows the wire is working.

It is important to know the battery life of all equipment. If an operation may last longer than conservatively anticipated, or the operation will last longer than the life of the batteries, make provision for battery replacement or charging.

MONEY FLASH OPERATIONS

Introduction

This is the most common type of operation used by undercover officers when a significant quantity of drugs and money is involved, although it is the most dangerous. The increased danger results from the possibility that the suspect(s) will attempt to rip-off (steal) the money from the undercover officer. Similarly, because the suspect has a large quantity of drugs, he or she fears a rip-off of those drugs and, therefore, is likely to employ countersurveillance strategies. Countersurveillance units present a hazard because they may identify law enforcement personnel involved in surveillance or other facets of the operation.

When a drug deal is arranged without having to show money beforehand, that is to law enforcement's advantage. Accomplishing that largely depends on the ability of the undercover officer to convince the dealer to participate in a deal without seeing money beforehand, although that is becoming increasingly difficult to accomplish.

People involved in the drug trade are usually in the business to create or maintain a lifestyle they believe is unattainable by legitimate means. They may feel inadequate, possess limited work skills, or they were attracted to drug dealing because of the enormous opportunities despite the increased risks associated with the lifestyle. Whatever their reason, they are motivated and sustained by the money generated from drug sales.

Many dealers will not hesitate to execute a rip-off if the opportunity presents itself. In fact, given the chance to keep the drugs and rob a buyer of his or her funds would be "right up their alley" so-to-speak, as there is little honor among criminals. The undercover officer must never forget that, to the suspect, they are just another criminal out to make a buck.

Paradigm is a word commonly used to describe one's perception, assumptions, or frame of reference. It is the way one "sees" the world in terms of perceiving, understanding, and interpreting. It matters little what officer's think about operational plans, and how well the undercover officer is "covered" during meetings; what matters is the suspect's paradigm as to the progress of a money flash and future negotiations. Officers should always try to perceive a meeting or deal from the suspect's paradigm and attempt to identify weaknesses that the suspect may attempt to exploit, thus minimizing opportunities for a rip-off.

Location Selection

The suspect will no doubt influence the selection of a location to conduct a money flash, although the undercover officer should dictate the money flash location and time. Whenever possible conduct the money flash on neutral ground in an open area, with space separating suspects from each other if possible. Parking lots or public areas are a good location, and at least two officers for every one suspect should be present. It is important that all officers, including the undercover officer, be armed, and provisions should be made to protect the undercover officer during the bust.

Hotel rooms, apartments, and other enclosed areas are a common choice for law enforcement because of the ease of wiring such locations for sound and video prior to the undercover officer meeting the suspect. Moreover, it is easy to position cover and support officers in adjoining rooms for quick undercover officer assistance in the event a problem develops.

Hotel rooms often provide officers a feeling of containment and control because they know they can protect the money. Unfortunately, although this facilitates protecting the money, the undercover officer remains vulnerable to attack and law enforcement can only react to the suspect's actions. The suspect's paradigm is that only the undercover officer(s) stand between him and the money. The suspect does not know the room is wired and that numerous officers are in position only feet away. They only perceive what their paradigm is. If a suspect chooses to execute a rip-off, he or she will most likely inflict injury or death on the undercover officers because the suspect enjoys the element of surprise, whereas the cover officers can only react.

When using enclosed locations for a money flash, the safety of the undercover officers is important, although that is difficult to achieve. There should always be an adequate ratio of officers to suspects. If the suspect brings an associate there should be at least four or more officers present. The officers should position themselves in different areas of the room so in the event of an attack, the suspect will be unable to direct gunfire in one general area.

These circumstances may be enough to deter a suspect from attempting a rip-off, if a rip-off was the intent.

Conducting a Money Flash

Once selecting a location to conduct a money flash, minimize the potential for a rip-off by careful planning. It is important to understand that there are criminals who set up drug deals with no intention of making the deal but set up the deal only to create the opportunity to rob the buyer of his or her funds.

The most dangerous point in this type of operation is when the suspect reveals the drugs and the undercover officer reveals the cash. Both are anticipating a possible rip-off, and the suspect has the additional fear of arrest and prosecution.

Proper strategy permits making the money flash in the safest manner. Proper strategy enables officers to retain the greatest tactical advantage, maintain officer dominance, and have firepower superiority. The following points illustrate historically successful drug investigation strategies, although officers should be creative and devise strategies consistent with circumstances. The only limitation is one's imagination when devising successful strategies. No single strategy will work in all instances, or work for everyone. Hence, the intention of the following list is to stimulate the imagination.

- Never use money flashes as a tool to persuade a suspect to make a deal. Forcing a deal can result in the suspect's arrest and seizure of the drugs, but it may result in the deal falling apart because the suspect may have misrepresented his or her capabilities, or the informant may have overrated the suspect's capabilities. The worst possibility is a rip-off, or a compromised operation. If the officer pushes the deal, so-to-speak, and deviates from valid tactics in an effort to secure a deal, the results can be disastrous to the case. Drug deals should progress relatively easy, and according to plan.
- Undercover officers should not be over anxious to conduct a money flash, especially if the suspect never asks to see the money. It is best if officers encourage the suspect to reveal his or her drugs before revealing money.
- Money flashes should be conducted only once, and involve only one suspect. There is no need for more than one suspect to see the money. Undercover officers should ensure they show the money to a suspect who not only is in control of the drugs, but who is not an intermediary (a middleman). If the money is shown to an intermediary who is bro-

kering the deal, and later during negotiation, the main suspect emerges, he or she will most likely desire to see the money. Officers should strongly consider refusing a second money flash. If a second money flash occurs, however, use a procedure different from that used during the first money flash.

- Conducting a surprise money flash is an excellent option when properly conducted. This tactic takes the suspect totally by surprise and can significantly minimize the potential of a rip-off. If the suspect demands to see the money a second time, it should raise doubt as to the suspect's true intentions, because there is no further need to prove the funds exist. When an undercover officer meets with a suspect to discuss a deal, a surprise money flash can be conducted. Once the suspect sees the money, the officer can demand to see the drugs prior to turning over the money for counting.
- After conducting a surprise money flash, the suspect may decide to flash a portion of his or her drugs. The suspect may also argue that he or she will sell the remainder of the drugs after given the opportunity to count the money when they meet later. This will provide officers two choices, either have the suspect arrested for the drugs he or she has revealed, or refuse to continue dealing with the suspect unless the entire quantity of drugs is shown prior to providing money.
- When planning a money flash, whether as a surprise or otherwise, it is important to avoid placing the undercover officer in a position whereby he or she can be taken hostage by the suspect or associates of the suspect. If the suspect believes the undercover officer has full control of the money, the officer is at risk of abduction and robbery. Alternatively, the suspect may force the officer to call the moneyman back to the scene. The kidnap risk diminishes, however, when the undercover officer portrays him- or herself as one who brokers deals, and does not have ultimate control of the money. Moreover, the undercover can specify certain conditions that must be in place before providing the money, such as the undercover remaining in a prearranged area alone for a certain period.
- Once flashing the money, remove it from the area as quickly as possible making sure that the suspect sees the money leaving. Ensuring that the suspect observes the money taken away is a safety issue, done to minimize the potential for an attempted rip-off–the suspect will not attempt to rob the officer of what he or she does not have.
- A good strategy is to arrange a meet with the suspect and then at a prearranged time a vehicle containing the money appears to conduct the money flash, immediately after which the vehicle leaves. If money is flashed from the undercover officer's vehicle, the officer should never

get into the vehicle and travel with the suspect, as this could result in a rip-off.

Indicators of a Rip-off

There are often indicators or so-called "red flags" that suggest a pending rip-off, the robbery of drugs or drug money. The following are clues suggesting an intended rip-off:

- The drugs are significantly cheaper than current street prices. If the deal sounds too good to be true, it probably is.
- The suspect insists that the deal take place at a location of their choosing.
- The suspect continually changes the plan and the location.
- The suspect attempts to persuade the undercover officer to meet at an isolated area to conduct the money flash.
- The suspect is adamant on having extra people at the site during the money flash, or during the flash additional suspects unexpectedly arrive.
- The suspect insists on recounting the money. Rarely do drug dealers recount money–if they express the desire to recount, they are often stalling while accumulating the courage to commit the robbery.
- The suspect is adamant that the undercover conduct the money flash alone.
- The suspect or associates are driving stolen vehicles. Other than smugglers who utilize stolen vehicles to transport drugs across remote sections of the Mexico-United States border, drug dealers rarely drive stolen vehicles because that increases their chance of being stopped and searched by the police.

Arresting theSuspect

Once the undercover officer has seen drugs, he or she should provide the verbal and visual signal to the arrest team. Properly planned and executed, the arrest of the suspect(s) is done while providing maximum safety to the undercover officer(s). When possible, the undercover officer should remove him- or herself from the arrest action. Environmental conditions and circumstances will determine the best approach and course of action for executing the arrest.

BUY BUST OPERATIONS

This type of operation is similar to a money flash operation, with the exception that the drug deal is actually completed and the suspect arrested. These are the most economical types of operations because officers usually recover the money from the suspect. Generally, officers purchase small quantities of drugs so in the event the suspect gets away, a large amount of cash is not lost. Large quantities of drugs generally involve a money flash, with the suspect arrested after showing the drugs but before exchanging them for money.

The primary advantage of utilizing this type of operation is the decreased risk of injury to the officer, as the officer will leave the scene after completing the deal. After the officer completes the transaction and leaves, an arrest team moves in to apprehend the suspect. The disadvantage of this type of operation is the possibility that the suspect will get away with the money, although if the suspect has been positively identified an arrest warrant can be obtained although the money is lost.

When possible, officers should maintain a covert approach to apprehending the suspect. A traffic stop conducted on the suspect after being followed a distance may arouse little suspicion, thus allowing an unassuming arrest. The suspect will probably not realize what has transpired until after taken into custody.

BUY AND WALK OPERATIONS

These types of operations consist of undercover officers making drug buys from suspects in an attempt to build cases on them for later charging. Officers usually permit the suspect to walk with the money, thus the buys are generally smaller quantities building up to larger quantities.

Because suspects walk with the money, it is important to identify them for later charging. Some situations do arise where officers do not have the suspect sufficiently identified, but the focus is on the suspect's supplier with the suspect simply serving as an unwitting accomplice.

These types of operations lend themselves to undercover officers fronting suspects with money to purchase drugs. This is not preferred, but today's drug market makes it difficult to obtain drugs without providing or showing funds. When fronting money, officers must consider the trustworthiness of the suspect, and surveillance teams must be prepared to follow the suspect if he or she takes the money and then leaves to obtain the drugs from a different location.

When an officer makes multiple buys from a suspect, a level of comfort develops between the officer and the suspect. This should not result in the officer becoming complacent, however, because the situation can turn dangerous without warning. Yet, when it comes time to order a larger quantity of drugs to conduct a buy/bust or money flash operation on the suspect, the deal is often easier to set up because the suspect's personality and methods are to some degree known.

REVERSAL OPERATIONS

Introduction

Reversal operations involve undercover officers assuming the role of a drug dealer instead of a buyer. There are different situations that lend themselves to these types of operations such as obtaining evidence for a search warrant, demand reduction programs (street level operations), and sales to buyers looking to acquire drugs. Many times informants identify potential buyers.

Because the officer assumes the role of a drug dealer, the officer must have a thorough understanding of *entrapment* issues. It is also beneficial to record conversations between the undercover officers and suspects because a recording will disprove later claims of entrapment when the case goes to court. Entrapment is discussed later in this chapter.

A persistent concern when conducting reversal operations is the possibility that undercover officers will find themselves unknowingly dealing with another undercover officer or an informant working for another officer. To avoid this potentially tragic situation, make an effort to identify the suspect attempting to purchase drugs and investigate his or her background. This problem can sometimes be eliminated, or at least minimized, if a system is in place that enables officers to determine if a subject or location is under investigation by another officer or agency. In the Phoenix, Arizona, metropolitan area, such a system has prevented conflict between agencies and investigators. The system has also assisted in bringing officers together who are investigating the same individual or location and has provided the means to exchange important information and avoid duplicated efforts.

Reversal operations are conducted in much the same manner as buy/bust or money flash operations, and carry many of the same risks. The potential exists that the undercover officer will be the target of a rip-off and, therefore, the same precautions are important to reduce that likelihood. Officers should also make use of the same tactics a dealer would employ against a rip-off as it pertains to money flashes and such, as these tactics are the norm rather than the exception, and may create suspicion if overlooked.

In reversal operations, the undercover officer must decide whether to provide drug samples to the suspect. Policies established by the officer's agency should address this issue. Many department heads and attorneys oppose this practice because it can create legal liability problems should use of the drugs result in problems such as a drug overdose or injury.

If department policy permits providing sample drugs, handle them carefully. Pre-weigh and package the drugs before giving them to a suspect, and if recovered from the suspect later, weigh them again. Reweigh undispensed drugs before returning them to the evidence locker.

Some agencies provide simulated drugs for these types of operations. Providing real drugs is troublesome because buyers usually try to swallow their drugs when being arrested. Drywall, soap, or peanut chunks are excellent choices for simulated crack cocaine, and are easy to obtain. If real drugs are used, they should be consistent in weight with one another and packaged in plastic to make it difficult to swallow.

Reversals at Search Warrants

After executing a search warrant for drugs at a specific location, officers frequently have the opportunity to set up a reversal operation as unwitting buyers arrive to purchase drugs. When implementing a reversal operation under such circumstances, implement procedures to provide for an efficient and safe means to conduct the operation and process each new suspect.

Officers will usually position themselves inside the residence to conduct the sales, although that will depend on the methods the suspects had been using. Usually the dealer makes sales through the door, opening the door only enough to see the suspect. This is an excellent opportunity for uniformed or plainclothes officers to experiment with drug sale negotiations, inasmuch the suspect most likely cannot see what the officer is wearing, especially if the interior is dark. The arrest team, wearing a police uniform or police raid shirts, is outside the residence in a van or outbuilding. They can also serve as spotters, advising officers in the house when vehicles arrive or subjects are approaching the door, window, or other location of drug sales. The arrest team should block potential escape routes. When possible, create video and audio recordings of the negotiations between suspects and the officer.

If undercover officers are outside the residence when making drug sales, a cover/arrest team should be close enough to render assistance should that be required. Moreover, make arrests with as little incident as possible. The undercover officer should wear clothing that is consistent with the area and conduct the sales in a manner consistent with that of the dealer. Two undercover officers working together are best because that reduces the likelihood of a rip-off or confrontation between a suspect and the officer. Additional undercover officers can rotate with officers making deals; that provides officers the opportunity to create quality notes for the subsequent report.

When suspected drug buyers knock on the door or approach an undercover officer to buy drugs, the officer should allow the buyer to initiate the conversation. This can alleviate entrapment issues. If the suspect knocks on the door, officers can crack the door, or open it if deals occur inside, and state, "What do you want?" If the suspect is at the residence to buy drugs, he or she will most likely say, "a twenty," "rock," "black," or in some way identify the drug desired.

Often, buyers will ask for a subject by name, asking for the person from whom they purchased drugs in the past. Officers can offer an explanation why they rather than the dealer are making sales, i.e., "I'm covering sales for him/her until their return."

After the suspect asks for a quantity of drugs, the officer should demand to see the money. Showing money demonstrates the intent to purchase illicit street drugs and arresting the suspect is justified. The charge is usually attempted possession, or conspiracy to possess whatever type of drug he or she was attempting to buy.

Once a buyer has purchased drugs, or attempted to purchase drugs, a bust signal alerts the arrest team and they affect the arrest. They should attempt to apprehend the suspect quickly and quietly to avoid the suspect running or fighting. The arrest team should identify themselves by announcing, "Police officers, you're under arrest!" When making the arrest, unambiguous commands let the suspect know what to do. Once arrested, escort the suspect to a secondary room of the residence previously cleared for weapons and drugs, a room then used to process suspects.

A team should be set up before hand to handle the booking paperwork and run records checks on the suspects. Depending on the location and the success of the operation, a room can fill up quickly with buyers. A procedure for keeping suspect funds, property, and purchases separate from one another is important. Ensuring adequate resources is important because the operation must discontinue when resources are exhausted.

SPECIAL CONSIDERATIONS. When setting up a reversal operation at the scene of a search warrant, officers must attempt to eliminate sources that may provide warning to potential buyers approaching the location. This can be very difficult in neighborhoods that have a large criminal element, or a disproportionate number of residents who are antipolice. Police must respect the civil rights of the people in such neighborhoods, but warning them that interference may result in arrest will often defuse them.

When the objectives of the search warrant have been satisfied, police may not "hold" the premises to conduct additional reversals. When concluding the search warrant investigation, discontinue the reversals. In this respect, officers should not prolong the search warrant investigation with the intention of prolonging the reversal operation, because so doing will leave them vulnerable to a lawsuit and dismissal of original charges.

Demand Reduction Programs

Demand reduction programs affect the demand side of the drug problem by targeting drug users buying at the street level. Calls for police service, obvious drug sales, or citizen complaints usually identify drug problem areas. This type of operation conducted simultaneously with other traditional drug enforcement efforts such as search warrants, undercover buys, and heavy police enforcement and visibility can effectively reduce widespread drug crime in an area.

Generally, during a demand reduction operation, undercover officers and informants conduct an extensive drug buying campaign, buying drugs from numerous individuals in an area over a predetermined period. The campaign culminates with the round up of suspects who sold drugs to undercover officers and informants, with search warrants simultaneously executed on sales locations. Officers then replace the suspects and pose as street dealers, and sell simulated or real drugs. Usually these operations occur where drug sales transpire in the open; thus, it is best to target locations such as parks, alleys, street corners, and apartment complex grounds. Many of the measures explained in the search warrant reversal section are used.

SPECIAL CONSIDERATIONS. During the round-up phase of the operation, it may not be possible to arrest all the dealers, and some may not have cases against them. However, police must deal with these individuals because they can pose a problem as the operation progresses.

A situation that occurred in Phoenix, Arizona, demonstrates the potential hazards that exist when offenders, who were not apprehended, arrive during the operation. Police identified a relatively small apartment complex as the location of numerous drug sales. The apartment complex featured no less than ten apartments from which dealers were selling drugs as well as supplying dealers on the grounds. Officers executed numerous search warrants and arrested dozens of street-level dealers. Undercover officers then set up in the complex to sell drugs. Cover officers were strategically located throughout the complex, which appeared natural since large numbers of people commonly loitered about the area. In addition to cover officers, a box van near the location of drug sales contained arrest teams. About midway through the operation, it must have been shift change time for the drug dealers because a crew of four men arrived in a car. The men challenged the undercover officers telling them they had no right to sell drugs in their territory but were quickly outnumbered and left. The undercover officers never identified themselves as police officers but radioed for the outer perimeter security to ensure they left the area. Unfortunately, the outer perimeter security team was not near the exit. Upon leaving the parking lot, the angered men drove along a road that paralleled the north side of the apartment complex and fired numerous rounds through a wrought iron fence in the direction of the undercover officers. Fortunately, no one received injuries, but the rear door to the box van containing the arrest team took numerous hits. The suspects then fled without being identified, or apprehended.

ENTRAPMENT

In addition to understanding *search and seizure* laws, when conducting undercover investigations, the officer must understand what constitutes *entrapment.* A clear understanding of entrapment is important to avoid unwittingly committing the offense, and to prevent a suspect, at the time of trial, successfully claiming entrapment as a defense. Failure to understand entrapment can result in the officer "going-too-far," so-to-speak, but it can also result in an officer unnecessarily stopping short and failing to obtain evidence that was in fact obtainable.

Although understanding what does and does not constitute entrapment from the perspective of the courts is important, the issue is often the subject of confusion; most civilians do not understand what constitutes entrapment, and many police officers have a poor understanding of the topic.

It is common to hear someone exclaim, "That was entrapment!" even though no entrapment occurred. Although the courts have ruled it permissible to deceive a criminal who has an unlawful intent to begin with, in an effort to build a case for prosecution, it is not permissible to manufacture crime for the singular purpose of prosecuting it. The court made that clear in *Jacobson v. United States.*

> In their zeal to enforce the law, Government agents may not originate a criminal design, implant in an innocent person's mind the disposition to commit a criminal act, and then induce commission of the crime so that the Government may prosecute. (*Jacobson v. United States,* 503 U.S. 540 [1992])

When deciding a case wherein the defense argues that the defendant was the victim of entrapment, and would not have committed the offense in the absence of inducement by law enforcement officers, the courts usually consider the question of the defendant's apparent *predisposition*. This is why an undercover officer will generally make several drug buys from a supplier before making an arrest, multiple buys establishing predisposition. Making multiple buys establishes that the person is in the business of selling illicit drugs, and did not do it just once at the urging of the undercover officer.

The defendant with one or more prior convictions for selling illicit drugs will have a hard time successfully using the defense of entrapment because the government's allegation of predisposition will be hard to dispute. Prior convictions for drug sales leaves predisposition reasonably inferred.

UNDERCOVER INVESTIGATIONS BY PRIVATE INVESTIGATORS

The following section is from the book, Siljander: *Private Investigation and Process Serving: A Comprehensive Guide for Investigators, Process Servers, and Attorneys*, Springfield, IL: Charles C Thomas Publisher, 2001.

The following information will provide police officers a better understanding of business and industrial undercover operations, conducted by private investigators. The understanding will help when police officers must work with undercover private investigators who encounter drug problems in the client firm.

What is an industrial undercover operation and who needs one? Such an operation is simply a private investigator going undercover to infiltrate the company's workforce by posing as an employee to detect a variety of internal irregularities. A variety of terms describes industrial undercover operations such as internal surveillance, internal intelligence, internal survey, or internal security. Reasons for an industrial undercover operation include:

- Internal problems are apparent or suspected.
- Periodic undercover investigations determine if there is an internal problem.
- When losses are apparent, but the source of losses unknown, a company will initiate an undercover investigation, and have accountants scrutinize business records.
- Undercover investigations run continuously for the purpose of early detection of internal problems. Internal problems, especially those pertaining to drugs and theft, are clandestine in nature and require clan-

destine methods of detection. Moreover, crews working swing and graveyard shifts generally have limited supervision and upper management has little way of knowing what actually occurs during those times.

A properly managed business and industrial undercover investigation provides many benefits, but is not an alternative to a well-conceived and properly implemented security and loss control program. Undercover investigations should supplement such a program.

Once the undercover investigator has infiltrated the company's workforce, he or she will be alert for and report on all irregularities such as theft, time card cheating (theft of time), malingering, destruction of company property, on-the-job drug use and/or sales, on-the-job alcohol use, safety hazards, quality of supervision, morale, and espionage, to name just a few.

The question often is not whether a company can afford an undercover investigation, but whether they can afford not to employ such methods. The *American Management Association* and the *United States Chamber of Commerce* report that almost one-third of all business bankruptcies are the result of undetected employee theft of money and property. The prevalent use of illicit drugs compounds the problem. Moreover, while a burglary or robbery loss is usually recoverable via insurance, shrinkage or "mysterious disappearance" is not. Recognize also that such losses detract from "net" profits (amount of revenues over expenses) and that can quickly bankrupt a firm; most firms operate at a 5-7 percent net profit. This means that if the net profit is 7 percent, the firm must sell $14,285 in goods or services to recover a $1,000.00 theft loss. A $50,000 theft loss means the firm sells the next $714,286 in goods or services without profit.

Organized theft rings do occur and can bankrupt a company very quickly! Nevertheless, while undercover investigations are often essential, are they ethical? Do undercover investigations violate the rights of employees? A properly administrated undercover investigation serves, not threatens, those employees who are properly doing their job, and employees have realized promotions because of favorable reporting by undercover investigators, diligent employees who otherwise would have escaped notice by upper management. Moreover, if almost one-third of all business bankruptcies are the result of undetected employee theft, then a properly managed undercover investigation protects the jobs that employee's depend on.

An undercover investigator affects infiltration of a company's workforce by obtaining a job within the client firm, usually using their real identity. However, a fictitious job history is usually developed. When developing a fictitious job history, just as when developing a fictitious name, the closer one can remain to the truth the better inasmuch as it is more likely to withstand scrutiny, and an inadvertent slip by the investigator is less likely to alert a subject.

When preparing a fictitious job history, one can accomplish it by such methods as claiming periods of unemployment living off savings, claiming periods of self-employment, and have a willing businessperson claim the investigator worked for them during a specified time. One can also have the owner of a now defunct business claim the investigator worked for them during a specified time. It is difficult to establish a fictitious job history that will withstand close scrutiny such as field interviews and examination of public and private records, but most companies do little more than make a few confirming phone calls and/or send out some inquiries by mail. Moreover, the job sought for use as a "cover" is usually a lower paying non-skilled position for which little applicant scrutiny usually occurs. If scrutiny will be diligent, the human resource manager may need to assist.

Low paying non-skilled positions are desirable because no special skill is required to obtain the job, and turnover is generally high making obtaining the job easier. Additionally, low paying positions often result in a lower level of productivity being tolerated, although the job must be done or a supervisor who almost certainly will not know the person is an investigator may fire him or her.

The investigator will be on the company payroll and paid for the job position he or she is using as a cover. Additionally, he or she receives an agreed amount for their investigative reports. The investigator is not just performing the cover job, however, but is devoting considerable effort getting to know people and establishing a rapport with them, developing information, and preparing reports. Moreover, the investigator is at risk. However, beyond all that, depending on the experience level of the investigator, management is paying for that as well. The saying, "you get what you pay for," is true. An inexperienced or poorly qualified investigator at half the price is not a bargain.

A list of employees, by department, is very helpful to the investigator. If the investigator hears someone say that Bob in a certain department did something, a check of the list can disclose that there is a Bob Thompson in that department. Alternatively, the investigator may have learned that Bob did something, but the speaker did not identify department and last name. A check of the list may disclose that there are three employees named Bob with the list identifying the department in which each works. That knowledge will make it easier to determine which Bob is at issue. If management does not provide the investigator with an employee list, he or she will begin compiling such a list, often taking the information from time cards. Depending on the size of the company's workforce, compiling an employee list that reflects employees by department can require a month or more to complete.

If a company has an internal drug problem (sales, purchasing, use), many problems accompany that situation. Some are:

- Incentive for employee theft
- Increased tardiness and absenteeism
- Increased on-the-job injuries
- Reduced productivity (less work, increased error rate)
- Diminished customer satisfaction

Police may do a stakeout and make arrests when drug sales occur on company property outside the buildings, but deeper problems will persist and police generally can do little about them.

Police cannot commit the resources necessary for an extended undercover operation to infiltrate the workforce. Management must employ private investigators for that purpose. Depending on circumstances, it may be necessary for more than one private investigator to infiltrate simultaneously, infiltrating different departments and/or shifts.

Undercover operations are long term, generally several months to a year or more. The results of such an operation are directly proportional to the investigator's ability to gain trust and establish a rapport with perpetrators. That takes time! Management must avoid the temptation to move the investigator from one department to another in a manner not characteristic of their normal practice. So doing does not leave the investigator in any one department long enough to develop useful information, and it arouses suspicion. If cost is an overriding concern and management therefore desires to get the investigator in and out quickly, they should not initiate such an investigation–the costs will be an expenditure rather than investment.

Industrial undercover operations are highly sensitive and require security measures reminiscent of a government intelligence operation. Only those with a legitimate need to know must be aware of the operation; their knowledge of the operation must be essential to its success. Those with a need to know must not confide in a spouse because people within a company socialize and for every person who is aware of the operation the potential for a leak increases significantly.

Managers and supervisors, if they are aware of such an operation, will often behave inappropriately and unwittingly jeopardize the operation. They will cruise through the investigator's work area more than is usual because of curiosity, and they often will attempt to speak with the investigator about the case. One assistant to a large firm's general manager at one point began asking the investigator questions about the investigation, in the presence of coworkers, by speaking in low tones and attempting to speak without moving his lips. That sounds bizarre but to such people, undercover operations are exciting and mysterious and what they know is limited to the fiction they have seen on television and in the movies. Moreover, there are cases where a supervisor or manager on some level will attempt to frustrate the investigation fearing that if the investigator finds internal irregularities it will reflect poorly on them. Anyone who is aware of the operation must be aware only because their having knowledge of the operation is essential to its success. No one is entitled to know simply because their position implies such a right; there must be a legitimate need to know!

Qualified industrial undercover investigators are extremely difficult to find. One of the problems stems from the fact that those who are highly qualified are often doing other things that they are reluctant to discontinue. For example, an investigator who has established a client base doing Worker Compensation fraud surveillance and photography will likely lose their client base if they take six months to a year or more to embark on an undercover assignment.

Typically, a detective agency, when they have a client in need of an undercover investigation, will hire someone and attempt to train them. The person is generally young and without experience, and often the person training them has limited undercover experience themselves. The ideal undercover investigator is one who has experience doing such investigations, and has prior law enforcement or government intelligence experience. They are familiar with the proper administration of an undercover operation, and they understand laws as they pertain to such things as entrapment, rules of search and seizure, and the proper handling of evidence. The later is essential if there is an internal drug problem and the investigator will be purchasing drugs and passing them on to law enforcement. Qualified undercover investigators are expensive, but a poorly qualified investigator at half the price is not a bargain.

When an undercover investigation first begins, for the first month or two, sometimes more, management may feel that things are off to a slow start. That is because the investigator begins by learning the job used as a cover, and letting coworkers become accustomed to him or her. However, what may appear to be a slow start is productive time and serves two very useful purposes.

- The better one learns the job used as a cover, the better they will be able later to devote effort to developing useful information. Moreover, other employees do not respect a poorly qualified coworker and establishing the necessary rapport will be difficult; the investigation will suffer.
- When infiltration is first accomplished, the investigator is a "new" employee unknown to others. It takes time to become familiar and trusted, for a rapport to be developed. During that process, the "new employee" must appear to be unconcerned about any irregularities that may be occurring to avoid arousing suspicion. Remember, what the investigator learns is the result of having developed a rapport with the

> right people much more than simply being on site to observe what is occurring. That is not to imply that the investigator will not initially be alert for and report on apparent irregularities.

The investigator, once having established a rapport with coworkers, will employ an interview technique called "roping." Roping is an interview technique whereby the investigator steers a conversation to a topic of interest, and attempts to elicit information from a subject, without the subject realizing it. Roping almost always involves use of a pretext, although a pretext does not always involve roping. Roping is a term characteristic of the private investigative field, and therefore it is common to hear private investigators speak about roping. Police undercover investigators use roping techniques, but they generally do not use the term roping. Hence, while the police do it, they do not refer to it as roping. While a traditional interview lasts only minutes to an hour or two, roping is generally a very long-term endeavor.

If an undercover investigator purchases drugs, he or she must forward them to the police. That being the case, it must be determined ahead of time how to handle such matters. All meetings involving the undercover investigator with police and company management must be at a secure off-site location where there is no risk that anyone working for the company will observe the meeting. When police receive drugs from the undercover investigator, they analyze them and secure them for use in court. It is advisable that a specified police officer act as liaison between the undercover investigator and the police department. This will ensure the officer is aware of the ongoing development of the case, the investigators involved, and suspects involved.

Often, drug sales or use will carry over to locations outside the confines of the business. When that occurs, law enforcement is usually better able to assist. However, when the undercover investigator, who is a private investigator and therefore a private citizen without police powers, anticipates making a drug purchase while at work, he or she should advise the liaison police officer before making the transaction. That is important because the undercover investigator is a civilian without police powers and therefore not immune from drug laws. Indeed, the civilian undercover investigator is not allowed to buy or transport drugs unless under direct control of law enforcement personnel, and should avoid partaking in drug transactions or negotiations unless law enforcement is aware of the situation.

Undercover operations are expensive in terms of time and money. Hence, one of the worse things a private investigator can do is fail to complete the operation. However, should the investigator's cover be compromised, they must withdraw from the case. Similarly, if without the undercover investigator's authorization someone in the client company's management confides to someone else such as a supervisor or manager the existence of the investigation, immediate withdrawal is justified if not recommended. A client who makes an unauthorized disclosure, for whatever reason, will likely make others. When that occurs, consider immediate withdrawal because undercover operations are dangerous enough without such breaches.

Clients generally make unauthorized disclosures for one of two reasons, aside from an unintended slip of the tongue. First, human nature compels some people to talk about that which they find unusual and exciting. Second, a manager will begin feeling guilty believing that some other manager or supervisor has a right to know, and failure to advise them is analogous to betrayal. It is important to discuss those concerns during an initial meeting to lessen the temptation.

Some of the detriments of unauthorized disclosure include:

- Undercover operations are expensive and compromising the investigator's cover will result in losing the investment.
- Morale deteriorates when employees learn management had them infiltrated.
- It will be much more difficult for a second investigator to infiltrate and gain the confidence of employees.
- The investigator could be injured or killed.

The investigator must be appropriate for the group he or she will infiltrate. A male investigator infiltrating a predominantly female workforce may not succeed and vice versa. Similarly, if there is a predominant language, the investigator must speak that language. Age appropriateness is also important.

Before commencing an undercover operation, there should be a remote location meeting involving all parties concerned to develop an understanding and agreement about the administration of the operation. The meeting must include the undercover investigator, his or her agency supervisor, and the client. If illicit drugs are a problem in the client firm, and the undercover investigator will likely make drug purchases, a liaison officer from the police department must attend the meeting to specify procedure.

During the meeting, it is important that all parties understand and agree that unauthorized disclosure of the operation will result in its immediate termination. Under such circumstances, the operation must end and knowing that termination will occur reduces the temptation, by anyone, to make an unauthorized disclosure. This is important because the temptation is strong. An unauthorized disclosure, made early, may go unnoticed by the investigator. However, once he or she has been in place for a month or two unauthorized disclosures are generally obvious. No matter how the person having learned of the operation tries to "act normal" their efforts almost never succeed. There will be a sleight but perceptible shift in their demeanor.

The undercover investigator should submit written reports in the third-person and avoid reflecting the name of the investigative agency, the client company, or the investigator. The client does not receive reports at his or her place of employment via mail, and not at home as a spouse may become aware of the operation. The client may obtain a Post Office box for that purpose. There will be no return address on envelopes containing reports. In the final analysis, how the client receives reports is not as important as it is security be maintained. Sometimes it is best for someone (never the investigator) from the investigative agency to hand deliver reports to the client at a secure location. Secrecy and security is vital!

UNIFORMED DRUG INVESTIGATIONS

When thinking of drug investigations one generally thinks of plainclothes and undercover detectives, even though uniformed patrol officers contribute in very important ways. Although frequently drug investigations begin in response to tips from area residents, drug investigations also begin because of information acquired by a uniformed police officer under circumstances such as:

- The officer observes something significant while on patrol
- The officer acquires useful information during a field interrogation
- The officer receives a tip from an informant
- The officer discovers illicit drugs during a traffic stop
- The officer discovers illicit drugs on the person or in the vehicle of a detainee and/or arrestee

The uniformed officer can also perform *knock-and-talk* investigations when sufficient evidence to justify a search warrant does not exist, but there is reasonable suspicion of illegal activity. An example would be suspicion of illicit manufacturing of methamphetamine.

Uniformed police officers in marked patrol cars, in addition to being fundamental in interdicting drug and cash couriers, can provide essential support for undercover drug officers by completing tasks the undercover officer cannot such as, but not limited to, the following:

- Conduct traffic stops for the purpose of arresting or identifying suspects, or briefly seizing a suspect's vehicle for installation of a tracking device. For example, depending on circumstances, a patrol officer can take a subject into custody long enough for detectives to install a tracking device.

- Run interference by making a pretext traffic stop if a subject begins approaching a premises while electronic surveillance devices are being installed.
- Stand-by in the area to offer rapid back-up support if needed by plainclothes or uniformed officers conducting a knock-and-talk, or undercover officers conducting a drug buy.

In addition to assisting plainclothes and undercover drug enforcement officers as described above, many uniformed officers do drug investigations themselves. In many small departments, which are the majority of police departments in the United States, there are no plainclothes detectives and uniformed officers do all investigations.

HIGHWAY INTERDICTION

The Origin of the Drug Courier Profile

The 1980s set in motion a major challenge for law enforcement because vehicle use for the interstate transportation of illicit drugs and money increased. Drugs traditionally transported into Florida by air and water began being smuggled into the United States through Mexico. In fact, estimates suggest that sixty-five percent of the cocaine smuggled into the United States now comes across the United States-Mexico border (DEA). Drug enforcement investigators, in an effort to identify couriers of illicit drugs and/or money, developed profiles.

Relative to those persons involved in the interstate trafficking of drugs via vehicles, a drug courier profile was developed. Those persons falling between the ages of twenty to forty-five demonstrated the highest incidence of drug use and therefore assumed to have a more intimate connection with drug dealers and, consequently, enforcement efforts focused on them. Persons displaying a "flashy" style of dress or wearing an abundance of large gold jewelry, also fit the profile.

As illicit drug/money courier profiles evolved, investigators identified other indicators as well. For example, interstate drug couriers often sported a couple days growth of facial hair, and displayed a general unkempt appearance, due to long road trips. Moreover, the couriers traveled interstate highways, often at night, and in large vehicles capable of carrying greater quantities of drugs. Couriers often used rental cars for their mechanical reliability and, in the event law enforcement made an arrest, a personal vehicle was not in use and therefore subject to seizure for forfeiture.

Using what became traditional profiling techniques, law enforcement disproportionately focused on ethnic minorities, usually blacks, Hispanics, and other dark skinned subjects. That occurred because experience suggested they were the distributors of most major illicit drugs. The El Paso Intelligence Center (EPIC), the federal clearinghouse for drug-interdiction data, has validated reports that on a nationwide level, blacks and Hispanics are represented at higher percentages than whites amongst those arrested for illicit drug trafficking. It is unclear, however, whether the imbalance is due to fair profiling practices or unfair racial discrimination. The imbalance can be the result of fair profiling if it is true that Mexican and South American drug cartels have integrated with Hispanic communities in the United States. This effect is evident in the Phoenix metropolitan area where undocumented Mexican citizens maintain control over most of the marijuana, methamphetamine, cocaine, and heroin smuggled into the United States from Mexico.

To put the issue of singling out dark skinned people into perspective, relative to racial bias, one can compare that situation with the Golden Triangle of Myanmar (formerly Burma), Laos, and Thailand wherein Asians are exporting heroin to the United States. Their distribution networks within the United States are predominantly Asian, as expected. Relative to trade associated with the Golden Triangle, profiling criteria focuses more on Asians than on Hispano-Latino people. That is because those in the countries of drug origin tend to utilize culture similar gangs or distribution networks within the United States. Hence, who becomes the primary suspect depends upon who is doing the trafficking, and the networks they cultivate. Naturally, language and culture are influencing factors.

Recently one of the authors attended a narcotics school taught by the United States Drug Enforcement Administration (DEA). A block of instruction was devoted to issues surrounding racial profiling as it relates to drug enforcement. For many years, the DEA taught law enforcement personnel useful techniques for intercepting drug and currency shipments on the interstate highways of the United States. The DEA has named this highway interdiction program "Operation Pipeline." This program is reminiscent of the teachings of the 1980s relative to the structure of drug distribution cartels, and methods of transportation. Many of these distribution organizations were predominately ethnic based.

Today, because of the controversy surrounding drug courier profiles and the controversial issue of so-called racial profiling, training emphasizes preventing the perpetuation of stereotypes that suggest only the members of certain ethnic groups' traffic in illicit drugs. Training is also "regionalized" so that officers learn about organizations operating in their jurisdiction, minority based or otherwise. The intention of "Operation Pipeline" was the reduction of drug and currency smuggling, and the reduction of other crimes that were associated with drug smuggling, distribution, and use. The Federal Bureau of Investigation (FBI) has reported that illicit drugs underscore 48 percent of all homicides, 60 percent of all assaults, and 80 percent of all property crimes in the Unites States. In addition to drug and currency seizures, officers are apprehending fugitives, locating missing children, and discovering other crimes unrelated to drugs. The program has been very effective in spite of the controversy that surrounds it.

The class attended by the author was in the southwestern United States, and thus the training focused on organizations that operate in that area. Training discussed Arizona in detail due to its close proximity to Mexico, and the large amount of illicit drug and currency seizures that occur in the state. Arizona, California, Texas, and New Mexico are transshipment points for drugs smuggled from Mexico. That traffickers in Mexico contract with traffickers in South American countries such as Bolivia, Columbia, and Peru to hold drugs for shipment into the United States, and to smuggle drugs into the United States using distribution networks established by Mexican cartels is well documented. Due to the ethnicity of the cartels, being Mexican, many of the smugglers arrested or implicated in drug smuggling are of that ethnicity. That, however, does not mean that other ethnically based drug smuggling organizations escape law enforcement attention.

Profile Stops

Introduction

Criminal profiling is often practiced when drug and money smuggling is suspected. This is not to be confused with so-called *racial profiling*, which is nothing more than selecting a target based on race or ethnicity with no other indicators of criminal activity being present.

A profile stop is only as valid as the indicators comprising the profile that underlies the reason for the stop. When considering a vehicle or pedestrian stop and detention, *reasonable suspicion* is the determining factor governing whether a court will accept the stop as legitimate and therefore legal.

Drug Courier Profiles (Vehicles)

Often, motorists will capture the attention of patrol officers, who suspect them of transporting illicit drugs, for one or more reasons. Sometimes the reasons are obvious, but sometimes they are subtle. Police officers working the highways and city streets have learned there are certain indicators that suggest a vehicle may be transporting drugs or money. Naturally, the greater the number of indicators, the greater the likelihood that drugs or money is in fact being transported. Officers must avoid the tendency to concentrate solely on vehicles conforming to what have proven to be reliable indicators of drug trafficking, while ignoring others because not all drug couriers display the same indicators.

Rental Cars

During the 1980s, drug traffickers began using rental cars and still use them today, although in over half the cases, personal vehicles are used (Remsberg, 1995). Rental vehicles offer reliability against mechanical failure thus reducing the potential of an undesirable roadside contact with law enforcement. Furthermore, a mechanical breakdown requiring repairs increases the likelihood that a mechanic will discover the drugs or cash in the vehicle while servicing it and alert law enforcement.

Drug organizations also use rental cars to distance themselves from the drugs and the courier in the event police stop the vehicle and arrest the driver, discovering drugs and/or cash in the process. For example, many organizations park a vehicle at a location with drugs or cash hidden inside. The driver receives a key to the vehicle that often only operates the doors and ignition, but not the trunk. Many times the only instruction the driver receives is to drive to a general destination and, after arriving, receive instructions as to where to park the vehicle and exchange it for another. If police stop and question the driver as to the origin and intended destination of the drugs, little information results because the courier knows only from where he or she picked up the vehicle, and the general destination. The renter usually uses a false name when renting the vehicle leaving his or her identity difficult to determine.

Rental cars provide advantages, as explained, but "compartmentalization" is another advantage they provide. Compartmentalization is effective in the event police stop the driver because, if the driver has only a key to the door and ignition, not the trunk, granting consent to search leaves police unable to access the trunk. If police do access the trunk and find drugs and/or cash therein, the driver claims no knowledge of the contents suggesting that a previous renter must have left them. Unlike personal vehicles, rental cars are not subject to seizure for forfeiture.

Many drug couriers do not know that they are transporting drugs, as was the case with Hasidic Jews in New York City, discussed under the subheading "Airport Drug Interdiction." Unwitting senior citizens often receive a generous fee to transport motor homes across the country, often unaware that drugs or cash is in the vehicle. However, sometimes they do know.

Police have recently discovered senior citizens crossing the Mexican border into the United States smuggling drugs. When questioned, the senior citizens often report that the allure of receiving the motor home as payment for driving it across the border was too hard to resist. Police recently arrested a man in his eighties who confessed to smuggling the drugs found in his vehicle.

Personal Vehicles

Personal vehicles used for transporting drugs offer couriers the opportunity to construct hidden compartments within the vehicles, and then use them repeatedly to transport drugs and/or cash. That is reminiscent of the tanker cars used to transport illicit (bootleg) alcohol during prohibition.

Purchasing vehicles using a false name makes it nearly impossible to identify the owner, and temporary registration is also an effective means of making it difficult for law enforcement to determine the origin of the vehicle while in transit. The courier sometimes receives the vehicle, if not intended for repeated use, as payment after making the drug or cash shipment.

Vehicles originating from a drug source state, such as Arizona or California, observed in an eastern state along with other indicators, may sometimes display the characteristics of a drug courier vehicle. For this reason, many couriers carry license plates for each state through which they pass.

Contradiction between indicators such as to the state of origin of a vehicle and the state of the license plate can give rise to suspicion. For example, a vehicle featuring a dealer logo or decals from one state while featuring a license plate from another may become suspect.

In Phoenix, Arizona, a Mexican drug organization utilizes VIN switched stolen vehicles with hidden compartments to transport drugs. In one case, a drug enforcement detective conducting surveillance of a drug house followed a vehicle from the house to a parking lot in a strip mall where he observed a package transferred to another vehicle. He subsequently followed the driver receiving the package and stopped him for a traffic violation (pretext stop). The driver granted consent to search the vehicle, but the officer found nothing in the passenger compartment. A more thorough search resulted in the discovery of a hidden compartment in the shifter compartment of the center console. The officer arrested the driver, charged him with possession and transportation of illicit drugs for sale, and seized the vehicle for forfeiture. Further investigation revealed the vehicle to be a VIN switched stolen car. Indeed, the Mexican organization was well aware of the benefit of utilizing stolen vehicles, hidden compartments, and vehicles registered to third persons.

A recent trend in Phoenix, Arizona, is for Mexican drug cartels to utilize stolen sport utility vehicles (SUVs) to smuggle large quantities of drugs into the United States across the Tohono O'odham Indian Nation that stretches 90 miles across the southern boundary of Arizona and actually extends into northern Mexico. The cartels utilize vehicles stolen from dealerships prior to an inventory count, or acquire vehicles by traditional auto theft methods. The vehicles are driven into Mexico and loaded with drugs and then driven across the Indian Reservation and into the U.S. in a caravan formation, usually late at night and at high speeds. The cartels employ the use of spotters on mountaintops to advise the smugglers of law enforcement presence on the desert floor below. The cartels equip the smugglers and spotters with night vision goggles, radios, scanners, cell phones, and automatic weapons. If law enforcement attempts an interdiction, one or more of the vehicles in the caravan breaks off and attempts to elude the officers while the caravan continues into the U.S. or retreats back into Mexico. Once the SUVs arrive in the United States, the drivers park them at prearranged locations for pickup by other members of the organization.

As stated, drug couriers often modify vehicles to conceal drugs or currency. However, the vehicles often display various indicators commonly associated with drug courier vehicles. Indictors of a drug courier vehicle are often subtle but meaningful if one is aware of them. Drug courier vehicles often display the following indicators:

- Rear end riding low (sagging under a load)
- Spare tire or luggage in the back seat to make room for more drugs in the trunk
- Tinted windows
- Windows down during unusually hot or cold weather, weather wherein windows are usually up
- Modifications to the vehicle
- Very little luggage, if any at all (out of state vehicles)
- "Good-guy" decals such as religious symbols, pro-police stickers, or anti-drug stickers
- Lifestyle statements such as drug paraphernalia, decals of drugs, or decals of rock groups such as the Grateful Dead
- Multiple deodorants used to mask drug odors
- Dirty vehicle with clean license plate, clean vehicle with dirty license plates, and/or clean tail light lens on a dirty vehicle
- Unusual driving habits such as driving abnormally slow, weaving, or driving that is too perfect

When considering the above indicators, keep in mind that courts have generally held that stopping a vehicle solely because the vehicle fits a drug courier profile is unconstitutional because the vehicle of many innocent travelers will display such indicators.

BOOK LERNIN' vs. STREET SMARTS

For the police officer, formal education is important, especially in the disciplines of psychology and sociology. So-called "street smarts," however, are just as important, and especially so for the undercover officer. Unfortunately, too often, the demands of our daily life cause us to be stuck in a routine that results in failure to look curiously beyond the boundaries of our daily life. Too often, we fail to expose ourselves to experience outside the parameters of our socialization circumstance.

For many people, travel has not been a significant part of their life, and when taking vacation, the tendency too often is to travel the interstate and visit so-called "tourist traps," instead of getting off the beaten path and getting to know people living in conditions different from their own. Similarly, there is a tendency to board a plane such as in Cleveland, Ohio, disembark in California, stay in a motel and visit places such as Disneyland, and then return home the same way. Travel of this nature does not significantly nurture a global perspective. It does little to enhance cultural and geographic awareness.

It is possible to travel without really traveling, as described. Alternatively, one learns a great deal when traveling by vehicle, off the so-called beaten path, and demonstrates the initiative to visit with people along the way. Take time to converse with the homeless and dine with them at a mission, perhaps also spending a night in the mission. Watch, listen, and visit with people while dining in sole-proprietorship restaurants in various ethnic communities, not omitting restaurants located in impoverished neighborhoods.

The point of all this is simply to break with convention, get out of the proverbial box and experience what is going on in the world. Discover how the people of other cultures, subcultures, and economic strata live. America offers so much variety that is worthy of experience considering she really is not the so-called "melting pot of the world," but a tossed-salad wherein the ingredients remain distinctly unique and identifiable.

So-called street smarts are important and enable the officer to apply experience-based logic in situations where overlooking details can result in an unsuccessful investigation. For example, an undercover police officer once failed in his effort to mingle inconspicuously with homeless people near a shelter and soup kitchen because, in spite of wearing disheveled clothing, he sported well-groomed hair, clean fingernails, and well-polished shoes.

Overlooking those details let homeless people instantly know he was not one of them but, almost certainly, a police officer.

The Calgary Police Service, Calgary, Alberta, Canada, includes a novel and valuable exercise when training new male and female undercover investigators. Constable Paul Wozney described the training program this way.

"Here is how our undercover officer-training program works. The undercover course is eight consecutive days in length, and features daytime classroom study and evening exercises on the street where the students experiment with and apply the concepts studied during the day in class.

"Each class features both male and female students, with the class divided into groups of 6-7 people each, each group featuring male and female students who work together as a team during the course of their training.

"During the eight-day training period, during the day students learn skills such as how to establish a cover and corresponding cover story, and they learn drug jargon. In the evening, they may begin practicing newly acquired knowledge by attending a bar to finagle a free drink from someone, and they will bum smokes on the street. By the third or fourth day of training, the students' knowledge and skills have advanced to the point they are successfully making purchases of illicit drugs on the street.

"By the sixth or seventh day, the students have mastered many of the undercover skills they will need on the job, at which time they are transported to a community an hour or two from Calgary. There they are stripped of all identification, all money, and they are forbidden to admit to anyone they are police officers. During this phase of their training, they must maintain their cover stories at all times, even if a local law enforcement officer detains and questions them.

"This phase of their training is intense and represents a culminating experience wherein they must successfully execute a number of daytime tasks, and nighttime tasks. For example, I require my students to purchase a disposable camera with which to take pictures to verify completion of various tasks. One such task required the students to obtain a new vehicle for test drive from a local dealership without providing any identification and have their picture taken with the vehicle in front of a local landmark, and another was to obtain pictures of each other begging for money. Remember, the students begin this phase of training with no money, yet they must purchase the camera, food, and secure a motel room for the night.

"The knowledge and skills the students acquire during the eight-day undercover course are amazing. For example, it is not uncommon for a group to earn as much as $300-$400 dollars ($200 U.S.) by begging during this culminating phase of training."

Chapter 6

MANAGING INFORMANTS

INTRODUCTION

An important element of drug investigations is the informant. The informant may be a suspect "working-off" a case, a "career informant" working for money, a frustrated resident living next to a drug house, a career criminal seeking to eliminate competition, or someone seeking revenge against another person. Developing and maintaining a professional working relationship with informants is challenging and sometimes frustrating, but it can be rewarding.

This chapter discusses the origin and development of informants in drug investigations. Also discussed are the various motivations of informants, and the legal issues that govern the use of informants in various situations.

WHY USE INFORMANTS?

Informants are excellent sources of information, often providing information that otherwise would be difficult or dangerous to obtain. They can often conduct covert surveillance in areas otherwise difficult for law enforcement to get into, and can provide the probable cause necessary for a search warrant and/or to make an arrest. Informants can set up drug deals for officers and introduce undercover officers to drug dealers.

TYPES OF INFORMANTS

Introduction

Depending on circumstances, terms such as nark, stool pigeon, snitch, and telltale identify informants. Street terms not withstanding, law enforcement officers generally refer to informants as CIs (Confidential Informants), or CSs (Confidential Sources). An informant, in the context of drug investigations is someone who informs or provides information to an officer about suspected criminal activity. Often the informant's identity remains a secret, but there are times when the informant is willing to testify in court, such as in the case of a retail employee or frustrated neighbor.

Officers investigating drug complaints will utilize the following three types of informants:

- Anonymous Informant
- Confidential Informant
- Past Proven Reliable Confidential Informant

A fourth type of informant that officers should not use is the so-called *blackballed informant*, blackballed by officers because of his or her past unreliability.

Although the term *informant* refers to anyone providing information to law enforcement, in the context of this chapter the term informant generally refers to someone who is confidential and to some degree reliable, and whose identity must be kept secret from the offender.

Anonymous Informant

The anonymous informant's identity is usually unknown to the officer. This type of informant will usually provide information in the form of a letter, e-mail, or by telephone, with the information sometimes relayed to the officer by a third party. Because the officer is unable to establish an anonymous informant's reliability, something that is always necessary when working with informants, it is necessary to verify the accuracy of information before acting upon it. Unless the officer verifies the accuracy of information received from an anonymous informant, when a case goes to trial the defense is likely to protest.

The following case studies illustrate the importance of validating anonymous information before acting on it.

Anonymous Tips Regarding Pedestrians

A case reviewed by the United States Supreme Court addressed the issue of acting on information received from anonymous sources. The case originated on October 13, 1995, when an anonymous caller reported to the Miami-Dade Police Department that a young black male standing at a particular bus stop, wearing a plaid shirt, was carrying a gun. Police officers went to the scene and observed a group of young black males standing at a bus stop as described by the anonymous caller. A black youth wearing a plaid shirt and fitting the description provided by the caller was among the group, but police could not discern whether he was carrying a gun. An officer approached the black male, asked him to put his hands up, and "frisked" him, finding a gun in his pocket. The officer seized the gun, arrested the suspect, and charged him with unlawfully carrying a concealed firearm and possession of a firearm by a minor.

Prior to the case going to trial, the suspect's attorney successfully convinced the judge to suppress the gun as evidence asserting that it had been seized illegally because the officers lacked reasonable suspicion to conduct the search and seizure. The suspect's attorney argued that the anonymous tip was unreliable because the police had no other information to verify that the suspect was carrying a concealed gun.

The prosecution appealed the trial judges ruling to the Third District Court of Appeals. The prosecution argued that once police arrived at the scene and saw that the anonymous caller had accurately described the person and location, the officers then had reasonable suspicion that the suspect was carrying a gun, and were therefore justified in conducting the "stop-and-frisk." The Appellate court reversed the lower court's decision allowing gun's admission into evidence. In 1998, however, the Supreme Court of Florida held the search invalid under the Fourth Amendment. The court found that anonymous tips are generally less reliable than tips from known informants and can form the basis for reasonable suspicion only if accompanied by specific indicia of reliability.

The State of Florida appealed the Florida Supreme Court ruling to the United States Supreme Court. The U.S. Supreme Court agreed with the Florida Supreme Court and held unanimously that an anonymous tip alleging that a person is carrying a gun is not enough to justify a police officer's stop and frisk of that person without further reliable information that the tip is credible.

Anonymous Tips Received by Letter

A case involving an anonymous letter, *Illinois v. Gates*, 462 U.S. 213 (1983), found its way to the United States Supreme Court. The investigation occurred in Bloomingdale, Illinois, a suburb of Chicago located in Du Page County. On May 3, 1978, the Bloomingdale Police Department received by mail an anonymous handwritten letter that read as follows:

> This letter is to inform you that you have a couple in your town who strictly make their living on selling drugs. They are Sue and Lance Gates, they live on

> Greenway, off Bloomingdale Rd. in the condominiums. Most of their buys are done in Florida. Sue his wife drives their car to Florida, where she leaves it to be loaded up with drugs, then Lance flys down and drives it back. Sue flys back after she drops the car off in Florida. May 3 she is driving down there again and Lance will be flying down in a few days to drive it back. At the time Lance drives the car back he has the trunk loaded with over $100,000.00 in drugs. Presently they have over $100,000.00 worth of drugs in their basement. They brag about the fact they never have to work, and make their entire living on pushers. I guarantee if you watch them carefully you will make a big catch. They are friends with some big drugs dealers, who visit their house often.

Officers corroborated the information by determining the suspect's address and learning that the husband made a reservation on a May 5 flight to Florida. A Drug Enforcement Administration (DEA) agent arranged for surveillance of the flight, and the surveillance disclosed that the husband took the flight, stayed overnight in a motel room registered in his wife's name, and left the following morning with a woman in a car bearing an Illinois license plate issued to the husband. The couple headed north on an interstate highway used by travelers to the Bloomingdale area.

Based on accumulated information along with a copy of the anonymous letter they had received, officers obtained a search warrant for the suspect's home and vehicle. The officers waited until the suspects arrived home, at which time marijuana and contraband were located in the suspect's home and vehicle trunk.

A suppression hearing prior to trial resulted in the evidence being suppressed because it did not meet the "two-pronged test" of (1) revealing the informant's "basis of knowledge" and (2) providing sufficient facts to establish either the informant's "veracity" or the "reliability" of the informant's report.

The Illinois Appellate and Supreme Court's also affirmed, holding that the letter and affidavit were inadequate to sustain a determination of probable cause for issuance of the search warrant under *Aguilar v. Texas*, 378 U.S. 108 (1964), and *Spinelli v. United States*, 393 U.S. 410 (1969), since they failed to satisfy the "two-pronged test."

The opinion of the United States Supreme Court, however, was that the letter, when corroborated by the police, created probable cause thus making the evidence admissible. Chief Justice Rehnquist issued the following statement regarding the *two-pronged test*:

> . . . The rigid 'two-pronged test' under Aguilar and Spinelli for determining whether an informant's tip establishes probable cause for issuance of a warrant is abandoned, and the 'totality of the circumstances' approach that traditional-

> ly has informed probable-cause determinations is substituted in its place. The elements under the 'two-pronged test' concerning the informant's 'veracity,' 'reliability,' and 'basis of knowledge' should be understood simply as closely intertwined issues that may usefully illuminate the common-sense, practical question whether there is 'probable cause' to believe that contraband or evidence is located in a particular place. The task of the issuing magistrate is simply to make a practical, common-sense decision whether, given all the circumstances set forth in the affidavit before him, there is a fair probability that contraband or evidence of a crime will be found in a particular place. And the duty of a reviewing court is simply to ensure that the magistrate had a substantial basis for concluding that probable cause existed. This flexible, easily applied standard will better achieve the accommodation of public and private interests that the Fourth Amendment requires than does the approach that has developed from Aguilar and Spinelli . . . Moreover, the 'two-pronged test' directs analysis into two largely independent channels -- the informant's 'veracity' or 'reliability' and his 'basis of knowledge' . . . There are persuasive arguments against according these two elements such independent status. Instead, they are better understood as relevant considerations in the totality-of-the-circumstances analysis that traditionally has guided probable-cause determinations: a deficiency in one may be compensated for, in determining the overall reliability of a tip, by a strong showing as to the other, or by some other indicia of reliability. (*Illinois v. Gates*, 462 U.S. 213 [1983])

This ruling illustrates the importance of applying the *totality of the circumstances test* in determining the overall reliability of a tip, rather than applying a set standard of rigid rules such as the *two-pronged test.* As we know, probable cause is fluid, and anonymous tips will lend themselves to various factors constituting probable cause. It is important, in any case, to corroborate anonymous information; anonymous information without validation is likely to be insufficient in establishing probable cause.

Confidential Informant

A confidential informant is a person who provides information to a police officer about suspected criminal activity. Although the officer knows the identity of the informant, the suspect does not have that information, and in fact usually does not know someone is providing information about him or her and his or her illegal activities.

Police usually confirm the identity of a confidential informant to substantiate that the person is who he or she claims to be, with identify confirmed via sources such as public and private records, fingerprints, and photographs.

When cultivating informants, officers create a *confidential informant file.* In instances where the informant has served as an informant in the past, the officer will scrutinize the quality of prior information the informant provided, a process that often includes contacting prior handling investigators.

Past Proven Reliable Confidential Informant

A *past proven reliable confidential informant* is one who has worked with one or more officers in the past, and provided information that established the informant as reliable. Courts usually accept this type of informant as being more credible because they have established a record of being reliable and consistent in the information they have provided. Although the courts tend to view these types of informants as having more credibility, it is still important for officers to validate the information they provide–do not base *probable cause* solely on the allegations of an informant regardless of how reliable he or she may appear.

Blackballed Informants

Officers should not utilize blackballed informants. A blackballed informant is one who has proven to be deceptive, implicated in criminal activity, or generally untrustworthy for any number of reasons. It can be difficult to identify a blackballed informant unless there is a system that identifies such informants.

In many instances, informants have previously provided information to law enforcement officers and, most often, such informants will advise the officer of that fact. However, the blackballed informant usually will not disclose his or her blackballed status, if he or she is even aware of it. Officers will discover that when they contact the officer who previously worked with the informant. This illustrates the importance of contacting officers who previously worked with an informant–those officers can provide valuable insight into the behaviors and psychology of the informant and, generally, the informant's degree of manageability and reliability. Additionally, the informant may have proven to be reliable in prior investigations. Establishing that fact will save the time usually required establishing the informant's reliability. However, the officer should still initiate a contract with the informant and maintain a file.

Problematic Informants

There are informants who are, or can become problematic. These informants are:

JUVENILES. Because of their minor status, legal issues can arise if parents or guardians are not aware of the arrangement the officer has with the youth.

In addition, most states do not consider a juvenile eligible to enter into a legal contract, which is required with most informant relationships.

DEFENDANTS ON PAROLE OR PROBATION. Individuals released from incarceration and placed on parole must comply with certain conditions–they are required to abide by various rules. In other instances, although the court convicted the informant of a crime, probation in lieu of jail or prison time resulted. In most instances, the conditions of parole or probation require an individual to avoid relationships with known criminals or activity that is illegal. It is difficult to utilize informants in a drug investigation without them violating the conditions of their release. If an officer believes it would be beneficial to utilize an informant who is on probation or parole, he or she should contact the attorney involved in the case, and the judge presiding in the sentencing, and discuss the situation. The overriding factor is the well-being of the informant, and his or her success in completing the probation and improving his or her life. It is often difficult for probationers and paroles to succeed if they continue to associate with criminals.

POTENTIAL DEFENDANT INFORMANTS. Informants implicated in prior criminal activity and currently cooperating with law enforcement can be difficult to manage because they must maintain a relationship with those against whom they are providing information. Moreover, depending on the circumstances, they may be required to suffer the consequences of their prior criminal activity. In some instances, however, depending on proper management and circumstances, such defendants will testify against others as well as being prosecuted themselves for similar crimes.

FEMALE INFORMANTS. Female informants can provide a wealth of information because men often trust and confide in them. Furthermore, women often communicate with other women more candidly than they do with men. Managing female informants can become problematic, however, if a male officer does not follow procedures, or fails to exercise appropriate precaution. The most frequent problem that occurs is a male officer becoming too close to a female informant, or giving the appearance to others of being closer to her than he really is. The other common problem is the female informant falsely accusing the officer of misconduct. The male officer can avoid those situations by following proper protocol when dealing with female informants.

Never should an officer become involved in a relationship with a female informant that is not professional and official in nature. Relationships outside professional or official boundaries will most likely by viewed as a conflict of interest and therefore deemed unethical. Officers should also refrain from becoming personally involved with someone they previously utilized as an informant. If possible, the male officer should never meet with a female informant alone–that will ensure that the relationship remains professional, and will prevent false allegations of officer misconduct. Meetings with female informants should occur in public places when possible.

UNWITTING INFORMANTS. The unwitting informant does not realize that police are using him or her as an informant. In drug cases, this usually results when the informant does not realize he or she is providing information to a police officer. For example, often an undercover officer will approach a street level dealer and ask where he or she can obtain drugs. In such instances, the street dealer/informant will provide the information, and often purchase the drugs for the officer. The officer can subsequently execute a search warrant on a specified location, or execute an arrest warrant based on the information received.

Another example of using an unwitting informant is the undercover officer who solicits information from a bartender and then leaves an uncharacteristically generous tip. The officer gives the bartender reason to believe the officer is involved in illegal activity. The problem with this type of informant is that they are generally time-consuming and difficult to control. The informant will often attempt to dominate the activity, although the officer can easily discontinue contact with them. The officer generally discontinues contact once the informant introduces the officer to the target suspect, and/or the necessary information obtained.

When using an unwitting informant, exercise care because he or she can be put at risk by being unaware of what he or she is doing. He or she will not know that he or she is compromising someone by providing the police with information. The unwitting informant may later contact the person they compromised not realizing that during court proceedings the person learned who compromised them.

INFORMANT MOTIVATION

Informants usually fall into specific categories depending on their motives. Many informants are working off charges in the court system, or doing it to receive money. Many are doing it for personal reasons such as to eliminate drugs and crime in their neighborhood, or they may have had a family member or close friend become involved with illicit drugs. Often there is more than one motivating factor. The officer must continually evaluate the informants' motivations because they generally provide information to benefit themselves, with the reliability of their information often affected by their motives.

Common motives of drug informants include:

- *Receive payment.* This informant seeks to profit monetarily by selling the police information about illicit drug activity.

- *Mercenary.* The mercenary, having obtained information about illicit drugs, seeks to determine who among local, county, state, and federal law enforcement will pay the most for the information.
- *Fear of prosecution or incarceration.* This person provides law enforcement with information about illicit drugs in an effort to avoid prosecution and/or incarceration, or in hopes of a lenient sentence.
- *Elimination of competition.* This person provides law enforcement with information about illicit drugs in an effort to have his or her competition arrested and jailed thus increasing his or her own market share.
- *Opportunist.* The opportunist does not go in search of information about illicit drugs, but having obtained information by chance will seek to sell the information to law enforcement.
- *Revenge.* This person provides information to the police to get revenge against someone for a real or imagined transgression.
- *Reformed criminal.* This person is a former criminal and often a former drug user trying to improve society by eradicating drugs and drug related crime.
- *Aspiring drug agent (wanna-be cop).* This person is acting on their desire to be a law enforcement officer, often more specifically a drug enforcement agent.

Informants who are working for pay, or to reduce or eliminate criminal charges against them have personal or secondary motives. Many times, an informant is seeking revenge on a person for real or imagined offenses. This can include an ex-spouse or lover, or an ex-friend or associate who is involved in criminal activity. In such instances, the informant may not be able to get close to the suspect, or purchase drugs from him or her, but he or she can provide in-depth information on the behaviors and habits of the suspect. The officer should act quickly on information received from such informants because any reconciliation between the informant and suspect will jeopardize the investigation.

Officers should keep in mind that often an informants' desire for retribution can be powerful, and may cause them to exaggerate information in an effort to get the officers attention, and in an effort to maximize the hurt they inflict on the other person. Officers should corroborate information received from informants who appear to be seeking retribution; however, their information can be extremely valuable and timely.

TIPS FOR HANDLING INFORMANTS

- *Maintain control of the informant and the case.* If the officer does not skillfully control his or her informant, the informant will try to control the case and attempt to influence its outcome. Furthermore, if informants are working off criminal charges, they will be selective against whom they provide information, often being reluctant to provide information against family, friends, drug sources, or individuals who are dangerous. If they are working for money, and are broke, they will tend to get anxious with the progress of the case. Sometimes their assertiveness can be problematic if it causes the case to move too quickly. Never permit informants to dictate the handling of a case; they must understand that is the officer, not them, who is in charge.

- *Limit the informant's exposure to undercover officers.* Many informants are working both sides of the law. Officers should not permit the informant to observe undercover vehicles or officers unless that is necessary, as that will compromise future investigations involving the informant.
- *Withhold information from the informant.* When officers speak with an informant, they should resist the temptation to provide information the informant does not know. Follow the need-to-know principle when providing the informant with information. If the informant asks questions and appears to be probing for information, officers should proceed cautiously and evaluate the informant's motives.
- *Maintain informant confidentiality.* The officer who agrees to keep an informant's identify confidential must make every effort to honor that agreement. Officers should be hesitant, however, to promise confidentiality in all circumstances. There may be situations that require the informant to testify in court, and thus their identity will no longer be secret. Those situations generally result when the informant has witnessed a violent or serious crime. Officers should also consider the possibility of dropping cases when the informant will be compelled to testify against his or her will, or when the defense attorney will cause revealing the informant's identify during a criminal trial. This is important if the officer intends to use the informant in the future, because identifying the informant will diminish his or her value. Revealing the informant's identify can also subject them to physical harm or death. Finally, while on the witness stand, the informant's credibility and motives are subject to challenge, and that can compromise the case.
- *Avoid making promises to the informant.* Officers should avoid making promises that he or she cannot honor. Promising to reduce or eliminate charges, but failing to do so, may result in court complications later. When discussing payment for information or evidence, avoid giving high estimates. Many informants are concerned for their safety and may desire relocation or witness protection. If that protection is not available under the circumstances, do not promise it. Officers should refrain from promising anything they cannot provide, or that is out of their control.
- *Officer and informant relationships.* Officers should treat informants with respect, and relationships should be professional. Over time, a bond

often develops between the officer and informant, but the bond must not develop into a friendship as that can taint the officer's judgment. Informants, once achieving friendship status, will attempt to use that standing for personal advantage, thus placing the officer in a situation where control on a professional level may be lost. Officers should also advise informants not to expect immunity for any crimes they commit, and in fact, committing crimes will often lead to the informant becoming "blackballed" and the officer/informant relationship terminated.

- *Informant control.* It is advisable that two officers control the informant, with one officer maintaining primary control. The officers should attempt to meet with the informant together whenever possible. When it is not possible for both officers to meet with the informant, ensure that another officer is present during the meeting. Two officers meeting with an informant is done for safety reasons as well as to prevent false allegations of officer misconduct.
- *Informant payments.* Officers should pay the informant as soon as possible after he or she has fulfilled the agreement. When making payment to an informant, have that act witnessed by another officer, and document it. Make payment based on the outcome of the information, rather than for the information only. For example, an informant receives payment for making a drug purchase for the officer, or having provided information utilized to obtain a search warrant. In the case of a search warrant, the officer can pay the informant for the information that justifies the search warrant request, or pay the informant based on the success of the search warrant, the latter being preferable. Paying for results will ensure against suspects being forewarned thus resulting in a "dry warrant." Paying for results will also encourage the informant to select targets that have a greater likelihood of successful police intervention. Officers should not put an informant on retainer because advancing them money will often lead to difficulties later when additional work is necessary.
- *Informant management policy.* Most agencies have a policy regarding informant management and officers must be familiar with that policy and honor it. Such policies commonly specify who may be used as an informant, and under what circumstances. Periodic reevaluation of informant management policies is important to ensure they remain consistent with current legalities.
- *Consistency and control.* The most important element of any relationship between an officer and an informant is control. Managing an informant will be much easier when there is a meeting of the minds. Early in the relationship, the officer must clarify the rules with the informant and insist on strict compliance. Officers must be vigilant in maintaining control and professionalism in every contact. Consistency is important, and if that is lost, the result will be a relationship that is difficult to control–

improving the situation will be difficult once complacency has set in. Officers must resist the temptation to get personal with the informant in hopes of gaining an advantage. A professional relationship is one of respect, trust, and professionalism.

RECRUITING INFORMANTS

Informants are worth cultivating. Indeed, many large and successful cases start with an officer taking the time to ask the right questions of a person, and cultivating them as an informant. One small bit of information from an informant can take the officer into cases beyond his or her imagination.

Informants come from a variety of sources and provide information for a variety of reasons, but as expected, their degree of reliability varies considerably. Whether the officer has an informant that he or she cultivated, or has acquired because the person initiated the relationship, it is important to ascertain their motive and degree of reliability.

Some informants initiate contact with law enforcement. They may or may not state their reason for desiring to provide information, but with proper questioning and acute listening, the officer can usually identify the informant's motives. It is important to identify his or her motive because making that determination helps to ascertain reliability and credibility, both of which can affect the outcome of a case.

Crime-stopper or *tip programs* also result in police officers acquiring informants. These programs often ensure informant anonymity with the officer not knowing who is providing information. Commonly, the informant receives an identification number, and receives pay based on the reliability of the information he or she provides, and the resulting success of the investigation. Effective marketing and efficient management have resulted in crime-stopper type programs being very successful.

Persons, once arrested, are excellent sources of information and often recruited as informants. In drug cases, the state, county, or city generally become the victims' and thus the issues of restitution and victims rights do not become an issue. These cases are generally the easiest to work with, having the defendant work off charges by providing information. When a victim is involved, however, it becomes more difficult for a defendant to work off charges. In spite of this difficulty, advising the victim of the process, and providing restitution, often encourages him or her to allow the defendant to assist law enforcement efforts.

Incarcerated subjects can become informants and provide useful information about individuals not currently incarcerated. After a sufficient period of incarceration, however, the information the informant provides may be stale (out of date). Check it for reliability. Usually the informant provides information because he or she is seeking leniency when sentenced. Hence, it is important to ensure that he or she provides information voluntarily and in the absence of having received promises. Many times the incarcerated person is facing the prospect of prison time with little hope of probation, with his or her only hope for leniency being the officer putting in a good word for him or her during sentencing.

In cases where the cellmate of a suspect provides information about the person's current or future drug dealing or other criminal activity within or without the correctional facility, restrictions on using informants generally do not apply. Conversely, when using a suspect's cellmate to acquire information about the crime for which the suspect is charged, and trial is pending, the suspect's right to counsel is a factor (Sixth Amendment to the United States Constitution). Information that does not pertain to pending cases in court is generally legal to acquire, as is information pertaining to pending cases if acquired without deliberate effort on the part of the cellmate informant. In essence, the cellmate must maintain a passive demeanor, i.e., listening and reporting, but not actively soliciting information.

Patrol officer contacts with people on the street can evolve into informant relationships. The ability to cultivate someone as an informant is especially likely in situations when the officer finds drug paraphernalia in the person's possession, but would not file charges anyway, but the person does not know that. These individuals can provide helpful information on drug dealers in exchange for the officer not arresting them or submitting charges. Officers should check their department's policy on these types of situations, and consult their prosecuting agency.

When an informant only provides information and there is no intention to use that person to make drug purchases, or to make undercover officer introductions to a drug dealer, an officer/informant contract is generally not necessary. The contact is more or less a street interview, after which the officer releases the person without charging him or her. If the officer intends to use the person to make drug purchases, or to make undercover officer introductions to drug dealers in order to avoid real or threatened charges, the officer should document the initial investigation in a written report, and in some cases have the informant enter into a written contract. Again, officers should check the policy of their department because policies vary considerably between agencies. The primary concern is to document the initial arrest or contact with the informant. That is important to defend against an informant later accusing the officer of coercion or intimidation to induce him or her to work off false charges. Many street-smart drug users are aware that drug paraphernalia charges will not go anywhere in the court system and therefore will not cooperate with the officer.

In instances when the officer develops an informant but most of the information the person provides pertains to activity in another jurisdiction, it may be prudent to turn the informant over to an officer in that jurisdiction. This reciprocal practice is an excellent means of acquiring informants.

ESTABLISHING INFORMANT RELIABILITY

The informant, once developed, must become *reliable* and there are various ways to accomplish that. Establishing informant reliability is nothing more than determining that there is a basis upon which to have confidence that he or she is trustworthy, credible, honest, and dependable. *The standard is that the informant is believable and can be trusted to provide accurate information.* One way to establish reliability is to have the informant make controlled drug buys. Controlled drug buys will usually not result in a prosecutable case, but will establish reliability on the part of the informant. Other ways to establish reliability include having the informant introduce an undercover officer to drug dealers, or provide information that leads to the seizure of contraband.

Officers can also establish informant reliability by determining the extent of his or her knowledge of illicit drugs. For example, the officer can question the informant about the practices and terms characteristic of the drug culture. In the case of an informant who has knowledge of drug manufacturing, when the informant accurately describes the manufacturing process, he or she is establishing reliability. If the informant provides information about past or present individuals, places, vehicles, or events, and the officer corroborates that information, reliability is established. Each case is circumstance specific and for that reason, circumstances determine what is required to establish informant reliability. Sometimes the officer corroborates information via physical surveillance, or with information from another informant who has personal and independent knowledge of the issue. When an informant's information results in an arrest and conviction, reliability is established.

As illustrated, there are numerous ways to establish informant reliability. One method is not necessarily best inasmuch as the appropriateness of each depends on the informant and the circumstances.

DEBRIEFING AND REGISTERING CONFIDENTIAL INFORMANTS

Debriefing Confidential Informants

During the initial debriefing of a new informant, there is information the officer should acquire to determine the capabilities, limitations, manageability, and potential reliability of the new informant. The officer should also scrutinize the informant's current life situation as it pertains to motivations, capabilities, limitations, and reliability. For example, the officer should ask if the informant owes money to a drug dealer for drugs fronted in the past; a delinquent debt such as this will affect capabilities and limitations. The officer may find it difficult to have an informant attempt purchasing drugs when he or she owes money to the dealer.

The officer should attempt to learn as much as possible about the drug dealer he or she will target using information the informant provides. When receiving information from a new informant, it must be independently verified and corroborated.

Other questions the officer should seek answers to include:

- What is the informant's relationship with the drug dealer such as family member or friend?
- How long has the informant been in business with the drug dealer?
- Has the informant introduced buyers in the past?
- Does the drug dealer challenge people unknown to him or her, and, if so, how and to what extent?
- Does the drug dealer insist that buyers use drugs in his or her presence?
- How does the informant contact the drug dealer?
- Does the drug dealer carry a weapon?
- What is the drug dealer's comfort level when dealing drugs, especially when interacting with people he or she does not know?
- Is the drug dealer paranoid and alert for surveillance, or comfortable and confident?
- Does the drug dealer use drugs? If so, what drugs and to what extent?

Learning the drug dealer's habits (modus operandi) is important in identifying the most successful means to obtain the evidence necessary for prosecution and conviction, with officer safety also an issue.

The important questions the officer should ask of new informants are not limited to the ones identified above, however. Every informant and every case is unique and the officer must tailor questions and manage the informant accordingly. Officers must guard against the tendency to develop a preference for one method for managing informants to the exclusion of others. When using informants, the officer must be flexible and utilize whatever method is necessary under the circumstances to accomplish the intended task.

Registering Confidential Informants

When registering a confidential informant (CI), it is important for the officer to be consistent and follow established policies. Maintain a separate and secure file for each informant, and maintain his or her anonymity. Do not disclose the informant's identity even to other officers. There have been occasions when another officer inadvertently revealed an informant's identity to other informants or suspects, causing much distress to the informant.

Reveal the informant's identity to other officers only on a need-to-know basis to reduce the likelihood of accidental disclosure.

Photograph and fingerprint informants and then run their fingerprints through the *Automated Fingerprint Identification System* (AFIS), when possible. This will corroborate the informant's identity if their fingerprints are in the system, and it may identify any outstanding cases in which the informant is implicated. Conduct an extensive criminal history check as well, and use whatever documentation exists to verify the informant's reliability.

The officer should explain the following requirements to the new informant, and emphasize that infractions are unacceptable:

- The officer, not the informant, is in control of everything that happens.
- The informant must not engage in any illegal activity outside that which the officer controls.
- The informant must honor his or her role as an informant, and follow the agreed upon guidelines.
- The informant must honor the procedure for officer/informant contact such as who will initiate contact, when and how.
- The informant must be punctual for all meetings.
- If arrested, the informant must not disclose that he or she is cooperating with police as an informant. Unauthorized disclosure will risk termination of the agreement.
- Indiscreet actions by the informant that compromise the investigation may result in termination of the agreement.

The informant must fill out the registration packet and all other applicable forms in the presence of an officer.

CONTROLLED BUYS

Introduction

Controlled buys usually entail the purchase of illegal street drugs, although other contraband such as firearms is often the subject of this technique. Informants make controlled buys under the direct control of law enforcement, to establish reliability or to obtain evidence against a suspect. The controlled buy can also establish probable cause for a search warrant.

Officers should not use informants to make controlled buys in those instances where the officer can personally infiltrate an organization to make buys. If, however, it would be difficult or potentially dangerous to an unacceptable degree for an officer to make buys, an informant may be better suited to infiltrate and make buys. Using informants in such instances does not imply that the life of an informant has less value than that of the officer. Use of informants, in such instances, reflects the fact that informants are often better equipped to accomplish the necessary task. For example, the informant may know essential people, talk the correct lingo (vernacular), and display an essential physical appearance. Often, the informant best equipped to make controlled drug buys is missing teeth, displays visible skin sores, skinny in an emaciated way, or in other respects fits the profile of the stereotypical drug user.

Planning a Controlled Buy

When planning a controlled buy, it is important for the officer to learn as much as possible about the suspect and the location where the buy will take place. If the informant cannot provide the officer the name of the suspect, or an address, the officer should have the informant point out the location personally. This practice is good to employ regardless, as it can minimize the likelihood of mistakenly investigating the wrong location. The officer should determine the nature of the informant's relationship with the suspect, and determine the best time and location to make the buy.

Prior to attempting a controlled buy, the officer should carefully brief the informant about the transaction and the expected outcome. If the objective is to obtain the probable cause necessary to obtain a search warrant for the suspect's place of residence, it may be best to attempt the buy at that location. If the suspect conducts business predominately by delivery, surveillance of the suspect's residence may be necessary. Surveillance often discloses whether the suspect transports drugs from the residence, or obtains them from another location prior to the sale.

When making controlled buys, paper currency should be marked and the serial numbers of bills recorded. That is important for the purpose of forfeiture if the subsequent serving of a search warrant at the suspect's place of residence results in recovery of the money.

Body transmitters are useful to document conversation between informant and suspect during the buy, and to ensure the safety of the informant. Officers should remember, however, that recorded conversations are evidence and will tend to reveal the identity of the informant when the case goes to trial. Furthermore, officers should consult the prosecutor prior to using body transmitters when making controlled buys because in some states, recording is not legal unless *all* parties to the conversation are aware of it and have consented to it. In many states, however, surreptitious recording is legal if at least one person, the informant or undercover officer in this case, is aware of it and has consented to it. This pertains to the "one-party consent" versus "two/all party consent" rule. Federal law embraces the "one-party consent" rule, but many states have adopted the "two/all party consent" rule. State laws may deviate from federal laws by being more restrictive, but they may not deviate by being less restrictive. It is important to ascertain the legality of body transmitters and recordings in one's state *before* engaging in the practice of using them.

Conducting the Controlled Buy

Prior to the informant making a controlled buy, officers should search the informant for contraband and remove personal funds. This will reduce the likelihood that an informant will fake a buy and provide the officer with drugs not obtained from the suspect. Moreover, by removing the informant's personal funds, there will be less likelihood of the informant using the wrong funds to make the buy, with this concern being especially important if marked money is used. Taking the informant's personal funds will also prevent him or her from paying more than desired for the drugs, or purchasing more drugs than agreed and surreptitiously retaining a portion for themselves. When the informant is fitted with a body transmitter, it is important to test the transmitter for proper operation before the drug buy takes place.

Before the informant makes a controlled drug buy, if he or she will be using his or her personal vehicle, search it for contraband, funds, and weapons. When possible, use the undercover vehicle to transport the informant to or near the buy location, although, understandably, many informants will resist this. When transporting the informant to the location of the buy, it is not necessary to drop him or her off in front of the premises if the officer can maintain surveillance while he or she enters and exits the premises. The informant can provide the suspect with the excuse that a friend dropped him or her off and will pick them up after he or she leaves.

When an informant makes a drug buy, the controlling officer must instruct him or her relative to what may or may not be done during the transaction. When the informant is fitted with a body transmitter, instruct the informant to talk slowly and count the money aloud when making the transaction. The informant must know that the officer will monitor all conversation. This is a legal issue pertaining to "participant and consensual monitoring." As previously stated, in many states it is legal to monitor and record a conversation if at least one person participating in the conversation knows about the monitoring.

Before the informant makes a controlled buy, the officer must instruct him or her to proceed directly to the suspect and not get involved in conversation or otherwise make personal contact with others at the premises. After making the buy, the informant must immediately return to the vehicle or a predetermined pick-up location. While making a controlled buy, the informant must not ingest drugs. There are exceptions, however, such as when the drug dealer threatens to injure or kill the informant unless drugs are ingested, this usually being done as a precaution to determine if the informant is a police officer.

Officers must also stress to the informant the importance of not compromising the investigation by being reckless or making promises to the suspect. Such promises could include the suspect promising something other than the immediate payment of money in exchange for contraband. The officer must also advise the informant to avoid setting up future drug transactions that may be impossible or difficult for the officer to honor.

If the informant is of the opposite sex of the suspect, caution him or her against inappropriate conduct during the controlled buy. It would seem that this point needs no mention, but it is important.

During the buy, keep the informant under constant visual surveillance whenever possible. The location of the buy should be under surveillance prior to, during, and after the buy to identify countersurveillance. If a listening device such as a body transmitter is used, monitor conversations closely to ensure informant safety. Closely monitoring the conversation is also necessary to be aware of what transpires because the recording, and testimony pertaining to it, may be required later during trial.

After the Controlled Buy

After making the buy, require the informant to initial the evidence to preserve the chain of custody unless they are to remain confidential. After a buy is attempted or made, again search the informant and his or her vehicle. Also, require the informant to provide a statement regarding the buy. To ensure against compromising the investigation, and to ensure informant safety, instruct the informant not to discuss the transaction with anyone. Although the officer has a working relationship with the informant, the informant receives no information about the investigation such as what will be done or when. The informant receives information only on a need-to-know basis.

After a successful buy, enter contraband, audio recordings, and informant statements into evidence as soon as possible, and do so in a manner consistent with departmental policy. If the informant receives payment for making the buy, document payment with a receipt and have a third party witness the making of payment. When a buy is successfully made, as soon as practical thereafter, update the informant's file to reflect the transaction and payment. Furthermore, document what occurred in a written report as soon as possible. The report must be restricted from public view, such as members of the news media, and restricted from the view of officers not associated with the case, at least until the case is completed.

Controlled Buy Summary

- When preparing for and conducting controlled buys the officers involved in the case make all the decisions, not the informant.
- The informant should never be trusted to the extent that the information he or she provides does not undergo corroboration by other sources.
- Always search the informant before and after he or she makes a controlled drug buy, and use the same search method in each instance. If the informant uses a personal vehicle, also search it before and after he or she makes a buy.
- Never provide the informant with information other than what they need to make the controlled buy. That helps to avoid compromising the case, and it helps ensure the informant's safety.

DANGERS AND DIFFICULTIES OF USING INFORMANTS

Introduction

Most informants utilized by police officers are criminals with varying degrees of experience and potential as an informant. Therefore, the officer must consider many things when using informants. Because most informants are criminals, they are often unpredictable when under pressure. Furthermore, during the officer/informant relationship, the informants become educated to law enforcement techniques and methods and will use that knowledge to further their criminal careers.

The following are common difficulties and dangers associated with the use of informants, although the difficulties and dangers are not limited to the issues discussed here. When working with informants, officers must be vigilant, resourceful, and flexible because every case is circumstance specific. Officers must always expect the unexpected and be ready to react accordingly.

The Double-Cross

One of the greatest dangers the officer faces when using informants is the informant who decides to double-cross (betray) him or her by providing information to suspects. This type of informant can put officers' lives in jeopardy, as well as create legal issues that can compromise a case. The double-crossing informant may function for some time as such before the officer realizes he or she is providing information to suspects.

Unpredictable Informants

Informants can be unpredictable when they are under pressure. They may decline to make a controlled drug buy or infiltration at the last minute after the officer devoted hours in preparation for the operation. Informants can become nervous, paranoid, or excited under various circumstances, thus making them ineffectual, with methamphetamine use magnifying these issues.

Other circumstances also contribute to unpredictability such as the informant who has an incentive to flee. The informant who has an incentive to flee, whether it is to flee from law enforcement or other criminals, may not be reliable. Such a person may unexpectedly disappear, or otherwise take unexpected risks, with this being especially likely if there is an increased level of paranoia.

Counter-Intelligence by Informants

An informant's life is often the proverbial rollercoaster ride characterized by pronounced ups-and-downs of fortune (vicissitudes). They have good days and bad days. Because drug use is part of the equation, informants can be extremely moody and unpredictable. At any time, if they are not already engaged in the selling of illicit drugs, they may begin doing so. For this reason, officers must be careful when discussing cases and the techniques of drug investigation in the presence of informants. Even when exercising caution and providing information to the informant in measured ways, on a need-to-know basis, they do obtain a grasp of many aspects of a drug investigation. In addition to learning the officer's operational methods, the informant learns the identity of the undercover officer as well as other officers with whom he or she comes into contact. With large law enforcement agencies, this may not be as serious a concern as it is with small agencies that have very few undercover officers.

Informant Prolongs the Investigation

Informants sometimes attempt to prolong drug investigations in an effort to obtain more money, with this being especially likely when they do not have legitimate employment. The reality of this concern causes one to revisit the issue of control; the officer must maintain control of his or her informants with the rules of the officer/informant relationship clarified early and reinforced as necessary.

Informant Criminal Activity

Informants who participate in criminal activity can be problematic for law enforcement. Informants involved in drug investigations are usually drug users themselves, and that is the reason for their recruitment and cultivation as informants; they are often good at buying drugs because they do it on a continuous basis. Although the officer may have no choice but to accept that his or her informant is using illicit drugs, the officer must not condone the activity or give the informant reason to believe that if arrested he or she will receive leniency because he or she is an informant.

Many informants who are working-off original drug charges become paid informants. The concern with such informants, however, is that they may expect leniency and anticipate working off future drug charges. They must understand that may not be the case. The officer must consider each informant and situation independently and determine if it is acceptable to continue using an informant if arrested. If the informant, once arrested, reveals his or her role as an informant and thereby compromises an investigation, his or her usefulness is usually history–he or she is "blackballed" with services as an informant discontinued.

The Rip-Off

Another area of danger when conducting a drug transaction, and this is an ever-present and serious danger, is the potential *rip-off*, the robbery of drugs or drug money. If a criminal can obtain money or drugs for nothing, he or she may attempt it. If the quoted price of the drugs seems lower than normal, or if the dealer fails to engage in negotiation, officers should anticipate a rip-off. When using an informant or undercover officer to buy drugs, orchestrate every drug transaction in a manner that minimizes the potential of a rip-off.

Suspects who insist on specifying the time and location of a drug transaction, who insist on having extra people in the vicinity during the transaction, or who insist that the informant arrive alone is suggesting a planned rip-off. Never permit a suspect to dictate the time and location of a drug deal, thus depriving the officer of his or her ability to prepare for and control the circumstances. If a suspect persists in his or her uncooperativeness, to an extent that deprives the officer of reasonable control, the potential for a rip-off is high–abort the plan.

When the informant has made a *money flash* and the suspect wants to see the money a second time, there is a good chance the intent is to rip off the money. There is no justifiable reason for a drug dealer to see the money a second time after negotiating a deal. When flashing money, a different person (the moneyman) arrives in a separate vehicle and flashes the money. After the flash, the vehicle leaves the area and returns only when the deal is to commence. This tactic is effective because the dealer does not know where the money is, and cannot target the informant at the scene or later by following him or her from the scene, because the informant does not have the money. When the transaction does commence, however, the informant may produce funds at that time, as the dealer did not know before that time where the funds were located. If a rip-off is the intent, nevertheless, it is insignificant when and from where the money appears, as the money is the target once produced. Hence, having the moneyman flash the money and then leave, returning only to consummate the deal, does not eliminate the potential for a rip-off, but does reduce the window of opportunity.

Drug transactions that involve large sums of money carry with them the increased risk of a rip-off. That is not to say that smaller amounts of money do not lend themselves to a rip-off, but it is not as common because it would tend to diminish a drug dealer's customer base. Ripping-off a small amount of money does not result in a gain sufficient to offset the loss represented by the diminished customer base.

Other indications of a planned rip-off include anyone on the suspect's team driving a stolen vehicle, the suspect trying to change the initial plan and lure the informant or undercover officer to a remote location, or suspects arriving unexpectedly during the transaction.

Foreign Nationals

When dealing with informants who are foreign nationals, the officer will find they usually exhibit a way of thinking that is different from that of American-born informants. Differences exist because of cultural differences. Informants from Mexico, for example, tend to have less trust of law enforcement than people socialized in the United States, their level of trust also being less in many instances than exists with people socialized in other countries. This can have a tremendous impact on officer/informant relations, as well as the eventual outcome of a case.

Foreign nationals also have different expectations of, and comfort levels with, violence. Some foreign nationals, depending on their country of origin, have experienced violence and death on a daily basis. For that reason, some foreign nationals have a greater propensity for violence than exists with those born and socialized in the United States. In addition, foreign nationals tend to feel more anonymous in the United States than American-born citizens, and they have the comfort of knowing they usually can return to their country of origin if desired.

When it is necessary to use an interpreter to communicate with a foreign-born informant, be sure the interpreter not only speaks the informant's native language, but also speaks the correct dialect. Furthermore, it is essential that the interpreter also understand the dominant American culture and that of the informant.

LEGAL ISSUES AND ETHICS

Maintaining Informant Confidentiality

Preserving an informant's confidentiality is a necessary and widely accepted principle, especially as it pertains to drug investigations. This confidentiality allows the uninhibited flow of information from private individuals to law enforcement officials. Depending on the jurisdiction, courts will view the disclosure of informant identity differently, as there are no fixed rules by which to abide. When a court withholds an informant's identity, thus denying the defendant his or her right to cross examination and confrontation, the denial generally does not violate the Sixth Amendment right of confrontation.[5] A practice referred to as the "informer's privilege" [6] includes a number of key factors that will keep an informant's identity confidential. These factors include officers testifying as to what foundation of reliability the infor-

---

5. "The Sixth Amendment to the United States Constitution guarantees the right of an accused in a criminal prosecution "to be confronted with the witnesses against him." This right is secured for defendants in state as well as federal criminal proceedings under Pointer v. Texas, *380 U.S. 400* (1965). [c]onfrontation means more than being allowed to confront the witness physically. "Our cases construing the [confrontation] clause hold that a primary interest secured by it is the right of cross-examination." Douglas v. Alabama, *380 U.S. 415, 418* (1965). Professor Wigmore stated: " 'The main and essential purpose of confrontation is to secure for the opponent the opportunity of [415 U.S. 308, 316] cross-examination. The opponent demands confrontation, not for the idle purpose of gazing upon the witness, or of being gazed upon by him, but for the purpose of cross-examination, which cannot be had except by the direct and personal putting of questions and obtaining immediate answers.' 5 J. Wigmore, Evidence 1395, p. 123 (3d ed. 1940). (Emphasis in original.)" (*Davis v. Alaska*, 415 U.S. 308 [1974]).

6. "What is usually referred to as the informer's privilege is in reality the Government's privilege to withhold from disclosure the identity of persons who furnish information of violations of law to officers charged with enforcement of that law. Scher v. United States, *305 U.S. 251, 254*; In re Quarles and Butler, *158 U.S. 532*; Vogel v. Gruaz, *110 U.S. 311, 316.* The purpose of the privilege is the furtherance and protection of the public interest in effective law enforcement. The privilege recognizes the obligation of citizens to communicate their knowledge of the commission of crimes to law-enforcement officials and, by preserving their anonymity, encourages them to perform that obligation. [353 U.S. 53, 60]

"The scope of the privilege is limited by its underlying purpose. Thus, where the disclosure of the contents of a communication will not tend to reveal the identity of an informer, the contents are not privileged. Likewise, once the identity of the informer has been disclosed to those who would have cause to resent the communication, the privilege is no longer applicable" (*Roviaro v. United States*, 353 U.S. 53 [1957]).

mant had, officers being subject to cross-examination by the defense, and the judge being satisfied that the officers are truthful and did not create a situation that mandates revealing the informant's identity. The *informer's privilege* does not require a jurisdiction to keep an informant's identity confidential. Rather, it provides that a judge is not guilty of unconstitutional conduct by allowing the prosecution to keep an informant's identity confidential, especially once ascertaining that the officer's testimony of the informant's information is inherently believable.

Maintaining the confidentiality of an informant is easier when the undercover officer accompanying an informant on a drug transaction ensures that the informant does not become a material participant of the transaction. If the informant simply introduces the undercover officer to the suspect, usually the informant will not need to testify. If the informant makes the buy or witnesses it, however, the informant may be required to testify.

Informant Involvement

Concealing Informant Identity

Whether it is necessary to disclose an informant's identity often depends on how much involvement the informant had in the case. If an informant sets up a drug buy, is present at its commission, or actually participates in the buy, expect the court to order disclosure. Hence, certain types of involvement, or too much involvement, can cause the defense to challenge the *informer's privilege.* In the final analysis, if the informant is a material witness to the offense for which the defendant is charged, and the informant's testimony is crucial in determining the defendant's innocence or guilt, the court may order *discovery,* thus revealing the identity of the informant. Hence, officers must consider the extent to which they involve informants in drug transactions.

In some cases, when the court orders disclosure, such as when there is a question about informant reliability, or there is doubt that the informant actually exists, an *in camera* hearing may take place. An *in camera* hearing generally occurs in the judge's chambers, and requires the prosecution to present the informant to the judge for questioning.

It is important that an informant's participation be limited if disclosure of identity is to be avoided, and there are ways to ensure limited participation. One method is to have the informant introduce an undercover officer to the drug dealer, with the undercover officer then purchasing drugs. Officers refer to this technique as an *introduction.* The informant is a material witness in such instances because he or she set up the deal, was present at its commission, and sometimes took part in the commission of the offense. In this type of scenario, however, the suspect is rarely charged; instead, the drugs are impounded as a *reliability buy* and the informant need not testify.

Once the informant introduces the undercover officer to the drug dealer, the hope is that the suspect will become comfortable with the undercover officer and consequently continue selling drugs to him or her. The officer can then begin making *case buys* against the suspect without the informant's involvement. Although the informant is not a party to subsequent drug buys, the buys that serve as a basis for prosecution, the possibility exists that the defense will demand revealing the informant's identity. Counter this by emphasizing that the informant was not present and did not participate in setting up the undercover officer's subsequent purchases. If the defense persists, the prosecutor can suggest that revealing the informant's identity will result in prosecution of the initial introduction purchase.

Other factors that affect when disclosure may be required include the availability of other witnesses or informants. The informant may also be required to testify when existing witnesses offer conflicting testimony, and there is a basis to believe the informant's testimony will clarify the issue.

Each case is unique and there is no prevailing standard by which to evaluate cases when determining whether to dismiss or proceed with prosecution when revealing the informant's identity is an issue. That is a decision for each officer and prosecutor to make based on the importance of the case, and the future usability of the informant.

When the possibility exists that the defendant knows the identity of the informant, the privilege against disclosure of identity may no longer be available.

The Informant and Probable Cause for a Search Warrant

Informants often provide the *probable cause* necessary to obtain a search warrant on a suspect's residence; informants typically will make a controlled purchase of drugs from the location of interest thus establishing probable cause. Although an informant purchases the drugs to establish probable cause, officers will not file the *sale case* to avoid making the informant material in the charge.

Informants can also provide the basis for a search warrant without anyone actually making a drug buy. For example, if a *past proven reliable confidential informant* has occasion to observe criminal activity at a location, or drugs in the possession of a specified individual, and informs the officer, probable cause sufficient to obtain a search warrant often exists. In instances where an exigency exists, such as the suspect being on foot or in a vehicle, officers can act on the information immediately without a search warrant and arrest and search the suspect. If no exigency exists, however, obtain a search warrant.

In cases such as those described above, it is not usually required that the informant's identity be revealed because the informant provided reliable information, based on firsthand observations, that drugs were in the possession of a certain person or at a specified location. Nevertheless, defense attorneys will sometimes argue for disclosure in hopes that the prosecutor will dismiss the case rather than reveal the informant's identity. If the defense is persistent in arguing for discloser of the informant's identity, the previously described tactic of suggesting the likelihood of an additional charge may neutralize the request. If discloser is forced, consider dismissing the case.

Entrapment

It is important for officers to understand what does and does not constitute *entrapment.* When setting up drug transactions using informants, understanding the elements of entrapment enables the officer to avoid creating a situation that enables a criminal defendant to invoke the entrapment defense. Refer to Chapter 5, subheading "Entrapment."

PROCEDURAL CONTROL

Introduction

Establishing guidelines regarding the proper use of Information Sources (confidential informants), and establishing procedures to monitor informant use are fundamental to efficiency and consistency. Policies should specify:

- The type of informants officers may use, and those precluded from use because of "blackballed" status.
- How informants are to be identified, contacted, documented, and used. The procedure should also specify the method for paying informants.
- Informant security procedures to ensure that the informant's identity is maintained in a system that is secure from those outside the agency as well as those in the agency that do not have a need-to-know the identity of informants.

Detailed Procedures

Introduction

Law enforcement personnel who utilize informants must be familiar with their agency's policies and procedures regarding informant management.

The policies should be in written form, and reviewed periodically and modified as needed. The following are the policies and procedures of a major southwestern metropolitan police department's drug enforcement unit. The policies and procedures address most aspects of informant management.

Master Name File

A master-name card file identifying *Information Sources* utilized by drug investigation officers is in a locked cabinet in a supervisor's office. If the unit has an administrative sergeant, he or she is often the most appropriate person to maintain the file. Supervisors assigned to the investigative unit should be the only ones with access to the information source name-file. Organize the master-name card file alphabetically using the information source's real name. The card identifying inactive, or "blackballed," informants goes in a separate section of the file.

The information source card should contain only the source's name (last, first, and middle), the information source number, and the case officer's name and serial number. If it is determined that the information source is unreliable, or is not going to be used before a number is assigned or an agreement is signed, this should be noted on the card and the card then placed in a file reserved for *inactive* information sources.

Informant Identification Form

Properly identifying a new informant and documenting informant information is the first step in signing up an informant–this is the responsibility of the controlling officer. Form 6-1, in the Appendix at the end of this chapter, illustrates *Information Source Personal Data Sheets.* These forms are permanent records and include identifying information such as a social security number and drivers license number, as well as why the source is informing. Assign the informant a source number, and create a manila folder file on the source. The folder tab should contain only the *Information Source Number.* The file will contain a recent color photograph of the source, a completed *Personal Data Sheet,* and the signed confidential informant agreement. Record the fingerprints of information sources who do not possess valid identification, and whose identity is unconfirmed; place the fingerprint card in the information source's file folder. As stated earlier, the administrative sergeant should maintain a locked file cabinet in their office to ensure the security of informant information.

Information Source Numbers

Officers who utilize confidential information sources on a continuing basis should issue informant identification numbers to facilitate keeping their identity secret. Information sources can than be referred to by number when discussing cases, or on documents such as payment receipts. The information source used on a one-time basis usually receives no number. A name card, however, is completed and placed in the Master Name File with a notation that the informant has no identification number. If the information source receives funds for services rendered or is involved in a controlled drug purchase, record that fact on the Informant Contact Record and file it under the Information Source's name.

Officers should issue consecutive numbers when assigning informant numbers. A practical method is to use the officer's agency's acronym, his or her serial number, and a consecutive number starting at 001, e.g., LAPD7515-001. If more than one officer is utilizing the information source simultaneously but independently from one another, they should each issue the source a different number. The name-file maintained by the administrative sergeant will indicate that two officers are independently using the information source.

Confidential Informant Agreement

Prior to the information source working, it is important that all parties involved sign the informant agreement forms once the appropriate entries are completed. Most general Confidential Agreement Forms, which are contracts, include questions that the officer should explain to the informant. At that time, the officer answers any questions the informant advances, and records the informant's answers to the questions on the forms. A form should include spaces where the officer can record the information source's answers, and the information source's initials can be included. Although the forms usually are completed and signed prior to the officer using an informant, pending that the officer is at liberty to elicit information and act upon it, or do it to establish reliability. Forms 6-2 and 6-3 in the Appendix at the end of this chapter illustrate general agreement contracts.

If an information source will receive leniency consideration as payment for cooperating with police after suffering arrest, being booked into jail, and charges filed, a signed agreement drafted by the prosecuting office will usually be required. This agreement goes into the information source's manila folder file previously discussed.

In some instances, a defendant (information source) charged with a crime requests a "free-talk" with the officer, the request made through the defendant's attorney. During a free-talk, any statements made by the officer or defendant, regarding the criminal investigation(s) involving the defendant and other co-conspirators, stays private. During a free-talk, statements made by the defendant are not subject to use during the criminal proceedings, except to impeach the defendant's testimony, if necessary, or for proceedings pertaining to perjury, false swearing, or the like. Moreover, the free-talk agreement applies only to the period of time that the agreement originally contemplates. Defendants, in hope of receiving consideration, in hope of reduced charges or penalties, often request free-talks. Incarcerated defendants may have limited ability to provide current information. Nonetheless, they often can provide detailed information about others involved in criminal activity.

Documenting Information Source Information

Officers who use information sources, whether confidential or not, should maintain a record of the information received. The information to be documented includes all relevant information, whether or not accurate, reliable, verifiable, trustworthy, or whether the officer follows-up on the information him- or herself, or refers it to some other agency for follow-up. Record the information on the *Personal Data Sheet–Record of Information Received.* Refer to the second page of the previously mentioned Form 6-1 in the Appendix at the end of this chapter. On the Personal Data Sheet, the officer records the information in sufficient detail. The information is dated, evaluated, and identified as verifiable/reliable (yes/no) after which the officer's supervisor reviews and initials the entries. Information should be as detailed as required and not limited to a few lines unless that is adequate. This is important because a record may span years, and if information is vague, recall of relevant facts, years later, may be impossible.

The Record of Information Received document, after supervisory review, should be maintained by the information source's control officer in a secure location, and be available for review upon a supervisor's request.

Documenting Credibility

The importance of documenting informant credibility lies in the fact that when testifying to an information source's credibility during trial, a judicial official must be informed of any past occasions that the information source's information was inaccurate. If documentation is absent or weak, it may be necessary to disclose the information source's identity, and credibility is subject to challenge.

Documenting Reliability

In court, officers can substantiate the reliability of an Information Source's information by showing that the information is entitled to a *reasonable inference of truthfulness* based on a history of receiving accurate information from the source. To the extent possible, the officer should verify the reliability of information received from an information source. Naturally, not all information requires corroboration, but corroborating sufficient information makes it possible for a judicial official to infer that unverified information is accurate. Information is subject to corroboration by surveillance, record checks, the observations of other officers, and information independently obtained by other information sources. When corroborating facts, they do not need to be criminal in nature, but can be innocent. The important point is to verify the accuracy of sufficient information so that there is a reasonable basis to trust the accuracy of unsubstantiated information.

Accepted definitions within the law enforcement community assist with assessing the reliability of information sources and therefore the trustworthiness of the information they provide. Information Source *reliability* can be classified into four categories:

- *Reliable.* The reliability of the source is unquestioned because of a history of unerring reliability.
- *Usually reliable.* The officer can cautiously rely on information as being factual because the majority of information received in the past proved reliable.
- *Unreliable.* The unreliable information source has a history of questionable authenticity, trustworthiness, or competency. In other words, the person was unreliable in the past.
- *Unknown.* The reliability of the source is unknown. Credibility of the person and validity of the information they provide remains unsubstantiated by experience or investigation.

Information *validity* can be classified into four categories:

- *Confirmed.* Confirmed refers to sufficiently corroborated information.
- *Probable.* Probable refers to information that possesses every indication of being accurate, but which has not been confirmed. Probable information is logical and agrees with other information on the same subject.
- *Doubtful.* Doubtful information is inconsistent with other information.
- *Cannot be judged.* The information in this category does not avail itself to corroboration.

Officers must remember that all documents pertaining to information sources are subject to a judicial "in camera" review. It is important, therefore, to write reports in a professional manner.

Informant Payment

All payments made to informants require a signed receipt. A receipt book that provides an original and two carbon copies works best. Forms 6-4A-D in the Appendix at the end of this chapter illustrates sample receipts for different informant services, followed by a blank receipt form.

Controlling officers should require informants to sign their real names and ensure that signatures are legible. A second officer should witness all disbursement of funds to an informant to avoid issues of missing or misallocated funds. The witnessing officer can also sign the receipt thus reducing the likelihood of misappropriated funds or allegations of under payment by the informant. Record informant payments and the witnessing officer's name on a money sheet that documents expenditures. The witnessing officer should also make an entry on his or her money sheet noting the informant number, the payment amount, the receipt number, and the disbursing officer's name. The disbursing officer should attach the original receipt to his or her money sheet and retain the pink copy for the officer's own records. The yellow copy should be given to the informant.

Money Sheets

Officers who use undercover funds must maintain a money sheet. A money sheet will account for daily expenditures made by the officer during the course of conducting drug investigations. The money sheet includes a running balance, usually adjusted weekly based on expenditures. The money sheet also documents drug purchases the officer makes, or controlled drug purchases made by the informant. See Forms 6-5A-B in the Appendix at the end of this chapter for sample money sheets.

Informant Use of Drugs Purchased with Undercover Funds

If an officer knows or suspects that an informant is using drugs purchased with undercover funds, or an informant admits to such acts, the controlling officer and his or her supervisor should immediately investigate the matter. Unless the informant can substantiate ingesting drugs because the seller compelled it, drugs ingested to avoid serious injury or death, deem the informant unreliable and "blackball" him or her.

Informant Inactivation

When inactivating or "blackballing" an informant, the control officer should document the facts leading to the inactivation in a memorandum, and place the memorandum in the informant's manila file. The administrative supervisor then relocates the manila file to the inactive section of the file, and relocates the name card in the Master Name File to the inactive section. Note the date of inactivation on the name card.

Information Source File Purging

The supervisor should inspect the Master Name File cards annually and remove Information Sources that have been inactive for five years or more. A responsible department head should review each file to determine suitability for destruction.

In-house personnel, ensuring complete integrity in the destruction of these files, should shred the files authorized for purging. Usually the administrative sergeant, who has maintained the files, is in the best position to complete this task.

DOS AND DON'TS WHEN USING INFORMANTS

Dos

- Use informants to lessen investigation time.
- Use informants to gain intelligence about criminal individuals and groups and the scope of the illicit activity.
- Develop and utilize policies and procedures for managing and using informants.
- Recruit informants from various sectors of society.
- Identify and remember informant motivations.
- Thoroughly debrief the informant.
- Ensure informant understands and signs an informant agreement.
- Corroborate informant information as much as possible using other sources.
- Control informant.
- Document all meetings with the informant.
- Maintain files on both good and bad informants.
- Be truthful with the informant.
- Whenever possible, protect the identity of the informant.
- Encourage informants to be lawful.

Don'ts

- Do not trust informants.
- Do not become an informant's friend.
- Do not meet informants alone.
- Do not pay an informant without a witness and proper documentation.
- Do not appraise an informant of an investigation except for safety purposes.
- Do not knowingly have two officers working an informant at the same time.
- Do not permit informants to control the investigation.
- Do not condone informant drug use.
- Do not make promises that cannot be honored.
- Do not make deals that cannot be honored, or if authority to make the deal is lacking.

Appendix

DRUG INVESTIGATION FORMS

The following forms are examples. Re-create them according to individual needs.

METROPOLIS POLICE DEPARTMENT
DRUG INVESTIGATIONS BUREAU

Personal Data Sheet – Information Source (Confidential Informant)

______________________ ______________ __________
Detective/Officer **Badge Number** **Date**

CI# DIB: __________ DATE: __________ CI NAME: __________

AKA: __________

ADDRESS: __________

SEX: __________ RACE: __________ DOB: __________

HEIGHT: __________ WEIGHT: __________ HAIR: __________ EYES: __________

GLASSES: __________ BUILD: __________ COMPLEXION: __________

MARITAL STATUS: __________ S.S. #: __________ D.L. #: __________

EMPLOYER: __________ ADDRESS: __________

OCCUPATION: __________ BUSINESS PHONE #: __________

DISTINGUISHING MARKS/SCARS: __________

____

PROBATION: YES ____ NO ____ P.O. NAME: __________

COMMENTS: __________

____

____

WHY IS THE SOURCE INFORMING?

WORKING OFF CHARGES: __________

WORKING FOR MONEY: __________

GOOD CITIZEN: __________

OTHER: __________

* Page 1 of 2 *

Form 6-1. A fingerprint card and identification photographs accompany this personal data sheet.

METROPOLIS POLICE DEPARTMENT
DRUG INVESTIGATIONS BUREAU

Personal Data Sheet – Information Source (Confidential Informant)

Record of information received from CI #DIB ______________________

______________________ ______________ ______________
Detective/Officer Badge Number Date

Date Information Received	Verified Reliable Yes – No	Synopsis – information received and how verified	Supervisor Initial Review

* Page 2 of 2 *

Form 6-1–*Continued.* Personal data sheet for information source (confidential informant)

METROPOLIS POLICE DEPARTMENT
DRUG INVESTIGATIONS BUREAU

Officer / Informant Contract Agreement

CI #DIB ______________________

I. **In exchange for the consideration described in Section II, paragraphs 1-3 of this agreement, Confidential Informant ______________________ agrees to the following terms and conditions.**

1. CI ____________ will fully cooperate with the State and the instructions of Detective ____________ and/or his or her designee/s in the investigation and prosecution of drug dealers and users as set forth in Section I, paragraphs 1-3. This cooperation will include truthful testimony at the request of Detective ____________, and the Prosecuting Attorney.

2. CI ____________, under the control and direction of Detective ____________ and/or his or her designee, shall provide information, and if necessary, testimony to investigate, charge, and prosecute at least ____ number of individuals engaged in narcotics, dangerous drugs, and/or marijuana trafficking in the Metropolis metropolitan area. The combined amount of cocaine, heroin, methamphetamine, or marijuana shall be ___ ounces, ___ ounces, ___ ounces, or ___ pounds respectively or a combination of cocaine, heroin, methamphetamine, and marijuana, which Detective ____________, in his or her sole discretion, deems to be equivalent in value and/or weight. In lieu of purchasing cocaine, heroin, methamphetamine, or marijuana, CI ____________ may arrange "reversals" (police controlled sales) of cocaine, heroin, methamphetamine, or marijuana, amounting to a total of not less than $______, if approved in advance by Detective ____________ or his or her designee.

3. CI ____________ will maintain regular contact with Detective ____________, in the manner agreed, and will provide information concerning current employer, residential address, telephone numbers, and description of vehicles over which he or she has control. CI ____________ will also provide biographical information including name, addresses, and telephone numbers of all family, friends, and business associates. CI ____________ will also provide a complete itinerary of his or her travel and visits outside the Metropolis metropolitan area prior to their occurrence during the term of this agreement.

4. CI ____________ agrees to not engage in illegal activity or associate with persons engaged in illegal activity unless instructed to do so by Detective ____________ or his or her designee/s. When so instructed, it is only to advance an official law enforcement criminal investigation.

5. CI ____________ will not at any time during this agreement possess or use any type of weapon.

6. CI ____________ will not identify him or herself as a law enforcement official or employee or volunteer worker of any government agency.

Informant initial ______

Page 1 of 2

Form 6-2. Officer/informant contract agreement.

Form 6-2–*Continued*

7. CI ________________ will not engage in any form of entrapment of any individual. To minimize the potential for entrapment, CI ________________ will provide, in advance of a "deal" or negotiation with any individual, all information requested of him or her by Detective ________________. CI will provide background information about the person to determine the individual's predisposition to commit the crime under investigation.

8. CI ________________ will not reveal to anyone except his or her attorney the existence or nature of this agreement, without the prior written approval of detective ________________ or his or her designee/s, or the Prosecuting Attorney.

9. CI ________________ shall complete all transactions within ____ days of signing this agreement. However, the agreement will remain in force throughout any resulting prosecutions.

II. **In exchange for the cooperation and information set forth above, the Metropolis Police Department agrees to the following terms and conditions.**

1. Use every lawful means to keep CI ________________ identity confidential, except (1) as may be required for prosecution of any cases resulting from this agreement, or (2) if he or she fails to abide by all of the conditions imposed by Detective ________________ or his or her designee/s.

2. Not file charges against CI ________________ relative to Metropolis Police Department Report Number/s ________________, and not file ________________ charges against CI ________________ for offenses occurring in the city of Metropolis prior to the date of arrest. This provision does not bar prosecution for any other kind of offense or for any offense in which a weapon was involved.

3. The State will not use information provided by CI ________________, against the CI in prosecution, except to impeach CI testimony, or for proceedings in the nature of perjury or false swearing. In the event that CI ________________ fails to fulfill every agreement contained herein, he or she loses all benefits and the State may charge and prosecute him or her for any offense it knows about.

Detective ________________, or his or her designee/s, may require the defendant to engage in particular conduct to confirm that he or she is complying with the terms of this agreement. For example, he or she may be required to consent to a search of his or her person, vehicle, or residence at any time without notice or cause. Failure to consent to any such request shall constitute a material breach of this agreement.

The parties, by signing and dating this agreement, attest to their understanding of and full consent to all provisions contained herein. The agreement will be effective and binding from the date the last party signs below. Alterations to this agreement will occur only in writing, and will be binding only when signed by all the parties or their designee/s or legal successors.

________________________	________________________
Date	CIs Signature
________________________	________________________
Date	Sergeant – Metropolis Police Department
________________________	________________________
Date	Detective – Metropolis Police Department

Page 2 of 2

Form 6-3. Agreement for confidential informant.

METROPOLIS POLICE DEPARTMENT
DRUG INVESTIGATIONS BUREAU

Agreement – Confidential Informant

Read this agreement to the informant. Explain each item, answer any questions the informant has, and record the session. The investigator will record the informant's answer in the space provided and have the informant initial it. If more space is needed write comments on the back of these pages, identified by the corresponding question number.

CI #DIB ______________________

1. Do you understand that you are not to break any laws during your association with the Metropolis Police Department? Yes __ No __

2. Do you understand that you are not an employee of the Metropolis Police Department? Yes __ No __

3. Do you understand that you are not to disclose your association with the Metropolis Police Department to anyone except as directed by your control officer or in response to a subpoena issued by a court of law? Yes __ No __

4. Do you understand that you are not to release any funds entrusted to you until you have first received the drugs for which you are negotiating on behalf of the Metropolis Police Department? Yes __ No __

5. Do you understand that you are not to purchase drugs from anyone that you cannot identify unless specifically instructed to do so by your control officer? Yes __ No __

6. Do you understand that you are not a police officer and you are not to carry any documents or equipment that indicate your association with law enforcement? Yes __ No __

7. Do you understand that you are not to affect an arrest of any type? Yes __ No __

8. Do you understand that you are not to use your association with the Metropolis Police Department to resolve personal matters? Yes __ No __

9. Do you understand that you are to confine your activity to that which is directed by your control officer? Yes __ No __

10. Do you understand that you are not to begin negotiations for any drugs without first notifying your control officer and receiving permission to proceed? Yes __ No __

11. Do you understand that during your association with the Metropolis Police Department you must keep your control officer informed of how to contact you? Yes __ No __

Informant initial ______

Page 1 of 3

Form 6-3–*Continued*

12. Do you understand that you must contact your control officer at least daily ☐ semiweekly ☐ weekly ☐ biweekly ☐ other ______ Yes __ No __

13. Do you understand that contact with this agency must be maintained until all investigations and prosecutions are completed and your control officer releases you? Yes __ No __

14. Do you understand that you are not to provide or offer to provide any quantity of marijuana, narcotics, dangerous drugs or prescription-only drugs to any investigative target unless specifically instructed to do so by your control officer? Yes __ No __

15. Do you understand that you may not carry any type of weapon while working as an informant with the Metropolis Police Department? Yes __ No __

16. A person is unlawfully entrapped if the intent to commit a crime did not originate in their own mind because they are an honest person, a person not predisposed to commit crime. The innocent person is unlawfully entrapped when they are persuaded to commit a crime they would not otherwise commit. Merely affording criminals the opportunity to commit crime is not unlawful entrapment.

    Do you understand that you are not to unlawfully entrap any person while working as an informant for the Metropolis Police Department? Yes __ No __

17. A reasonable effort will be made to ensure that your role as informant for the Metropolis Police Department remains confidential and that you do not become a material witness on a case.

    If the prosecutor believes there are adequate legal grounds to oppose a motion to reveal your identity, the State will oppose the motion. If, however, your involvement in a case is deemed to be material, the court may order that your identity be disclosed. If this happens, if you become material through events over which you had no control, the Metropolis Police Department will ask that the case be dismissed to preserve your confidentiality. If the case is not dismissed, your identity and association with the Metropolis Police Department will not remain confidential.

    Do you understand? Yes __ No __

18. Do you understand that if you become a material witness and required to testify or give an interview, that you must tell the truth regardless of whether it is unfavorable to you or anybody else including the State? Yes __ No __

I have reviewed the terms of this agreement with the control officer listed below, and I understand each requirement. I agree to honor the requirements.

______________________ ______________________
Date Signature (Informant)

Page 2 of 3

Form 6-3–*Continued*

I have reviewed the terms of this agreement and discussed them with the above named person. I have recorded all answers to the questions asked and believe that the listed person understands the agreement.

____________________ ____________________
Date Signature (Detective/Officer)

I have reviewed the terms of this agreement and discussed the facts of the case with the control officer. I approve the use of this informant and believe that using of this informant is consistent with the regulations of Metropolis Police Department and those of the XYZ County Attorney's Office. I also believe using this informant is consistent with good law enforcement practice.

____________________ ____________________
Date Signature (Supervisor)

Page 3 of 3

METROPOLIS, ARIZONA
POLICE DEPARTMENT
RECEIPT

DATE: *December 14, 20 04*

CONFIDENTIAL INFORMANT NUMBER (CI#): *CI DIB 4051-007*

RECEIVED FROM: *Det. Juan Alvarez #2315* $ *150.00*

CASH ☐ CHECK ☐ PAYMENT IN FULL ☐ PARTIAL PAYMENT ☐

FOR: *Payment for information leading to a Search Warrant at 2572 E. Double-cross Drive, Metropolis, AZ*

DEPT. REPORT NUMBER (DR#): *74563655*

DIVISION: *Drug Investigations Bureau*

WITNESS: *Det. James Smith #2816*

RECEIVED BY: *Sandy Snitch*

(Form Serial No.)
WHITE – CUSTOMER
YELLOW – ACCOUNTS
PINK – FILE

Form 6-4A. This is an example of a receipt for payment to an informant who provided information that resulted in a *Productive Search Warrant.*

METROPOLIS, ARIZONA
POLICE DEPARTMENT
RECEIPT

DATE: *December 14, 20 04*

CONFIDENTIAL INFORMANT NUMBER (CI#): *CI DIB 4051-007*

RECEIVED FROM: *Det. Juan Alvarez #2315* $ *150.00*

CASH ☐ CHECK ☐ PAYMENT IN FULL ☐ PARTIAL PAYMENT ☐

FOR: *Funds for an introduction and clean cocaine buy at 4236 E. Betrayal Blvd., Metropolis, AZ*

DEPT. REPORT NUMBER (DR#): *74563655*

DIVISION: *Drug Investigations Bureau*

WITNESS: *Det. James Smith #2816*

RECEIVED BY: *Sandy Snitch*

(Form Serial No.)
WHITE – CUSTOMER
YELLOW – ACCOUNTS
PINK – FILE

Form 6-4B. This is an example of a receipt for payment to an informant who introduced an undercover officer to a drug dealer, and then used the restroom thus enabling the officer to make a *clean buy* of cocaine from that dealer.

METROPOLIS, ARIZONA
POLICE DEPARTMENT
RECEIPT

DATE: *December 14, 20 04*

CONFIDENTIAL INFORMANT NUMBER (CI#): *CI DIB 4051-007*

RECEIVED FROM: *Det. Juan Alvarez #2315* $ *150.00*

CASH ☐ CHECK ☐ PAYMENT IN FULL ☐ PARTIAL PAYMENT ☐

FOR: *Funds provided to CI DIB 4051-007 to purchase evidence at 5732 E. Turncoat Terrace, Metropolis, AZ. Reliability for a search warrant.*

DEPT. REPORT NUMBER (DR#): *74563655*

DIVISION: *Drug Investigations Bureau*

WITNESS: *Det. James Smith #2816*

RECEIVED BY: *Sandy Snitch*

(Form Serial No.)

WHITE – CUSTOMER
YELLOW – ACCOUNTS
PINK – FILE

Form 6-4C. This is an example of a receipt for payment to an informant who performed a *Reliability Buy* from a drug dealer.

METROPOLIS, ARIZONA
POLICE DEPARTMENT
RECEIPT

DATE: ____________

CONFIDENTIAL INFORMANT NUMBER (CI#): ____________

RECEIVED FROM: ____________ $ ________

CASH ☐ CHECK ☐ PAYMENT IN FULL ☐ PARTIAL PAYMENT ☐

FOR: ____________

DEPT. REPORT NUMBER (DR#): ____________

DIVISION: ____________

WITNESS: ____________

RECEIVED BY: ____________

(Form Serial No.)

WHITE – CUSTOMER
YELLOW – ACCOUNTS
PINK – FILE

Form 6-4D. Blank receipt. Reproduce it as is after inserting the proper department name and serialized numbers, or modify it according to preference or need.

Form 6-5A. Expenditure log.

METROPOLIS POLICE DEPARTMENT
DRUG INVESTIGATIONS BUREAU
EXPENDITURE LOG

DATE

DETECTIVE – OFFICER (Print) BADGE NUMBER

BUREAU – DETAIL

MONEY TRANSFER			
UNIT	TO	UNIT	AMOUNT

DATE	RECEIVED FROM	AMOUNT
		$
		$
		$
		$
	TOTAL	

DATE	DISBURSED TO	AMOUNT
		$
		$
		$
		$
		$
		$
		$
	TOTAL	

DATE	ADVANCE (Explain on reverse side)	AMOUNT
		$
		$
		$
		$
	TOTAL	

DATE	ADVANCE RECOVERED	AMOUNT
		$
		$
		$
		$
	TOTAL	

Previous Balance	$
Money Received	$
Advance Recovered	$
Total	$
Money Disbursed	$
Advance Disbursed	$
Total	$
Expenditures	$
Balance On Hand	$

EXPENDITURE TYPE (Explain on reverse side)	SYMBOL	
Pornography	(P)	$
Gambling	(G)	$
Narcotics Reliability	(NR)	$
Narcotics Case Buys	(NCB)	$
Evidence Purchases	(EP)	$
Alcoholic Beverages	(AB)	$
Alcoholic Beverages/Other	(ABO)	$
Cover Expenses	(CE)	$
Investigative Food, Soft Drinks, Tips	(IF)	$
Investigative – Other	(O)	$
Information Source Payment	(ISP)	$
Information Source – Other	(ISO)	$
Witness Protection	(WP)	$
Special Programs	(SP)	$
Food – Official Business	(FOB)	$
Massage – Table Dances	(M)	$
Other Expenses	(OE)	$
	TOTAL	$

Signature Badge No. Approved by

∗ Page 1 of 2 ∗

Form 6-5A–*Continued*

METROPOLIS POLICE DEPARTMENT
DRUG INVESTIGATIONS BUREAU

EXPENDITURE LOG

DATE	LOCATION	TYPE	EXPLANATION	# DRINKS CONSUMED	AMOUNT

METROPOLIS POLICE DEPARTMENT
DRUG INVESTIGATIONS BUREAU
EXPENDITURE LOG

DATE	LOCATION	TYPE	EXPLANATION	# DRINKS CONSUMED	AMOUNT
5/18/04	1305 E. Shady Way	NR	CI DIB 4051-007 purchased one small	N/A	$40.00
			rock, believed to be cocaine, for $40.		
			Receipt #459101. Scott Reagent test		
			positive. Impounded for destruction		
			at 620 W. Washington. Search		
			warrant to follow. Det. Jones		
			witness.		
4/20/04	620 W. Washington	ISP	CI DIB 4051-007 paid $150 for	N/A	$150.00
			services which lend to productive		
			search warrant at 2572 E. Double-		
			cross Drive. Receipt #459102.		
			DR 20290421. 3 arrests, one ounce		
			(approx) of "crack," two handguns and		
			$852 in cash seized. Det. Jones		
			witness.		
5/21/04	2321 W. Willetten	NCB	Paid $20 for small rock, believed to	N/A	@20.00
			be cocaine from suspect Jim Carver.		
			Clean buy – on hold. DR20290652.		
5/22/04	620 W. Washington	ISP	Paid CI DIB 4051-005 $70 for clean	N/A	$70.00
			cocaine introduction on 5/21/04 at		
			2321 W. Willettn. DR20290652.		
			Receipt #459103. Det. Jones		
			witness.		

* Page 2 of 2 *

Form 6-5B. An example of how Page 2 of the expenditure log is used.

Chapter 7

CONSPIRACY INVESTIGATIONS

INTRODUCTION

Often, when discussing advanced drug investigations, the term "conspiracy" is used. The term is especially common with drug investigations because the drug trade at various levels generally involves more than one person. Conspiracy investigations are generally complex and feature advanced investigative techniques requiring tremendous labor, special equipment, and funding resources.

These investigations, often referred to as "wiretaps" or "title 3s," usually include electronic interception of wire communications by such devices as *Pen Registers* (Dialed Number Recorders–DNRs), *Trap-and-Trace devices*, and electronic monitoring of verbal and/or text communication. Yet many investigations, though complex, can be resolved utilizing traditional investigative techniques thus resulting in the dismantling of a criminal organization and successful prosecution of its membership. There are, however, circumstances when a criminal organization cannot be investigated and dismantled using only conventional techniques because of the clandestine nature and increased levels of sophistication of their operations. In such cases, it may be necessary to employ advanced techniques such as the ones discussed in this chapter.

This chapter will present various advanced investigative techniques commonly utilized in conspiracy investigations. Also examined is the proper development of a wire intercept case. Because of the complexity and sophistication of developing, managing, and concluding a wire intercept case, this chapter provides only a basic overview of wire intercept use in drug investigations. Officers are encouraged to seek additional reading and training on this matter. In addition, because these investigations occur in close concert with prosecutors, prosecutors can provide guidance and recommendations on the progress of a case–consult them early.

CONSPIRACY DEFINED

A conspiracy is an agreement between at least two people to commit an unlawful act by lawful or unlawful means. Persons participating in a conspiracy must be willful and knowledgeable participants to the unlawful act even though they may be unaware of the actions of other co-conspirators. A "formal" agreement is not necessary to complete the offense. An overt act, whether legal or illegal, follows the agreement. A conspiracy charge is a separate and distinct offense from the offense that forms the object crime of the conspiracy. In other words, in the case of illicit drug distribution, the perpetrators are subject to prosecution for drug distribution *and* conspiracy to distribute illicit drugs.

ELEMENTS OF PROOF

When considering the elements of a conspiracy, there will be (1) two or more persons (plurality), (2) a genuine agreement, (3) participation (criminal intent), and (4) an overt act in furtherance of the conspiracy.

PLURALITY REQUIREMENT

The plurality requirement is that two or more persons are required for a conspiracy. This cannot include the undercover officers or confidential informants. The persons involved in the conspiracy do not have to know other persons involved in the conspiracy or their involvement; however, as previously stated, each is responsible for the acts of others. A person is subject to prosecution for conspiracy even when the names of other co-conspirators are unknown to them. A husband and wife, or a corporation and its officers and employees, are examples that fulfill the legal requisites of plurality.

GENUINE AGREEMENT

The "agreement" in a conspiracy is a crime. It is a separate offense from the substantive act such as the purchase or sale of illicit drugs. A substantive act is the crime resulting from the conspiratorial agreement and is the best proof of the existence of a conspiracy. Substantive criminal violations, in drug organizations, usually are rooted in some conspiratorial undertaking. Thus, when evidence exists and prosecution is an option, both the substantive act *and* conspiracy violations are the subject of prosecution because they constitute separate chargeable offenses. Moreover, because the *agreement* is the essence of a conspiracy crime, it is immaterial if the conspiracy fails to accomplish its objective. In reality, effective utilization of conspiracy laws can ensure prosecution and provide law enforcement the ability to thwart the commission of the object unlawful act or acts.

PARTICIPATION (CRIMINAL INTENT)

To be a co-conspirator, the person is not required to have joined the conspiracy at its inception. By joining a conspiracy, the person accepts and therefore is an accomplice in the prior acts and statements of other co-conspirators, made in furtherance of the conspiracy. To be guilty of conspiracy, the prosecution must prove that the person had knowledge of the conspiracy and its chief objective. It is not sufficient only to show that a person furthered the conspiracy by association with co-conspirators or through the commission of lawful or unlawful acts. Vicarious liability is a legal principal often referred to when discussing involvement in conspiracies. In essence, it means that a co-conspirator can be charged with a substantive offense committed by others if the person was a member of the conspiracy at the time of the offense, was participating in furtherance of the conspiracy, and the consequence was foreseeable.

WITHDRAWAL

Persons implicated in a conspiracy may allege they withdrew from the conspiracy prior to the indictable period. The burden of proof in these circumstances is on the individual claiming withdrawal, and requires affirmative proof that he or she in fact withdraw from the conspiracy. To constitute withdrawal some affirmative action is required by the person such as their notifying other co-conspirators of their desire to withdraw, notifying law enforcement of the activities, refusing to commit additional crimes, or being arrested. A person will usually not be considered withdrawn if they merely become inactive or passive. Withdrawal does not relieve a person for unlawful acts that occurred prior to withdrawal.

OVERT ACTS

Overt acts include anything done to carry out the object of the conspiracy, and the acts can be either legal or illegal. Generally, to substantiate the existence of a conspiracy, at least one of the co-conspirators must commit an overt act in furtherance of the conspiracy. Examples of overt acts include renting or leasing locations for use as stash houses, renting phones or pagers, laundering money, or transporting money or drugs. Officers are encouraged to check the laws of their jurisdiction as to the requirements for proving an overt act–it varies by jurisdiction. In some jurisdictions, an "overt act" is not always required to establish the existence of a conspiracy.

Prosecution is not required on *all* the overt acts committed in furtherance of a conspiracy–prosecuting and proving one act is sufficient. Moreover, proof against only one of the co-conspirators is necessary. The jury will decide questions as to whether the overt act was in furtherance of the conspiracy.

CONCLUDING A CONSPIRACY

The venue in a conspiracy prosecution is generally the jurisdiction where the agreement took place, or where overt acts in furtherance of the conspiracy are committed. In the event of telephone calls between two jurisdictions, venue can lie in either jurisdiction, if the call is purported to have been an overt act in furtherance of the conspiracy.

When the objectives of a conspiracy are completed, or fail, the conspiracy ends.

STATUTE OF LIMITATIONS

The time limit to prosecute a person for conspiracy is five years from the last overt act, or at the conclusion of the conspiracy, whichever occurs last.

TYPES OF CONSPIRACIES

There are different types of conspiracy investigations that include, (1) historical (past), (2) present (ongoing), and (3) Continuing Criminal Enterprise (CCE).

Historical Conspiracies are the most common and involve acts previously unknown to law enforcement. The investigation involves compiling evidence to support the theory that a conspiracy occurred prior to the commission of a crime.

Present Conspiracies involve situations that have not yet reached the object of the conspiracy. These cases generally involve undercover officers or confidential informants and can lead to wire intercept investigations.

Continuing Criminal Enterprise (CCE) conspiracies, also referred to as "Drug Kingpin" operations, fall under federal statutes. The "Drug Kingpin" statute, or running or operating a Continuing Criminal Enterprise is defined as *a person* working in concert with at least five others, occupying a supervisory position, and obtaining substantial income or resources from trafficking in controlled substances. A conviction under the Continuing Criminal Enterprise statute carries a minimum prison sentence of twenty years and a maximum sentence of life in prison. A second offense is thirty years to life. This is the most severe conspiracy charge against a drug dealer and often results in the defendant accepting a plea agreement. The "Kingpin" need not personally commit a series of three or more drug felonies–he or she must only qualify as a "Kingpin" under the statute.

THE PROS AND CONS OF CONSPIRACY INVESTIGATIONS

There are advantages and disadvantages to conducting a conspiracy investigation. The advantages include the ability for law enforcement to dismantle organizations that would otherwise be difficult to investigate and dismantle. Another advantage is that during the prosecution stage, there is greater latitude of evidence, especially as it pertains to hearsay evidence. Sentences are generally more severe, often requiring mandatory minimums. The cases are also harder to defend against and defendants often plead out rather than face more severe sentences. Conspiracy investigations are also generally more effective against suspects who have become educated to traditional methods of drug interdiction by virtue of education or through being the subject of prior enforcement efforts.

There are disadvantages to conspiracy investigations. Usually, they are extremely time consuming, and they may involve multiple venues requiring careful coordination. Conspiracy investigations require a team of investigators and support personnel, often including electronic surveillance personnel, as well as the support of management and a commitment by the prosecuting agency. For these reasons, conspiracy investigations are very expensive and usually involve overtime costs. Depending on circumstances, a conspiracy investigation may also require expensive computer equipment and software, those items often necessary to effectively and efficiently manage the incredible amounts of information that require processing in preparation for court. Another disadvantage to a conspiracy investigation is the use of more witnesses.

INVESTIGATIVE TECHNIQUES

Various investigative tools apply to conspiracy investigations, many discussed in other chapters. The tools include:

- Informants
- Co-conspirators
- Surveillance (physical and technical)
- Mail Covers
- Pen Registers and Trap-and-Trace Devices
- Wire Intercept (title III's)
- Undercover Operations
- Trash Rips (Trash Runs, Trash Covers)
- Grand Jury
- Public Records
- Search Warrants
- Subpoenas
- Asset Seizures
- Photo Line-ups
- Utilizing and coordinating with other agencies

ELECTRONIC SURVEILLANCE

Criminal drug organizations, by the nature of their business, are usually most vulnerable in their communications. It would be difficult, if not impossible, for a sophisticated drug trafficking and distribution organization to function without communicating via electronic means. In 1968, the Omnibus Crime Bill, passed and enacted into law, gives federal investigators the authority to intercept telephone communications pursuant to extremely stringent rules and procedures. More recently, the "Patriot Act" has expanded options available to investigators.

Drug dealers today have at their disposal various electronic tools to facilitate drug trafficking and distribution. No longer is a person's landline (conventional telephone) the only means of communicating, and in fact is usually used less by those involved in criminal activities. Mobile phones provide a person involved in criminal activity mobility and often anonymity, as many cellular companies do little to confirm a person's identity or address. Computers connected to the internet, facsimile machines, and pagers are other electronic tools used by suspects to communicate with others. Calling cards, although not electronic tools, have also become extremely popular with drug dealers.

Prior to utilizing electronic surveillance as an investigative tool, it is necessary to take and document preliminary investigative steps. The steps include:

- Available Information Sources have been interviewed and it has been determined that the information sources are incapable of obtaining the information necessary to conclude the investigation successfully unless electronic surveillance is utilized.
- The primary investigator has checked with other officers in his or her agency, as well as other area agencies and confirmed that they do not have information or access to information regarding the primary suspect's activities that will result in successful dismantling of the suspect's drug operation.
- Extensive surveillance on the primary suspect's activities failed to result in essential evidence.
- Informants or police officers have unsuccessfully attempted to infiltrate the target organization. Conversely, if infiltration would be impossible or unreasonably dangerous, documenting that fact is necessary.
- Officers analyzed the primary suspect's phone toll records in an attempt to develop other leads.
- Convincing evidence from information sources indicate that the target suspects are utilizing the telephone in furtherance of their criminal enterprise.
- If information exists that establishes probable cause for a search warrant, then executing a search warrant is an option. If, however, the serving of a search warrant would not lead to the seizure of evidence necessary to effectively dismantle the organization, or may injure the case, this must be completely documented.
- A court recently ruled that police must attempt to acquire appropriate evidence via trash runs before electronic surveillance is permissible.

The above steps, if unsuccessfully attempted or are unnecessarily dangerous or unreasonable to attempt, and documented as such, demonstrate that the only effective means to investigate a suspect or organization is by the use of wire intercept. Wire intercept should not be the initial goal of an investigation, yet the investigation must proceed with the realization that the case may progress to such a level. Document accordingly! If documentation is weak, and the investigation reaches the level where a wire intercept is necessary, obtaining authorization may be difficult and time consuming.

Essential evidence to support the request for court authorization may be gone, or difficult or impossible to obtain.

Once a court issues the appropriate warrant, officers may install a pen register (dialed number recorder) on the primary suspect's telephone, or a telephone that is determined most likely to provide necessary evidence. In most agencies, a detailed memorandum will be prepared documenting the completion of the prerequisite investigative steps and forwarded through the chain of command to the police chief and the agencies legal advisor requesting authorization to submit an affidavit to a court requesting authorization to use a pen register.

Upon approval by the appropriate head personnel, the primary investigator, or affiant, will prepare an affidavit requesting authorization to conduct electronic surveillance by utilizing a pen register device. Authorization ultimately must come from a court of competent jurisdiction.

TRAP AND TRACE DEVICES AND PEN REGISTERS

Trap and trace devices, installed at the telephone company, target a specific telephone number and record the number from which all incoming calls originate. *Pen registers*, also installed at the telephone company, target a specific telephone number and record the destination number of all outgoing calls regardless of whether the connection is successful. Neither device records conversations.

Federal law requires law enforcement to obtain a court order for utilization of a trap and trace device or pen register[7] even though the courts have recognized that a person does not have a *reasonable expectation of privacy* in regards to telephone numbers dialed, or the telephone number from which incoming calls originate. As always, police officers must know the state and federal laws pertaining to the use of electronic surveillance devices. Requests for installation of both devices on a target telephone may be incorporated together in the same memorandum, affidavit, and court order–officers are cautioned to ensure that all necessary language is included.

Readers may wish to refer to *Smith v. Maryland*, 442 U.S. 735 (1979), an excerpt and footnote of which appear below. The case can be found by going to www.findlaw.com.

> The telephone company, at police request, installed at its central offices a pen register to record the numbers dialed from the telephone at petitioner's home.

---

7. United States Code; Title 18–Crimes and Criminal Procedure; Part II–Criminal Procedure; Chapter 205–Searches and Seizures.

Prior to his robbery trial, petitioner moved to suppress 'all fruits derived from' the pen register. The Maryland trial court denied this motion, holding that the warrantless installation of the pen register did not violate the Fourth Amendment. Petitioner was convicted, and the Maryland Court of Appeals affirmed.

[Footnote 1] 'A pen register is a mechanical device that records the numbers dialed on a telephone by monitoring the electrical impulses caused when the dial on the telephone is released. It does not overhear oral communications and does not indicate whether calls are actually completed.' United States v. New York Tel. Co., 434 U.S. 159, 161 n. 1 (1977).

WIRE INTERCEPT

Once pen registers and/or trap and trace devices result in evidence suggesting use of targeted telephones in furtherance of a criminal enterprise, police may submit a request for a warrant authorizing electronic wire interception of communications. Usually the police chief and the agency's legal advisor receive a request from the investigator for authorization to seek a warrant for wire interception. Hence, it is important that agency heads be informed of various aspects of the investigation such as:

- The name of the affiant officer(s), and the detail conducting the investigation.
- The target date the investigation is to begin and its anticipated length.
- Telephone numbers to be intercepted, addresses if landlines, and names of subscribers as received from service providers.
- The primary subject of the investigation, and all suspects involved including their suspected criminal activities.
- Whether the primary suspect, or others in the organization have been the subject of prior wire intercept by the officer's agency or other law enforcement agencies.
- Reason a wire intercept is necessary. The affiant should document all investigative avenues exhausted.
- Objectives of the investigation.
- Anticipated use of extra resources as well as cooperation expected from other agencies.
- Identify the prosecuting attorney responsible for reviewing the documents to be presented to the court authorizing the interception.
- The name of the agency's legal adviser reviewing the preliminary information and verifying that the agency's interests are protected.
- The projected costs of the investigation including personnel overtime, equipment, and associated fees.

Upon approval by appropriate head personnel, the primary investigator, or affiant, will prepare a detailed affidavit requesting issuance of a court order authorizing officers to conduct electronic intercept. If the subject has no telephone, other eavesdropping devices remain an option. The affiant prepares the court order for the magistrate to sign.

INVESTIGATION OBJECTIVES

Once having obtained the necessary court order to intercept communications, the investigators must discuss and plan the entire investigation. The main point of discussion is the objective of the investigation. Many times, when conducting these types of investigations, other individuals or groups involved in criminal activity become apparent and the temptation to "spin off" onto other cases will exist. It is important that officers stay focused on the primary target organization and adhere to the general objective of gathering sufficient evidence to indict the principal(s) for the suspected crimes listed in the affidavit. It is important to establish and honor the geographical, jurisdictional, and operational parameters of the investigation. As the investigation progresses, these factors must be under constant evaluation and revised if necessary to fulfill the objectives of the investigation.

It is not possible to emphasize too strongly the importance of quality planning and communication. All personnel involved in the investigation must know and understand the investigative objectives and the strategy for their achievement. Supervisors charged with overseeing the investigation are responsible for terminating the wire interception once achieving investigative objectives.

CONCLUSION

Electronic surveillance of suspected drug traffickers and distributors can provide valuable evidence for law enforcement. In fact, in many cases, electronic surveillance is the only effective means of dismantling an organization. However, in spite of its importance, the subject of electronic surveillance entails much more than has been provided here–the topic justifies an entire book. The authors hope, however, that a general understanding of the capabilities of electronic surveillance will leave readers knowing when electronic surveillance is appropriate and necessary.

It is vitally important, when assessing the capability of a target, that officers do not become emotionally involved in the case because that can cloud judgment and lead to a target being targeted inappropriately. If it becomes apparent a target was selected in error, officers should conclude the investigation and proceed with the evidence obtained up to that point. It is much too costly to continue an investigation of a subject who does not warrant the investigation just for the sake of following through with initial desires. There is no limit to the availability of worthy targets for electronic intercept, so do not waste time with a target of dubious value.

ASSET FORFEITURE

Introduction

Many drug investigations result in the seizure of property used in the manufacture, transportation, and sale of illicit drugs, seized property used as evidence at the time of trial. Asset seizures are civil actions and need not be the result of criminal charges. When property is seized under civil asset forfeiture laws,[8] the seizure offers two conspicuous benefits in addition to its use as evidence. First, seizure provides the government with ownership of assets such as currency, equipment, vehicles, and real estate. Personal and real property, when legally forfeited to the government, provides the government with cash once sold. Alternatively, instead of liquidating property for its cash value, the government may elect to use it. Second, when the government seizes the assets of a drug organization, thus depriving them of the benefit of their investment, the organization tends to suffer economic emasculation.

Civil Forfeiture Actions

When a criminal trial ends with a conviction, the subsequent sentence serves as punishment. Conversely, the purpose of a civil forfeiture action is to deprive the defendant of the assets used in the commission of a crime, that is to say, anything that facilitates the manufacturing or selling of illicit drugs. The intent is also to prevent a subsequent offender using the same assets.

There are two types of civil actions allowing for seizure of assets for forfeiture, those being actions against property, and actions against a person.

---

8. When it is determined that property such as money, securities, and real estate was used in the commission of a crime, or that such property was acquired from the proceeds of crime, the government may seize it for forfeiture under certain federal and state statutes, i.e., RICO and Controlled Substances Acts. RICO is an acronym for *Racketeer Influenced and Corrupt Organizations Act.* RICO laws facilitate the investigating, controlling, and prosecuting of organized crime by imposing strong sanctions and forfeiture provisions. Numerous criminal offenses fall under RICO.

The first type of civil action, *In rem forfeiture*, is a civil action brought against property, property obtained with intent for use, or actually used, in the commission of specific offenses that include drug sales and/or drug transportation. The second type of civil action is an action against a person for the harm caused by the commission of a specific offense, or for the financial gain enjoyed by the perpetrator, a gain that resulted from the commission of a specific offense that include drug sales and/or drug transportation.

Asset forfeiture actions pertain to property, not to the liberty and freedom of those who own property. Civil forfeiture actions allow for the seizure of property and funds used directly, or indirectly, to commit crimes, crimes such as the distribution and sales of illicit drugs. The assets, once legally forfeited to the government, serve to compensate the government for the cost of investigating violations of anti-drug laws, and for the costs associated with drug prevention. Hence, seizure of assets shifts the economic burden from the taxpayer to the criminal. Asset forfeiture laws are useful in the war on drugs because they serve to destroy the economic foundation and infrastructure of a criminal enterprise, and they diminish the ability to operate profitably (Rankin, n.d.).

U.S. Federal Forfeiture Law vs. State Forfeiture Laws

Federal forfeiture laws concentrate on property, but they take into consideration the culpable mental state of the property owner. Many states have adapted civil laws that provide for remedial action (seizure) directed at the property, but seizure for forfeiture requires proof of culpability on the part of the property owner. Many states created their forfeiture laws to accomplish the following:

- Remove the assets used to commit or facilitate certain offenses including violations of anti-drug laws.
- Compensate the government for the costs of investigation, enforcement, and prevention of drug-related crimes.
- Shift the social and economic costs of drug offenses from the taxpayer to the criminal.

Chapter 8

CLANDESTINE DRUG LABORATORIES

INTRODUCTION

The demand for illicit drugs and the ease of manufacturing some drugs are circumstances that result in clandestine drug laboratories posing a persistent threat to the community, environment, and police officers. The danger lies in the fact that the manufacturing of illicit street drugs involves the use of hazardous materials.

Many states have seen a dramatic increase in the number of emergency responses to clandestine drug laboratories, drug chemical storage facilities, and waste abandonment sites. Responding to and managing these often complex scenes requires adequately trained and equipped law enforcement personnel.

Investigating clandestine drug laboratories is a multi-disciplinary endeavor involving several government departments. Working together to manage clandestine laboratory incidents are police officers, firefighters, emergency medical providers, public health officials, and environmental quality regulators.

A clandestine drug laboratory is both a crime scene and a hazardous materials scene, requiring teams of investigators with specialized training. The majority of emergency responders, both police officers and fire personnel, do not routinely assume management responsibilities of clandestine drug laboratory scenes. That occurs because they respond to a variety of emergencies and often lack the specialized training to recognize clandestine drug laboratories and waste disposal sites. Because they lack specialized training and experience, they often fail to recognize a dangerous situation.

Because the drug problem has reached epidemic proportions, it is essential that emergency responders receive proper training. Proper training will enable police officers to recognize a clandestine drug laboratory, be aware of its hazards, and manage the incident properly.

CLANDESTINE DRUG LABORATORY DEFINITIONS

Clandestine Drug Laboratory: A secret illicit process whereby a sufficient combination of equipment and/or chemicals have been, or could be, used to manufacture a controlled substance.

Clandestine Drug Laboratory Hazardous Waste Disposal Site: A disposal site is a location where chemicals and/or equipment used to manufacture controlled substances, or hazardous waste produced during the manufacturing process have been disposed of.

TYPES OF CLANDESTINE DRUG LABORATORIES

Introduction

Clandestine laboratories are capable of synthesizing a variety of drugs. The focus of this section, however, will be methamphetamine laboratories because they are the most frequently encountered. Although they generally are the most frequently encountered, the availability of chemicals and drug user demographics affect the types of drug laboratories police officers are most likely to encounter.

Other laboratories the officer may encounter include Methcathinone (Cat), phencyclidine (PCP), Gammahydroxybutyrate (GHB), MDMA or MDA (Ecstasy), and lysergic acid diethylamide (LSD). However, the officer will rarely encounter LSD production, and indications suggest that a small group of individuals is responsible for the majority of LSD production in the United States.

DEA Clandestine Drug Laboratory Seizures (2002):		
	Methamphetamine	589
	Amphetamine	1
	Methcathinone	1
	MDMA	4
	GHB	3
	PCP	1
	Other	3

Methamphetamine Laboratories

The use of methamphetamine has reached epidemic proportions in the United States, with no indication that the situation will soon reverse itself.

Because of the prevalence of this drug, methamphetamine laboratories comprise the majority of drug laboratory seizures by law enforcement. Although the number of incidents will vary somewhat by region, methamphetamine production occurs throughout the country. In 2001, law enforcement seized methamphetamine laboratories in forty-six states.

In the western United States, predominately California, Mexican-based criminal organizations operate large-scale methamphetamine laboratories known as "super laboratories" capable of producing ten or more pounds of methamphetamine in a twenty-four-hour cycle. Law enforcement officials estimate that "super laboratories" operating in California produce more methamphetamine than all other laboratories in the United States combined, although methamphetamine production is limited in the eastern states. Because of the availability of chemicals and recipes, nearly anyone can manufacture methamphetamine.

A recent trend has emerged, most notably since the September 11, 2001, terrorist attacks on the United States. The trend reflects the decentralization of "super laboratories" in the west to "super laboratories" being strategically operated in various areas of the country. This strategy reduces the risk of drug seizure during transport to drug markets, as well as taking advantage of minimal law enforcement resources in remote areas of the country.

Along with the decentralization of "super laboratories," Mexican-based criminal groups have moved methamphetamine production into Mexico, usually near the United States border. This has resulted primarily because of increased enforcement efforts by United States authorities, and the increasing difficulty of obtaining the necessary chemicals for production. Once manufactured, the methamphetamine is smuggled into the United States utilizing established smuggling routes.

Methamphetamine Production Methods

Ephedrine/Pseudoephedrine Reduction. The following processes utilize ephedrine or Pseudoephedrine as the principal chemical, and through a chemical process, the laboratory converts the ephedrine or Pseudoephedrine into methamphetamine.

Hydriodic Acid/Red Phosphorus. Hydriodic acid and red phosphorus are the primary chemicals utilized. This method is most often associated with Mexican drug cartels and yields high quality d-methamphetamine. The following is a summary of the process:

- Ephedrine, red phosphorus and hydriodic acid are placed in a glass container, usually a round bottom flask. A condenser column is commonly used with this process (see Figure 8-1).

- Heat is applied and reflux takes place, usually for three to seven hours. The solution will be amber, purple, or brown in color after refluxing. The red phosphorus may also have crept up the sides of the flask.
- After cooling, pouring the liquid through a filter into a second glass container removes any red phosphorus not consumed in the cooking process. The remaining red phosphorus, captured by the filter, is discarded or saved and used during a subsequent "cook."
- The liquid, very acidic at this point, is made basic by adding sodium hydroxide (lye). This creates an exothermic reaction that can be volatile. An oil layer (methamphetamine oil) will form on top of the water.
- A solvent is added at this point and the liquid is mixed, thus insuring that all the methamphetamine moves into the solvent layer. Freon works for this purpose, but its use is rare because it is expensive. Two layers or phases will form, the solvent layer being on top.
- The layers are separated with the solvent layer retained. This can be accomplished by using a separatory funnel.
- Hydrogen chloride acid gas is bubbled through the solvent solution, and white crystals form. The crystals are hydrochloride (HCL) methamphetamine.
- The solvent containing the crystals are poured through a filter and collected.
- The crystals are dried.

Iodine/Red Phosphorus. Iodine and red phosphorus are the primary chemicals utilized. This method relies on the iodine reacting with red phosphorus in water to produce hydriodic acid. The subsequent manufacturing steps are the same as the hydriodic acid/red phosphorus method described above. This is the method of choice in the west for manufacturing methamphetamine and yields high quality d-methamphetamine.

Iodine/Hypophosphorous Acid. Iodine and hypo phosphorous acid are the primary chemicals utilized. This process is known as the "Hypo" method and relies on the iodine reacting with hypo phosphorous acid in water to produce hydriodic acid. The subsequent manufacturing steps are the same as the hydriodic acid/red phosphorus method described above, although filtering is unnecessary because red phosphorus is not used. This is a popular alternative method from the traditional iodine/red phosphorus method and yields high quality d-methamphetamine. This method became popular when red phosphorus became more difficult to obtain.

Nazi or Birch. Anhydrous and either sodium or lithium metal are the primary chemicals utilized. This process does not produce significant quantities of methamphetamine, but does produce a greater yield of high quality d-methamphetamine in a substantially shorter time. This is the prevailing

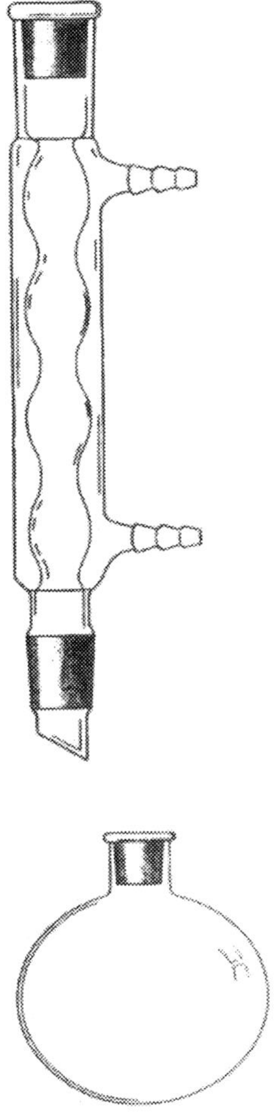

Figure 8-1. Condenser column and round bottom flask commonly used for methamphetamine production.

method of manufacturing methamphetamine in the Midwestern United States and is usually executed by independent operators. The following is a summary of the process:

- Ephedrine or pseudoephedrine is dissolved in a solvent and the solution is added to liquid anhydrous ammonia in a container. Some "cooks" just add crushed ephedrine or pseudoephedrine pills to the anhydrous ammonia liquid which results in the pill binder freezing. This is known as "crush and rush."
- Small pieces of lithium, sodium, or potassium metal are added to the mixture until it turns blue and the color remains.

- Water is added to the mixture until the blue color disappears.
- After the remaining ammonia evaporates, additional water is added resulting in the solvent layer containing the methamphetamine to separate from the water.
- The solvent layer is separated from the water layer.
- Hydrogen chloride acid gas is bubbled through the solvent solution causing white crystals to form. This is hydrochloride (HCL) methamphetamine.
- The solvent containing the crystals is poured through a filter and the crystals collected.
- The crystals are dried.

Phenyl-2-Propanone. Phenyl-2-propanone, aluminum, methylamine, and muriatic acid are the principle chemicals in this process. This process does *not* utilize ephedrine or pseudoephedrine in the production and results in an inferior form of methamphetamine called "prop-dope." It was a popular method of manufacturing for outlaw motorcycle gangs in the past but is rarely used today because of the end product being dl-methamphetamine, a form of methamphetamine that is unpopular. In 2002, only 25 laboratories utilizing this process were seized.

Ephedrine/Pseudoephedrine Tablet Extraction

In order to use ephedrine or pseudoephedrine tablets or pills in the manufacturing of methamphetamine, the active chemical must be extracted from the tablet or pill. Cold medicine containing HCL pseudoephedrine is selected, as it converts to d-methamphetamine. Sometimes manufacturers mistakenly use norephedrine (phenylpropanolamine), and end up manufacturing amphetamine. The following is a summary of the process:

- Tablets are crushed or chopped into a powder using a food blender or coffee bean grinder.
- The pulverized pills are mixed with water, alcohol, or ether. The latter two are most common as they evaporate more quickly than water.
- The solution is then poured through a filter that collects the pill binder.
- The liquid is evaporated by heating, leaving the ephedrine/pseudoephedrine residue.

Glassing or Washing Methamphetamine

A practice of glassing or washing methamphetamine has become more popular in recent times. It takes approximately six grams of powder to make five grams of "glass," and although the finished product looks cleaner, the drug is no more potent, and contains the same byproducts as the original substance. The process is done purely for marketing purposes, which is evident from the increased sales price of the product. The following is a summary of the process:

- Methamphetamine powder is combined with acetone in a glass container and sometimes heated to assist in dissolving the powder.
- After methamphetamine has dissolved into the acetone, the solution is placed in the freezer to slow the evaporation of acetone. This results in crystals forming that have the appearance of rock candy, glass shards, or crystals.

Methamphetamine Chemicals

There are numerous chemicals commonly used in the manufacturing of methamphetamine, most being suitable for substitution with one another in the various processes. Most of the chemicals, even though some are common in homes, are dangerous and toxic, especially when combined with other chemicals. These combinations of chemicals can create explosive, toxic, and corrosive environments. It is crucial that the officer recognize the chemicals immediately upon encountering a methamphetamine laboratory and know the dangers the chemicals pose.

The following is a description of the chemicals most often used when manufacturing methamphetamine. Space does not permit considerable detail about the hazards associated with these chemicals although some hazards are identified.

Acetone. Acetone is a colorless, flammable liquid with a mildly pungent and sweet-smelling odor. It can be purchased from hardware stores in gallon quantities. Fingernail polish remover is also a source of acetone. Acetone is generally used for "washing" or cleaning finished methamphetamine, and creates a crystal appearance referred to as "ice" or "glass" on the street.

Alcohol. This can include methyl, denatured, or isopropyl alcohol. Methyl alcohol is flammable and usually derived from gas-line antifreezes such as Heet. All products can be obtained from various retail outlets.

Anhydrous Ammonia. Liquid with a strong ammonia odor. It is extremely toxic and can freeze body tissue on contact. Anhydrous Ammonia is used commercially as a fertilizer but is stolen from storage tanks at agricultural or chemical supply centers, or stolen from tanks on farms. The liquid is often stored in twenty-pound propane tanks or in igloo style water coolers with the covers wrapped in duct tape. Recently a process has been discovered whereby suspects make anhydrous ammonia utilizing ammonia sulfate, Red Devil Lye, dry ice, and water.

Coleman fuel. A colorless flammable liquid available at hardware and grocery stores.

Ephedrine/Pseudoephedrine. An over-the-counter cold medicine with bulk quantities available from black market sources generally originating from Canada.

Hydriodic Acid. A colorless liquid that turns yellow to brown upon exposure to light and air. A corrosive acid causes severe tissue burning. Vapors are irritating to the respiratory system, skin, and eyes. It is not easily obtained from chemical suppliers because it is controlled and regulated by the Controlled Substance Act (CSA). For that reason, it is rarely encountered, although organized criminal groups such as Mexican cartels do use it. Usually, iodine and red phosphorus are used in place of hydriodic acid.

Hydrochloric Acid. Commercially referred to as muriatic acid, hydrochloric acid is a colorless to slightly yellow highly toxic and corrosive liquid that causes burns and irritation to the tissue, eyes, and respiratory tract. Because hydrogen chloride gas is difficult to obtain from chemical suppliers because it is controlled and regulated by the Controlled Substance Act (CSA), it is most often made by combining muriatic acid and aluminum foil, or sulfuric acid and rock salt.

Hydrogen Peroxide. A colorless odorless liquid usually found in a 3 percent solution. It is available at grocery and drug stores as an antibacterial solution. It is used to extract iodine solids from tincture of iodine when manufacturing methamphetamine.

Hypophosphorous Acid. This acid is usually encountered as a liquid, and is used during the "hypo" method of methamphetamine manufacturing. It is a strong reducer and will irritate and burn the skin, eyes, and respiratory tract.

Iodine. A blue or blackish chemical found in liquid or crystal form. It has a unique odor with a sharp acrid taste. It produces a violet corrosive vapor that is irritating to the respiratory system and eyes. The solid form irritates the eyes and can burn the skin. It is available from feed stores, although the DEA scrutinizes crystal iodine purchases. Liquid tincture of iodine (usually 7%), however, can readily be purchased in gallon jugs with crystals obtained from the liquid by a process involving hydrogen peroxide. Hydrogen peroxide is also available at various retail outlets.

Kitty Litter. Used for capturing fumes during the cooking process to minimize the telltale odor.

Lithium Metal. Metal ribbon or chunks that are water reactive; they will ignite on contact with water. Drug manufacturers generally obtain lithium metal from lithium batteries either purchased or stolen. The battery is peeled open and the metal ribbon removed.

Red Phosphorus. Red phosphorus is a red to violet powder, the availability of which has diminished because of federal controls. Smaller independent manufacturers have resorted to extracting red phosphorus from matchbook striker plates. This is extremely time consuming and requires an enormous quantity of matchbooks. Approximately 10,000 matchbooks are required to obtain one ounce of red phosphorus. Waste removal companies in Albuquerque, New Mexico, and Phoenix, Arizona, have reported numerous dumpster and waste-removal truck fires caused by large trash bags containing matches. Red phosphorus is extracted from striker plates by soaking them in acetone or alcohol and filtering the liquid. Flare strikers are also a source of red phosphorus.

Sodium Hydroxide. A white substance found either in solid or liquid form available from various retail outlets. Most often, Red Devil lye is the brand of choice. It is very corrosive to human tissue and causes severe burns. It is used to neutralize the acidic mixture after the initial methamphetamine reaction.

Sodium Metal. A silvery metal obtained from chemical supply outlets, but it can be homemade using sodium hydroxide (lye), a skillet, and a 12-volt battery. Sodium metal is water reactive; ignition occurs on contact with water. It is stored in a liquid, often kerosene.

Sulfuric Acid. Sulfuric acid is a colorless, odorless, oily liquid that is extremely corrosive to human tissue and thus causes severe burns. It is available in diluted concentrations from retail outlets. When combined with rock salt, hydrogen chloride gas is generated.

Toluene. This chemical is a flammable liquid with a benzene-like odor. It can irritate and burn mucous membranes, eyes, and the respiratory tract. It is available from retail outlets, although regulated by the Controlled Substance Act (CSA).

Phenyl-2-Propanone (P2P). A clear liquid that is irritating to human tissue and the eyes. This chemical is controlled by Schedule II of the Controlled Substance Act (CSA) as an immediate precursor in drug manufacturing. This chemical, used in the legal manufacturing of amphetamine and methamphetamine, is diverted to the illegal market. Since 1980, when it became controlled, its use declined drastically. Ephedrine has replaced this precursor as the most widely used in methamphetamine production.

Methamphetamine Glassware and Equipment

Methamphetamine laboratory equipment can vary from chemistry grade to home cookware. Most commonly, however, officers encounter the latter because it is cheaper and easier to acquire. As a methamphetamine cook becomes more proficient at manufacturing, he or she may obtain more elaborate glassware and equipment. This is generally the case if the methamphetamine cook is producing greater quantities as household glassware often will not accommodate the increased quantity of chemicals. Curiously, there is a stigma attached to a methamphetamine cook who utilizes chemistry grade glassware and equipment.

The following is a list of glassware and equipment used by persons manufacturing methamphetamine clandestinely. This list is not exhaustive, however, because cooks often devise equipment that will facilitate manufacturing, although the manufacturing process rarely deviates from the norm.

Glassware

Pyrex or Corning
Dishes
Jugs/bottles
Mason jars
Beakers
Glassware
Condenser columns
Separatory funnels
Gallon ice tea jars
Flower vases

Equipment

Pails/buckets
Duct tape
Turkey baster
Plastic soda or sports drink bottles
Plastic gas cans
Hand or electric blenders
Plastic tubing
Kitchen utensils
Coffee filters
Cotton balls
Towels or washcloths
Pillowcases or sheets
Hot plate
Electric vacuum pumps
Plastic funnels
Electric or propane stove
Ph strips or electric ph tester
Aluminum foil
Measuring cups
Scales
Rubber gloves
Air respirators
Plastic storage containers

CLANDESTINE DRUG LABORATORY LOCATIONS

Clandestine drug laboratories are located in both urban and rural locations, and along transportation routes. They are commonly located in residences, industrial and commercial complexes, and self-storage facilities. Police frequently encounter the components of a drug laboratory broken down and in a container while being transported by vehicle to a different location (see Figure 8-2). In some instances, clandestine drug laboratories are in operation while being transported such as in motor homes and travel trailers. Tunnels, abandoned mines, and other subterranean areas have also been sites for drug laboratories.

Figure 8-2. Police officers often find the components of a methamphetamine laboratory broken down and in a box or crate. The discovery may occur at a location the officer is searching, or in a subject's vehicle. This illustration is a methamphetamine laboratory found in a crate located in the trunk of the subject's vehicle.

CLANDESTINE DRUG LABORATORY RECOGNITION CLUES

External Clues

There are usually *recognition clues* that a clandestine drug laboratory may be present at a location. Examine the exterior of the location for indications such as unusual structures or an assembly of equipment that seems unusual. Such indicators may suggest a clandestine laboratory. In addition, methamphetamine cooks frequently try to conceal or camouflage where manufacturing occurs, so be alert for evidence of that, and they often fortify the location and install security systems and/or surveillance cameras. The intent of camouflage is primarily to avoid detection by police, with security measures primarily intended to protect themselves and their drugs, chemicals, and money from a rip-off perpetrated by other criminals. Other recognition clues include chemical caused discoloration of the structure, pavement, or soil. The discoloration often has a bleached, tarnished, rusted, or corroded appearance.

There are odors associated with drug manufacturing, which vary depending on the drug in question and therefore the chemicals used. Most often, odors will be chemical in nature, and sometimes strong or unusual for the area. The odors are generally associated with common solvents, ether-like (anesthetic, sweet), ammonia, pungent, acrid, or sour. The odors may cause irritation to the nose, eyes, and throat.

Illicit drug manufacturing can be extremely dangerous and pose a great threat to the cooks. If the cooks are conscientious, they may employ methods to reduce the likelihood of themselves and their associates becoming victim to toxic air emissions, and explosion and fire. For example, individuals may exit the building to smoke cigarettes. People smoking outside may suggest the presence of a laboratory, smoking being done outside for safety reasons, or it can be that someone inside prefers smoking be done outside. People exiting the building to smoke may also suggest countersurveillance, an effort to detect law enforcement surveillance of the location.

On one occasion, a drug investigator in Phoenix, Arizona, was conducting surveillance of a hotel room suspected of containing a clandestine methamphetamine laboratory. The detective observed a suspect carry a large glass iced tea jar to the room. A short time later, the detective observed people smoking on the balcony of the hotel. The strongest indicator of unusual behavior was when someone opened and closed the room door repeatedly in a fanning motion, as if attempting to air-out the room. The detective walked by the room a short time later and could detect a strong chemical odor consistent with methamphetamine manufacturing, the smell emanating from the room. The detective executed a knock-and-talk that resulted in the immediate seizure of a clandestine drug laboratory and the arrest of seven individuals.

Internal Clues

Various chemicals, glassware, and assorted equipment located in the structure can indicate illicit drug manufacturing (see Figures 8-3 & 8-4). However, items appropriate for illicit drug manufacturing exist in many residences although knowledge and good judgment will usually enable the officer to determine if the items suggest drug manufacturing. For example, in many instances the nature of the items and their location leaves the nature of their use obvious.

Figure 8-3. Police officers found this typical methamphetamine laboratory in a subject's garage while conducting a knock-and-talk. Many items observed here are typical of the methamphetamine laboratory such as the flask sitting on a hotplate, the recipe/note book, and a surveillance monitor that was in operation.

If an officer uses the definition of a clandestine drug laboratory or waste abandonment site as a guideline, there will be a greater likelihood that the officer's assessment of the situation will be correct. If an officer must go around the residence gathering items to "make" a laboratory, the case will likely be questionable. On the other hand, persons involved in manufacturing drugs, especially methamphetamine, often attempt to separate chemicals and equipment into different areas of the residence to avoid detection. If that appears to be the case, the officer should identify other indicators of manufacturing such as the state of the chemicals and equipment, staining, odors, or intermediate products created from manufacturing.

Other internal indicators include, but are not limited to, police frequency scanners, surveillance camera monitors, drugs or drug paraphernalia, literature about drug manufacturing, and locked rooms.

Figure 8-4. Police found this display model of a methamphetamine laboratory in a motel room after receiving information from an estranged friend of the subject. The subject had decided to make a business of selling commercial quality methamphetamine laboratories, and assembled this laboratory in a motel room as a display model to promote sales.

FIRST RESPONDER ACTIONS

Introduction

When police officers respond to a possible clandestine drug laboratory, the foremost operational thought must be the safety of the responding officers, the suspects, and any civilians at the scene. The tendency, however, is for emergency personnel to rush in, secure the scene, thus saving the day. This can result in first responder exposure to significant hazards.

First responders are also concerned with preserving evidence to support criminal charges against the persons responsible for the drug laboratory. Nevertheless, while preserving evidence is vitally important, safety is first on the list of priorities. Officers must ensure that the potential spread of contamination is limited, and do what is necessary to minimize exposure to physical and chemical hazards by all investigative personnel, suspects, and the public. Officers must remember that investigating clandestine drug laboratories requires specialized training, and there are federal guidelines relative to the removal of hazardous materials (evidence).

Safety Procedures

At all times, think safety, safety, safety! Clandestine drug laboratory incidents are manageable if everyone takes the time to follow safe procedures, but complacency develops when officers get comfortable investigating clandestine drug laboratories and begin taking shortcuts. Most hazardous-exposure injuries occur because officers fail to take the necessary precautions when investigating drug laboratories. Moreover, supervisors may encourage officers to expedite the process to reduce labor expenses that often occur because of the time consuming nature of these incidents.

It is important for agencies to have a clandestine drug laboratory policy in place to provide guidance to first responders and certified laboratory investigators. Such policies are intended to provide guidance relative to minimum safety standards (equipment and procedures) required by law to insure the safety of citizens and investigators.

The clandestine drug laboratory policy must specify appropriate procedures for safe response to a laboratory (see Figures 8-5 & 8-6). The policy must also address procedures for the safe dismantling of a laboratory, and quality documentation to facilitate the successful prosecution of the persons responsible for a clandestine laboratory. The safety of citizens and the public will be the prime consideration in laboratory procedures with the development of a viable criminal case being a secondary although important consideration.

Figure 8-5. Tactical entry team equipped with personal protective equipment (PPE) including *self-contained breathing apparatus* (SCBA) preparing to execute a search warrant. Tactical entry teams commonly feature six personnel (Courtesy of Jackie Mercandetti Photography).

Figure 8-6. Tactical entry team, during a training exercise, outfitted with *personal protective equipment* (PPE) including *self-contained breathing apparatus* (SCBA) executing a search warrant. Tactical entry teams commonly feature six personnel; note that the officer on the right is providing cover (Courtesy of Jackie Mercandetti Photography).

Isolation and Scene Control

Officers must have a positive attitude about safety. When officers first arrive on scene, they should assess whether or not persons are exhibiting signs of injury or illness resulting from exposure to the drug laboratory chemicals. Request medical assistance immediately if indications of injury exist. Officers should then ensure that exposure to the drug laboratory is minimized to the officer and others at the scene. If suspects are detained at the scene, they should be in custody a safe distance from the laboratory, and upwind.

Officers should not attempt to shut down the lab, or ventilate the building. Turning off power can result in shutting down cooling systems intended to keep the heated chemical reaction from drying out or burning, resulting in the production of deadly phosphine gases.

The scene must be secured and access restricted as quickly as possible, but done using a tactically safe approach. Immediately block roads leading to and from the scene, and string barrier tape to cordon off areas where public access must be restricted. The use of barricades, barrier tape, cones, and vehicles is encouraged to ensure a well-defined crime and hazardous materials scene. Establish an initial perimeter larger than seems necessary because it is easier to reduce the size of the scene than to later increase it.

A command post is required by OSHA (Occupational Safety and Health Administration), and should be situated upwind from the drug laboratory. Expect wind shifts and be prepared to move the command post if necessary.

Officers should not eat, drink, or smoke at the scene, and should not touch or smell anything suspected to be chemicals or laboratory equipment.

Notifications

Once initial first responders stabilize the scene, they must notify the agencies that will assume the investigation. These agencies will include specialized clandestine laboratory investigation teams, fire service hazardous materials teams, environmental and public health agencies, and emergency medical service providers. Support agencies and organizations can include explosive and firearms technicians, animal control, child protective services (CPS) or public social services agencies, and hazardous materials clean-up companies. Depending on the circumstances, other resources may also be necessary.

CLANDESTINE DRUG LABORATORY OPERATIONS

Introduction

Effective management of the scene depends on various personnel working together to achieve common goals, the goals being the successful preservation of evidence, the minimizing of injury, and protection of the environment. A clandestine drug laboratory is not the time or place for power struggles between agencies. Each agency has a function to perform that is specific to its expertise, needs, and objectives.

Before officers may enter an identified clandestine drug laboratory, they must have Drug Enforcement Administration (DEA) certification. Certification requires forty hours of initial training, and eight hours of annual training is required to maintain certification. Because of the extensive training and knowledge required to investigate clandestine drug laboratories, this section is brief. The intent of this section is to familiarize officers with drug-laboratory scene operations. Officers are encouraged to read additional material, and avail themselves to courses on clandestine drug laboratory operations.

Initial Response Actions

Initial response actions include preserving evidence while stabilizing the incident. Officers generally have three choices from which to choose when responding to an incident. They are:

- Non-intervention–take no direct action other than to isolate the scene and deny entry
- Defensive–contain the scene and restrict the spread of hazardous materials
- Offensive–hazardous material release is controlled or stopped

It is generally wise to progress from a non-intervention, to defensive, and then offensive posture when resources and the capabilities of personnel are consistent with strategy. Officers are not encouraged to intervene when so doing is unsafe, when no threat to life exists, or resources or personal protective equipment (PPE) are lacking.

Protective Actions

Protective actions include evacuation and sheltering of citizens who have been, or could be, exposed to chemicals or other hazards at the clandestine drug laboratory scene. Such circumstances as the following determine the appropriateness of various protective actions.

- Chemical materials involved
- Population threatened
- Officer resources and capabilities relative to an action
- Time factors
- Weather conditions
- Ability to communicate with the public

Drug Site Assessment

After stabilizing a drug laboratory scene, an assessment is essential to identify the most effective means to investigate the crime safely and effectively. During the site assessment, officers must honor search and seizure laws to ensure that a prosecutable case can be prepared and submitted for charging.

Some incidents will fall under exigent circumstances initially, but stabilizing the scene may leave it necessary to obtain legal means to continue a search of the location. This may require a search warrant or the subject's consent to search.

Carefully assess the quantity of chemicals and equipment involved, and evaluate the characteristics of the structure containing the items. Also, query the initial responding officers or tactical entry personnel regarding what they observed and smelled at the location. Determine if they observed equipment, chemicals, waste, or contamination.

Identify and designate the contaminated portion of the site as a "hot zone." Only certified clandestine drug laboratory investigators may enter a hot zone. Identify points of entry and exit, and designate specific points of entry and exit for removal of chemicals and contaminated items. If points of entry and exit are limited, determine whether the scene qualifies as a confined space per OSHA.

The condition of the site is important because it can be just as hazardous as the chemicals encountered. A cluttered site features trip-and-fall hazards, and wet surfaces are a slip-and-fall hazard.

Air Monitoring

Prior to investigating officers entering a drug laboratory site, an assessment of the air quality must be completed. The data collected from air monitoring may be critical to various phases of field operations including the selection of personal protective measures and the establishment of site control.

If an air quality assessment does not provide sufficient information to identify hazards, "Level B" personal protective equipment (PPE) should be the minimum used for site entry. An air-monitoring instrument should be capable of measuring the *Immediate Danger to Life and Health* (IDLH) of hazardous materials as well as *Lower Explosive Limits* (LEL), *Upper Explosive Limits* (UEL), and oxygen deficient atmospheres. If unknown chemicals are encountered, or chemicals have undetermined IDLH properties, additional air monitoring equipment should be brought to the scene.

After site assessment and air monitoring are complete, a Site Safety Officer (one who has received DEA Site Safety certification), can determine PPE to be worn during the investigation. If a site safety officer is unavailable, certified clandestine laboratory officers can determine PPE to be worn (see Figure 8-7.)

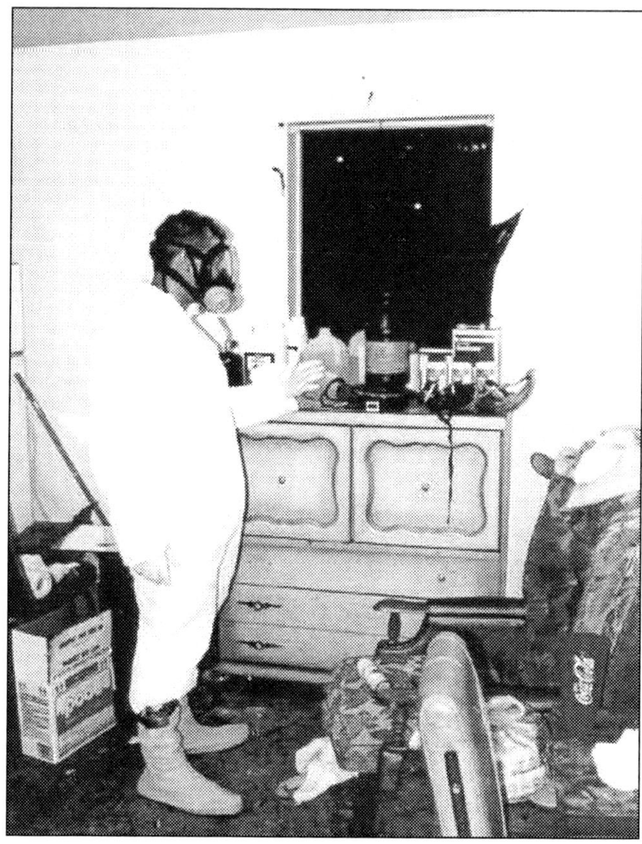

Figure 8-7. Illustrated is a drug enforcement officer wearing Level C *Personal Protective Equipment* (PPE) while searching the scene of a methamphetamine laboratory. Note the hotplate and containers of chemicals on the dresser. The lab was not in operation when discovered inasmuch as the plastic bottle on the hotplate is there for storage not cooking. When police raided this second story apartment, the subject dove headfirst through the window in an effort to escape–serious injury resulted.

Air monitoring should be performed periodically during the course of an on-site investigation. Air monitoring should also be done when work begins in a different area of the site, when new chemicals are encountered, when leaking or open chemicals are encountered, or when containers are opened. A clip on air monitoring device will provide constant air monitoring, and should be used when moving, sampling, and packaging chemicals and contaminated equipment.

Protective Zones

Classify clandestine drug laboratory scenes into zones. This is fundamental to the site control intended to prevent or reduce the spread of contamination by establishing artificial and/or physical barriers that isolate various hazards from potential targets. Implement site control by establishing work zones, decontamination and communication procedures, and safe work practices. This will prevent non-certified personnel inadvertently entering contaminated zones, ensure containment of chemical exposures, and prevent cross-contamination. The scene features three zones: the Hot or Exclusionary Zone, the Warm Zone, and the Cold Zone.

- *Hot or Exclusionary Zone.* The immediate area where the laboratory has been cooking, or chemicals and contaminated items located. This zone should be large enough to contain the area and limit inadvertent exposure to others. Only certified personnel are permitted in this zone.
- *Warm Zone.* This is the immediate area around the hot zone, although it can include other areas where chemical contamination was discovered, but identification of the chemicals is pending. The warm zone can include the yard surrounding a structure. This zone will also contain the decontamination station.
- *Cold Zone.* This includes all areas outside the hot and warm zones.

Site Safety Briefing

A site safety officer is one who has received specialized training in clandestine laboratory site control, and is responsible to the employer for site safety and health. If a site safety officer is on scene, he or she should give the site safety briefing before any work at the site commences.

The briefing will include a written plan or map which identifies work zones, emergency alert communications, and the nearest medical facility. This is usually prepared on a dry erase board and posted near the drug laboratory operations site in the cold zone. Identified chemical and physical hazards should be reported as well as the initial and assessment team findings. The PPE to be worn and equipment to be utilized will be stated as well as emergency procedures, site control, and decontamination. Operations and personnel assignments will be given and proper chemical handling procedures specified. During the course of the investigation, new information or changes in work practices should be posted to the safety plan/map and personnel appropriately briefed.

Evidence Processing Area

The Site Safety Officer and chemist should designate an area to process items of evidence (if a chemist is used), with the area located near the edge of the Hot Zone. Use plastic tarps to contain any chemicals that may spill and contaminate the ground. Use two tarps, one for processing evidence and the other for items that will be disposed of.

It is always best to remove chemicals to a central processing point rather than process the chemicals in place. There are several reasons for this. There is a greater chance of a chemical chain reaction when processing chemicals in an enclosed environment. Should a mishap occur, chemical fumes would not be trapped in a confined space. There is usually less room to work in a drug laboratory scene, and working indoors requires wearing a higher level of personal protective equipment (PPE) for a longer time. Removing chemicals to a central processing point will also allow for easier segregation of chemicals for processing by investigators and the hazardous materials waste removal personnel. By removing items from the lab, hazardous waste removal personnel can work without interfering with evidence processing, and their activities are more easily monitored to ensure compliance with OSHA rules such as all glassware being destroyed prior to removal from the scene. This is important because corrupt employees of the firms have diverted chemicals and equipment from legitimate hazardous material removal companies to illicit drug manufacturers.

During and after the investigation, hazardous waste removal personnel collect all gloves, protective suites, rubber boots, and general trash and remove them according to procedure.

Lobby

This is the location for monitoring personnel as they enter and exit the drug laboratory scene. The lobby officer is a scribe who keeps records in a log. The lobby officer notifies the site safety officer when it is time to rotate officers investigating the scene. Typically, the investigators wear PPE such as air respirators, self-contained breathing apparatus (SCBA) equipment, and protective clothing that will put tremendous stress on the body. For this reason, they must be closely monitored and notified when established work time limits are met.

The scribe also monitors outside air temperature and records pulse, temperature, and blood pressure of investigating personnel. Lobby officers are also useful for researching unknown chemicals found at the scene, referring to the National Institute for Occupational Safety and Health (NIOSH) guide, the National Fire Protection Association (NFPA) book, and clandestine laboratory field guides. Lobby officers can notify the clandestine laboratory incident commander if additional resources are needed to conclude the operation safely.

Additional officers can be assigned to such duties as assisting with the donning of PPE, measuring pulse rates and blood pressure, inspecting equipment prior to its use, refilling SCBA bottles, and monitoring the vitals of personnel while on break.

Rehabilitation and Support

Arrange for rehabilitation and support services prior to executing a search warrant on a clandestine laboratory, or commencing an investigation at a clandestine laboratory. Rehabilitation service includes supplying water and/or sports drinks, and quick energy snacks such as energy bars to personnel. Avoid soda drinks and high sugar foods because they can be diuretic and create unstable sugar levels.

A toilet facility along with a hand washing station are beneficial. This reduces time away from the scene, and minimizes issues of decontamination. Shade and chairs are ideal in hot climates. A command type vehicle or motor home that can provide warmth or cool air depending on climatic conditions is ideal.

Support trucks can provide SCBA refills, a generator for electricity, air evacuation fans, and lighting. Fire department personnel and vehicles are usually well equipped for clandestine drug laboratory operations because firefighters receive training and equipment for fire and hazardous material events. It is beneficial to establish a close working relationship with fire department personnel because they can provide resources and services often difficult to obtain elsewhere because of limited funding.

Decontamination

Fire department personnel possess the training and equipment necessary to handle decontamination procedures, so using their services is prudent.

Using fire service personnel will also free-up police personnel who would otherwise provide decontamination services. If it is necessary to assign police personnel to decontamination, assign two officers. They should be equipped with PPE that is one level below the laboratory entry officers.

Place a plastic sheet at the hot zone exit and secure it with traffic cones to hold it in place and to identify the area as a hot zone. Using different colored cones makes it possible to designate the hazard level of each zone, i.e., red for hot zone, yellow for warm zone, and blue for cold zone.

The decontamination station should be equipped with a step tub with a bucket and brush, tri sodium phosphate (TSP) soap or detergent, two trash receptacles, and two chairs (see Figure 8-8).

Decontamination should be set up so that all personnel must pass through decontamination when they exit the hot zone. Decontaminate boots, gloves, and any other clothing or equipment that might be contaminated. Decontamination personnel can assist officers with scrubbing and removing PPE.

A water source is necessary–obtain water from a residence, fire hydrant, or the water supply in a support vehicle. Once the operation is complete, officers should ensure that wastewater and PPE are properly disposed of. Water can be ph tested to ensure that it is neutral, and sometimes conveniently disposed of on site.

CLANDESTINE DRUG LABORATORY HAZARDS

Introduction

The combining of, or movement of, chemicals at clandestine laboratory incidents by suspects, or done accidentally by officers may produce life threatening gases such as phosphine and/or hydrogen chloride gas. Other deadly gases may also be present that lack a chemical odor. Lack of an odor does not mean life-threatening gases are not present. In addition to life threatening gases, there are other hazards that can affect one's health, such as toxic chemicals and structural and environmental hazards.

Clandestine drug laboratories present multiple hazards. Other than the hazards of the chemicals, officers must deal with criminal suspects. Individuals involved in the manufacturing of drugs are often armed and under the influence of drugs, a deadly combination–methamphetamine cooks who use the drug themselves can be extremely dangerous. Cooks who also use methamphetamine are usually extremely paranoid, and tend to become violent with little provocation. Moreover, they usually have defen-

Figure 8-8. Illustrated is a decontamination station featuring a portable shower and pool (Courtesy of Jackie Mercandetti Photography).

sive systems in place to protect themselves and their drug assets from theft. Although booby traps are not common, officers should always assume they exist. In Phoenix, Arizona, police discovered a methamphetamine laboratory in a secret basement that contained a light bulb filled with a flammable liquid. Fortunately, officers could not find the light switch to turn the light on. Had they turned the light on as intended, it could have had a devastating effect on any officers near the bulb when activated. Of greater concern, however, was the fact that bomb technicians had cleared the location and provided the proverbial "green light" to enter.

Motion sensors and surveillance cameras are common with clandestine methamphetamine laboratories. Thorough scouting and surveillance should identify these hazards prior to executing a search warrant.

Surveillance cameras are sometimes blatantly visible, but concealed cameras are more common. Cameras are found concealed within the structure or in objects placed near or on the building. Plastic owls used to deter pigeons and rabbits have been a popular item to conceal surveillance cameras, and it appears that word spreads rapidly among drug manufactures because so many employ the use of the owls to conceal their cameras. One or more surveillance cameras at a location where manufacturing is suspected has always been a strong indicator in the southwestern states that drug manufacturing is in fact taking place, because many laboratories are found to contain surveillance cameras.

Traditional alarm systems are not common at methamphetamine laboratories, although drug manufacturers often install motion sensors to turn on a light or activate a noise in the house if someone approaches.

When investigating a location for suspected drug manufacturing, it is important to identify what type of animals are present because dogs can be dangerous, and they can alert suspects that officers are on foot in the area. It is common to encounter dogs at methamphetamine laboratories, and it is important to deal with them swiftly when executing a search warrant. A carbon dioxide fire extinguisher may be adequate to scare the dog, or the use of non-lethal weapons can be effective. However, as unfortunate as it seems, it is sometimes necessary to dispatch the dog. This is a decision the team executing the search warrant must make.

Chemical Hazards

The chemicals used when manufacturing drugs pose a serious hazard to anyone who may be exposed. Many of the chemicals encountered will be unidentifiable because they will be in secondary containers or the labels may be removed or illegible. Chemical hazards include flammables or combustibles depending on flashpoint, reactive, corrosive, toxic, or any combination thereof. Illicit drug manufacturers often demonstrate unsafe storage practices, and they often improvise equipment for manufacturing. Improvised equipment is often unsafe and increases the risk of chemical exposure, fire, and explosion.

Chemicals found at drug laboratories are often improperly stored–chemicals are often in containers that are inappropriate for the chemical and incompatible chemicals are often stored together. Moreover, electronic devices are often intrinsically unsafe, and power supplies are usually of a makeshift variety thus increasing the possibility of fire or explosion.

When chemicals are in improper containers, when incompatible chemicals are stored together, and unsafe electrical devices are used, there is an increased danger of fire and/or explosion, and an increased danger of toxic fumes. In the final analysis, drug manufacturers rarely follow correct protocol when handling hazardous chemicals and associated waste.

Structural Hazards

Officers familiar with how the typical methamphetamine addict lives appreciate the hazards associated with the conditions in and around the location of their laboratories. When searching a laboratory, it may be necessary for officers to recover chemicals and equipment from confined spaces such as crawl spaces, tunnels, and attics. The flooring can be uneven or unstable and there is usually an abundance of junk, making it hard to navigate through the structure. Laboratory equipment, often improvised, features inferior workmanship and duct tape. Improvised electrical wiring and alternate power supplies to operate the drug laboratory are common. Water supplies for manufacturing are usually crude, utilizing makeshift plumbing that leaks, increasing the chance of electrocution and a slip-and-fall injury. Top all that with an improvised cooling and ventilation system and it spells disaster for those persons living in the structure, and police officers who are required to investigate the drug laboratory.

Environmental Hazards

Environmental hazards include toxic air emissions, soil and water contamination, hazardous waste accumulation, and usually irreversible damage and contamination to the structure that contains the drug laboratory.

PERSONAL PROTECTIVE EQUIPMENT (PPE)

Introduction

Personal Protective Equipment (PPE), previously illustrated, is essential to preventing or at least reducing the danger of chemical exposure. OSHA requires PPE, OSHA being the regulatory agency of the federal government that determines the levels of chemical exposure to which workers may be exposed. Officers should consider PPE as important as wearing a ballistic vest.

Chemicals enter the body through four routes:

- Inhalation
- Absorption
- Ingestion
- Injection

Inhalation allows for the most effective and rapid absorption of a number of compounds. The lungs are also the only organ system to receive the entire output of the heart as compared to the other organs that receive only a fraction of the output of the heart. Knowing how chemicals affect the body and their routes of entry helps to determine the type of PPE needed. Space limitations prevent going into all the chemicals an officer may encounter at a drug laboratory, although many chemicals were identified earlier. Rather, officers are encouraged to familiarize themselves with the chemicals they may encounter and the types and levels of PPE required.

Levels of Personal Protective Equipment

There are four types and levels of personal protective equipment:

- *Level A.* Best respiratory and skin protection. Level A consists of a self-contained breathing apparatus (SCBA) and fully encapsulated chemical protective suit. *Used in unknown atmospheric environments, or when handling unknown or skin absorptive materials.*
- *Level B.* High level of respiratory protection but a reduced level of skin protection. Level B consists of a SCBA and hooded chemical resistant clothing. *Used in atmospheric environments with less than 19.5 percent oxygen and/or gas or vapors are unidentified, and there is a low skin absorption hazard.*
- *Level C.* Lower level of respiratory protection and reasonable skin protection. Consists of a full- or half-mask air purifying respirator (APR)

and hooded chemical resistant clothing (see Figures 8-5, 8-6 & 8-7). *Used when there is no skin absorption hazard, no unknown atmospheric hazards, and there is a sufficient oxygen environment.*

- *Level D.* Regular work uniform that provides minimal protection. Coveralls or battle dress uniforms (BDUs) with appropriate boots and eye protection is encouraged. *Used when no hazards are evident.*

Selecting Protective Equipment

When officers know what types of hazardous materials are on scene, i.e., vapor, liquid, or solid, selecting personal protective equipment is easier. Knowing the extent of the hazard, such as the length of exposure and skin absorption qualities, is also important. Other factors to consider when selecting equipment include oxygen levels, work activity, and chemical compatibility. However, because of the many different processes for manufacturing illicit drugs, officers entering a clandestine laboratory cannot always anticipate what chemicals they will encounter. Hence, proper selection of chemical PPE can be difficult–it is best to err on the side of caution.

The primary limitation first responders face is the lack of chemical protective clothing. Firefighters may incorrectly assume their *turnouts* are chemical protective clothing, which they are not. Even when utilizing an SCBA, they are at Level D. Police officers often wear clothing that will absorb hazardous chemicals. It is important to outfit emergency responder personnel with the minimum levels of PPEs to reduce potential exposure. It is not only fair–OSHA requires it!

With the increased awareness and preparation for a weapons of mass destruction (WMD) attack, many agencies have outfitted their first responder personnel with equipment that is also appropriate at a clandestine laboratory. Officers must ensure that the PPE they utilize will effectively protect them from the chemicals they may encounter. This is an important point because PPE is often specialized relative to specific chemicals.

HEALTH EFFECTS

Introduction

Toxicology is the field in which the adverse effects of chemicals on living organisms are studied. Toxicity is the inherent ability of a substance to cause injury to a biological tissue. Toxic agents are classified in terms of such things as the target organ, use, source, effect, physical state, etc.

In toxicology, a hazard is defined as the likelihood that injury will occur in a given situation, whereas safety is defined as the probability that harm will not occur under specified conditions. The conditions of exposure are comprised of several factors that include the dose, the route of exposure, and the frequency of exposure. Other factors include the type of toxin, personal tolerances, and variables such as sensitivities, age, medical history, gender, health condition, personal habits, and medical conditions.

It can be said that, "The dose makes the poison." All substances are poisons, only the dose determines whether they are toxic. In toxicology, one of the most important principles to learn is the *dose-response relationship.* This correlation prescribes that as a toxin's dose is increased, a percentage of the population will exhibit an increased response to the dose. Although not all segments of the population are equal, those that respond to the lowest dose are categorized *hyper-responsive*, and those that respond to the highest *hypo-responsive.*

An officer's exposure to toxins at clandestine drug laboratories will be dependant on the various factors discussed above. Understanding one's physical limitations in combination with environmental conditions are crucial factors in limiting toxic exposures. In addition, an important factor is whether exposures are acute or chronic in nature.

Acute vs. Chronic Exposure

Acute exposure is a one time, limited, or short-term exposure and the effects may not manifest themselves immediately. The effects can range from death within minutes, to injuries, illness, or central nervous system damage. Many substances cause medical problems that do not show up for hours or sometimes days after an exposure.

Chronic exposure is frequent or long term. The toxic exposure may not be evident for years but can cause death, injury, illness, or central nervous system damage.

Hazardous materials cause damage to biological tissue by chemically affecting target organs. Some examples include:

- Carcinogenicity (development of cancer)
- Hepatotoxicity (liver damage)
- Neurotoxicity (nervous system damage)
- Nephrotoxicity (kidney damage)

DRUG ENDANGERED CHILDREN (DEC)

An increasing number of children suffer exposure to clandestine drug laboratories and the toxic chemicals they produce. In 2002, out of the 2023 children residing in seized methamphetamine laboratories, 1373 were exposed to toxic levels of chemicals. Of those children, twenty-six were injured, two died, and 1026 were taken into protective custody (DEA).

The long-term health risk to children is substantial because a child's developing brain and organs are more susceptible to damage at specific maturation levels, and children may be less able to process and eliminate chemicals than adults. Acute and chronic diseases such as cancer and organ damage may result, and emotional and behavioral problems are more common with children who have lived in a home where methamphetamine was produced. There is also the risk of chemical burns to tissue, eyes, and the respiratory tract, and poisoning from ingesting chemicals and drugs. Clandestine drug laboratories also present a serious explosion and fire hazard.

As increasing numbers of children are found at drug laboratory sites, law enforcement, medical, and social service personnel are combining their resources to address the welfare of these children, and many states have enacted laws increasing the punishment of offenders who violate child abuse and endangerment laws. By combining resources, professionals can intervene and break the cycle of child abuse and endangerment.

The Drug Endangered Children (DEC) Program originated in Butte County, California, in 1993 to improve the safety and health of children endangered by drug production, distribution, and abuse. The program brings together law enforcement personnel, social workers, public health nurses, and district attorneys in a cooperative effort to remove children from homes where methamphetamine is produced and to safeguard the children from further abuse and neglect. The DEC program is an excellent model that agencies can use to learn how to negotiate the legal, medical, and social issues associated with children being present at methamphetamine laboratories, and other hazardous drug production and abuse environments.

The development of a strategy, and formulating a specialized team comprised of professionals who can respond to clandestine drug laboratories and treat and care for children, as well as assist with the criminal prosecution, would be beneficial for any agency. Indeed, this is a problem affecting all communities, as most will have occasion to attend to children located at a drug chemical site.

The number of children found at drug manufacturing sites continues to rise, and is expected to continue at an even higher rate. These children will continue to suffer physical and psychological effects associated with exposure to hazardous chemicals, and cases of abuse and neglect will no doubt rise as well. This will be an ongoing challenge for law enforcement agencies, medical personnel, and social workers as they struggle to develop innovative solutions to address this problem.

Numerous publications are available that provide useful information for developing prevention and response strategies. One such publication, produced by the Department of Justice, is titled, *Children at Clandestine Methamphetamine Laboratories: Helping Meth's Youngest Victims* (DOJ, 2003).

CONCLUSION

This section was by no means exhaustive, but provided to acquaint the reader with the various aspects of drug manufacturing. The processing and investigation of clandestine drug laboratory scenes is multi-faceted, and is dependant on a number of professionals working together.

Much focus in this section was on methamphetamine laboratories because 99 percent of the drug laboratories in operation are producing methamphetamine. Although there is much to be said about the various processes and methods of drug manufacturing, and although there are many different drugs, it is safe to say that one will most likely encounter a methamphetamine laboratory.

If the reader has grasped the essence of this discussion, he or she will almost certainly recognize a clandestine drug laboratory when he or she sees it, and be able to implement safety measures to prevent injury to persons in the vicinity.

Chapter 9

SOURCES OF INFORMATION

INTRODUCTION

The very nature of investigations requires obtaining information from a variety of sources, and although there are numerous sources and as many methods by which officers attempt to exploit them, all information sources fall into one of three general categories, exclusive of evidence recovered from a crime scene. They are:

- Interviews and interrogations
- Record checking
- Physical surveillance

As for records, many information sources are accessible by computer, some by telephone, some in writing, and some require the officer to visit the location of the records. There are cases where a person in possession of private records, such as an apartment manager, for example, is willing to provide information but requires verification of the identity of the person making the request and will not provide the information over the telephone. Hence, a personal visit is required.

PUBLIC AND PRIVATE RECORDS

Introduction

People create numerous records during their journey thorough life between birth and death, and often beyond by virtue of probate court records. When properly exploited, public and private records provide considerable information. As a person goes through life, they engage in various activities that result in records that include, but are not limited to, the following:

- Birth certificate
- Medical records
- Educational records
- Social Security records
- Credit reports–financial records
- Vehicle operator's license
- Vehicle registration
- Voter registration
- Military service
- Club and/or church membership
- Trade and professional associations
- Trade unions
- Various licenses
- Divorce records–wealth of information
- Marriage License application
- Business ownership records
- Civil court records
- Criminal court records
- Telephone service
- Utilities; water, gas, & electricity
- Rental records; habitation
- Property ownership records
- Moving company records
- Insurance applications and policies
- Death certificate
- Probate court records
- Last will and testament
- Employment records, including
- Employment applications

Some of the records that result from the above activities are public and can be examined by anyone, while others are private and cannot be accessed without first having cultivated an inside contact, a confidential informant. The latter occurs, for example, when records are not open for public inspection because of a company policy. When records are not open for public inspection, if the officer tactfully requests permission to examine them, the custodian of the records may grant permission, while in other instances, a warrant will be required to access the records.

Historically, law enforcement officers have not cultivated public and private information sources to the extent characteristic of private investigators because the nature of most criminal investigations does not require information from such sources, not to the extent that was characteristic of civil investigations, but that is changing. The complexion of crime is changing and for that reason, today's law enforcement officers are making more use of public and private records.

When searching records and documents, one should always access first those sources that are the easiest to access, the least costly to access in terms of time and fees, and those that are the most likely to provide the desired information. There have been cases where considerable effort was devoted to locating someone when all along, the person was a telephone subscriber and listed in the telephone directory. *Always, when attempting to locate someone, first check the telephone directory and call directory assistance to determine if there is a current telephone listing.* If it is determined that the person has an unlisted telephone number, learning that fact has value inasmuch as it tends to confirm that they reside in the area, which is helpful information if that was not already known. Once knowing that, his or her address can be determined via telephone company records, which may require an inside contact (informant) or obtaining a warrant.

Confidential Information Sources

As stated, many records are private and not available for examination simply by requesting to see them because there is a policy prohibiting disclosure. In such cases, their access is generally possible only by means of a confidential informant, by having first cultivated an employee with access to the records that will make the disclosure. In some instances, a person with access to the records, who had not been previously cultivated, will make the desired disclosure if properly approached. In some cases, a warrant will be required to obtain the information.

Government Records: Local, County, State, and Federal

Governmental entities on the local, county, state, and federal levels all feature many departments with each maintaining a variety of records. Some of the records are of interest to officers while others are not, and some are open for public inspection while others are not.

The number and types of departments a government entity features, and what departments maintain certain records, varies depending on the size of the population served. For example, a large city will have more departments than a small town. Similarly, a county serving a large population will feature more departments than a county serving a limited population. In addition, the specific name of each department may differ somewhat from one jurisdiction to the next although their names are generally indicative of their area of responsibility and therefore the types of records maintained. The officer who has a general understanding of the types of information each political subdivision maintains will not experience difficulty locating desired records.

One of the quickest and easiest ways to determine what government entities feature what departments, and therefore what type of records, is to examine the telephone directory government section. The records that are accessible without a warrant, because they are open to public inspection, will vary by department and from one government entity to another. Similarly, one city or county may permit examination of records that another city or county may not. The same holds true from one state to another. The federal government, however, is uniform from one state to the next inasmuch as their policies are uniform throughout the country.

With time, experience will result in a familiarity with what government department maintains what kinds of records and which are open for public inspection and which are accessible only via a warrant. The inexperienced officer, for educational purposes, may visit the various government departments and ask what records they maintain and which ones are open to public inspection.

Some government records, which are open for public inspection, are accessible at no cost while others require a fee. Additionally, although some government records are accessible via the computer, some only go back a certain number of years beyond which manual inspection is necessary.

Directories

There are numerous directories published each year that provide valuable information and officers should be aware of them. In fact, there are so many directories that there is a directory listing directories–*Directories in Print.*

Commonly, directories list such things as Public Companies, Manufacturers, Wholesalers and Distributors, Technology Companies, Big Businesses, Colleges and Universities in the United States, Attorneys in the United States, City Directories, Cross Reference Directories, Telephone Directories, Who's Who Directories, etc. If one is not familiar with the variety of directories available at the public library, a day should be devoted to browsing their collection.

Other sources must validate information obtained from directories because directory information quickly becomes dated, and the information may not have been accurate to begin with. Most directories suffer a 15-40 percent change yearly with the overall average being 25 percent. The amount of change that occurs will, of course, depend on the type of information, with some directories suffering more change than others do. Old directories are often useful for research purposes.

Research Using the Computer

Computers have become so essential to officers that without them, many phases of an investigation would suffer. Not long ago, when checking records during an investigation, it was necessary to commute to the location of various records. Naturally, that was time consuming. Although many records still require personal examination, increasing numbers of records are becoming accessible by computer.

Because computer technology is advancing so rapidly, and because of the ever-increasing sources of information that can be accessed via the computer, little will be offered here relative to specifically what records can be accessed by computer. Rather, it is important to know what useful records exist, regardless of whether they are accessible by computer, because as sources previously requiring manual inspection become accessible via the computer, officers will become aware of that fact.

Today, one can use the computer to locate people, determine who a person's neighbors are, determine who else has resided at a subject's address, whether someone owns aircraft or watercraft, do vehicle license plate searches, do Vehicle Identification Number (VIN) searches, drivers license searches, civil and criminal court record searches, bankruptcy searches, worker's compensation claims searches, property searches, etc. The list could go on.

A great deal of information is available at no cost via the computer, and there are very good databases that offer access to information for a fee. With time, as more of the various databases link up one with another, the information resources will expand proportionately. Some databases are accessible only by law enforcement and licensed private investigators, and they are valuable.

TRASH RUN

Trash runs, also referred to as a *Trash Rip* or *Trash Cover*, are the surreptitiously obtaining a subject's trash and examining it for information and/or evidence. Depending on the nature of the case, inventorying someone's trash can provide a great deal of valuable information. For example, officers may find evidence of drug manufacturing, sales, and use. Other information often found in someone's trash includes, but is not limited to, the following:

- Where a person banks
- What credit cards they have
- Where they shop, what they purchase, and method of payment via sales receipts
- Personal interests via magazines
- Personal letters and envelopes reflecting a name and return address

Before attempting to obtain someone's trash, identify the best time and method for acquiring it. One method for acquiring someone's trash is to obtain an empty trash container from an unoccupied home that is for sale and switching it with that of the subject. A pickup truck or van may be used, and the switch is quick when three officers are involved. There have been cases, when confronted with a highly cautious subject who does not place trash at the curb until the sanitation truck is approaching, that the sanitation department has acquired the trash for police by surreptitiously segregating it from other trash at the time of pickup.

When making a trash run, one must honor the laws of the jurisdiction. There was a time when the courts considered a person to have a *reasonable expectation of privacy* relative to trash that had been disposed of, the rationale being that a person had a legitimate expectation that their trash would be lost to obscurity in a landfill. Many jurisdictions have more recently ruled that once trash is no longer on the subject's property, it constitutes abandoned property and seizure may occur without a warrant. In the latter jurisdictions, police officers must have a warrant to seize trash from someone's property but are free to seize it without a warrant once it has been set at the curb and is therefore abandoned property.

Caution! The contents of trash are unknown and it is important therefore to consider personal protective equipment/clothing needs when inventorying trash being alert for hazards such as hypodermic needles and razor blades.

CITIZEN COMPLAINTS

Citizens are excellent sources of information as they are often in a position to see, hear, and gather information on potential suspects that would otherwise escape law enforcement observations. Many large investigations originate from a neighbor who is conscientious enough to call law enforcement when suspicious activity is observed.

Citizens will be more cooperative with law enforcement if they are confident they will remain anonymous, that the suspect will not learn they were providing law enforcement with information. Offering assurance of anonymity is usually possible because citizens' fall under the same protections as a confidential informant would. In the southwestern United States, the Phoenix metropolitan area to be more specific, many drug trafficking activities (i.e., stash houses, processing centers, etc.) occur within communities that are largely comprised of Hispanic residents. This is not all-inclusive, but correlates with the fact that Hispanic drug trafficking organizations are well integrated into the communities. Many Hispanic residents of the community are aware of the illicit activities but fear harsh retaliation by the drug traffickers if they provide information to the police, and perpetrators discover that fact. If properly cultivated, these citizens can provide invaluable information on drug activities, but police must protect the information sources identity to the extent of dropping a case if the information sources identity is subject to revelation, or testimony would reveal them.

Citizens, just as informants, have reasons for providing information to law enforcement. In most cases, it is because the illicit drug activity deteriorates the quality of life of the neighborhood, and they simply want the activity to cease. Other times the motives may not be so benign. Neighbor disputes can result in false accusations perpetrated by both parties involved in a dispute. It is unfortunate that anyone uses law enforcement in such a manipulative fashion, but it does happen. If an officer conducts a thorough background of the location and the persons involved, such a situation should be identifiable. Usually there will be a list of incident reports, calls for service, etc., that involve the complainant and the alleged suspect of criminal activity. If a neighbor dispute is suspected, it does not rule the information invalid, and in fact the information may be very accurate and the dispute a result of the suspected illicit activity. Officers should attempt to determine the accuracy of the information by thoroughly debriefing the complainant. An interview will usually reveal if the complainant has a personal vendetta against the alleged suspect and is therefore embellishing allegations of illicit activity.

The mentally imbalanced citizen can be very convincing and difficult to handle. These citizens will be suffering from some type of mental disorder and are convinced they are observing drug activity or in the case of methamphetamine laboratories, smelling chemicals from drug manufacturing. They will claim illness and will in fact many times be experiencing illness as they have convinced themselves that what they are experiencing is real. Again, a thorough background check and interview will often reveal this type of complainant. Many times the officer will still need to conduct a preliminary investigation to (hopefully) satisfy the complainant, and support the fact that the activity being reported is inaccurate. Mentally imbalanced complainants will usually continue believing criminal activity is occurring regardless of information to the contrary.

In Phoenix, Arizona, a drug enforcement detective received a complaint from a husband and wife about chemical odors believed to be from a nearby drug laboratory that was reportedly permeating the residence, resulting in the wife experiencing severe illness. The wife was adamant there were chemical smells, and her husband supported her ill feelings. The husband also told the detective that his wife was hyper-sensitive to chemical odors and in fact he had to remove all odors from the home including soaps, detergents, shampoos, etc., and seal the house from outside odors. Both the husband and wife suspected the drug manufacturer was their new neighbor. The chemical smells were reportedly getting stronger and the wife had to leave the house and sleep in a camper trailer. This behavior did not seem sensible because the camper would be more susceptible to chemical fumes than the house. The detective suspected that the chemical fumes alleged by the women were a figment of her imagination, but she believed it and continued make telephone complaints to various officers in different details. Detectives decided to do a trash run and nighttime surveillance during the times of the alleged activity, which was virtually every night. The surveillance would occur without the complainant's knowledge to confirm or dispute reliability.

During the first night of surveillance, detectives conducted three walk-bys of the suspect residence, which was next door to the complainant. No odors were evident. The next day the case detective called the complainant and asked if any odors were apparent the previous evening. As suspected, the complainant reported strong odors and difficulty in sleeping. Detectives then conducted a second surveillance. During surveillance, a detective observed the elderly female carrying blankets and pillows to a camper trailer parked on the side of the house. Again, the following day, the woman reported smelling strong chemical odors the previous night. Detectives decided that a quick and easy remedy to the situation was to conduct a knock-and-talk at the alleged perpetrator's residence. During the knock-and-talk, the alleged suspects reported that the neighbors (complainants) probably reported them as drug manufactures because the neighbors did not like them. The accused volunteered this information without the officers having disclosed the source of the complaint.

In conclusion, it is important that officers not accept information from citizens as unquestioned truth, but attempt to corroborate it and identify the motivations the citizen for reporting the information. In most cases, the information will be valid, but the cases based on false allegations often result in a futile expenditure of time and resources that take away from other cases, and unnecessarily put a location or persons under law enforcement scrutiny, when there is no reason for it.

OTHER LAW ENFORCEMENT AGENCIES

Law enforcement agencies gather information on persons relative to the needs of the agency. The Drug Enforcement Administration (DEA) has computer systems that can cross-reference various data such as vehicle license plate numbers, names, addresses, and telephone numbers. This information can be important when trying to establish criminal associations among various individuals that are involved in drug activity. The El Paso Intelligence Center (EPIC), and the Special Operations Division of the DEA are excellent resources as well, being able to provide valuable information to officers involved in investigating drug organizations. The Rocky Mountain Intelligence Center (RMIN) is yet another source. Many of these organizations do the same thing–gather data on criminals, and criminal organizations, but they all have unique objectives that make them distinctive from one another, and experts at acquiring and processing the vast data they collect. Many of these organizations provide inexpensive, often free, drug training to law enforcement agencies of various sizes, on various topics. Seasoned veterans provide the training.

Chapter 10

PHYSICAL SURVEILLANCE, VISUAL AIDS, AND SURVEILLANCE PHOTOGRAPHY

PHYSICAL SURVEILLANCE

Introduction

During a drug investigation, essential information is often not available from conventional sources such as public and private records, interviews and interrogations, and physical evidence. When that occurs, physical surveillance often becomes necessary. Physical surveillance is the watching and following of people. Accomplishing this may involve observing activity at a given location, referred to as *stationary surveillance* or *stakeout*, or following a person as he or she moves about the community by vehicle, public transportation, or by foot, this form of surveillance referred to as *moving surveillance.* The officer conducting surveillance is the *surveillant*, and the person observed is the *subject.*

The investigation of drug-law violations commonly requires considerable physical surveillance. However, because treating the topic of physical surveillance comprehensively requires more space than can be devoted here, the reader is encouraged to refer to the book *Fundamentals of Physical Surveillance.* The book features 368 pages and 160 illustrations.[9]

The purpose of this chapter is simply to emphasize the importance of physical surveillance during the investigation of drug law violations, and to acquaint the reader with the importance of visual aids such as binoculars, and photographic equipment. This chapter will leave the reader with an appreciation for the tremendous distances from which meaningful observations are possible using optical aids, and the tremendous distances from which a subject can be photographed using either still or video equipment.

Although one commonly thinks of moving surveillance and stationary surveillance as if they were two different operations, with a case calling for either one or the other but not both, moving surveillance always features both. Moving surveillance, whether done by vehicle or on foot, begins with

9. Siljander, R., & Fredrickson, D. (2002). *Fundamentals of Physical Surveillance: A Guide for Uniformed and Plainclothes Personnel (2nd Edition).* Springfield, IL: Charles C Thomas.

stationary surveillance wherein one waits for the subject to appear and begin the commute, at which time moving surveillance begins. Stationary surveillance resumes when the subject reaches a destination.

Identification of the subject is the most important element of any surveillance. Doing everything correctly from start to finish will avail nothing if the wrong person is followed. That is why it is important to obtain all identifying data pertaining to the subject, including a recent photograph, before surveillance is attempted.

Stationary Surveillance

Almost all drug-related surveillance operations will require stationary surveillance at some point. Some cases require an operation that consists almost entirely of stationary surveillance, but many require both stationary and moving surveillance.

A *preliminary survey* precedes stationary surveillance to facilitate selecting a good *vantage point.* When selecting a vantage point, one is seeking a location that offers an unobstructed view of the area of interest while, at the same time, providing sufficient cover so that the subject does not become aware of the surveillance.

When selecting a vantage point to serve as a prelude to vehicle surveillance, the officer must consider the directions by which the subject may leave the area and the appropriate course of action in each instance. This is important because in many instances, when a subject is lost, it occurs within the first few blocks because of poor planning and positioning on the part of the officer.

Foot Surveillance

The officer will endeavor to follow a subject by foot when the subject travels by foot. When conducting foot surveillance, the officer must anticipate the possibility of the subject using some form of public transportation and be prepared to meet fare requirements. In addition, it is important to carry an ample supply of expense money, including plenty of small change, and a mini-binocular or monocular.

Although a lone officer can do foot surveillance, assigning two or more officers will enhance effectiveness. When working as a team, each officer has a specific position in relation to that of the subject and other team members. A well-coordinated surveillance team can be highly effective, but if a team is not well coordinated, the results are generally poor. Preplanning and practice are essential.

Vehicle Surveillance

There are many techniques for vehicle surveillance, the appropriateness of each depending upon circumstances. Many factors determine the most appropriate technique, so the officer must have a clear understanding of the merits and limitations of each to apply appropriate variations. This is important whether a lone officer is attempting surveillance, or whether he or she is part of a multiple-vehicle surveillance team.

A preliminary survey of the area in which surveillance will occur or at least begin precedes vehicle surveillance. The preliminary survey enables the officer to:

- Select a suitable vantage point from which to wait for the subject to appear and depart.
- Make a quality choice as to the most suitable type of vehicle and style of dress.
- Anticipate difficulties that direction of departure may present.
- Determine equipment needs such as binoculars.

The most appropriate vehicle will generally be a vehicle of common make such as a Ford or Chevrolet, reasonably new, no distinguishing features, and a subtle color that is also consistent with the majority of vehicles in the area. As for dress, casual clothing will generally be the most versatile.

The most appropriate distance to be maintained between the officer's vehicle and that of the subject can vary from little more than one car length during heavy inner-city work traffic, to distances of half a city block or more on suburban streets that are almost void of traffic. On freeways, the distance often will be greater, depending on traffic volume, and in rural areas, distances as great as one-half to one mile are not uncommon.

Assigning two officers to one vehicle will allow the driver to concentrate on the important task of driving while the second officer concentrates on the subject, directs the driver, and records field notes. The second officer can also conduct foot surveillance if necessary when the subject reaches a destination, leaving the driver free to watch the subject's vehicle. The second officer is the *foot person.*

When watching for evidence of detection, realize that a wary subject will often execute routine maneuvers in an effort to detect or lose anyone who may be following; some officers call that making a "heat run." Many subjects will routinely engage in such activity as a precautionary measure. In fact, during surveillance, officers should be alert for indications that they themselves have become the subject of surveillance, and when concluding surveillance officers should make a heat run to ensure that they are not followed home or to the office.

Vehicle Tracking Systems

For many years, officers have used vehicle locating and tracking systems commonly referred to as *bumper beepers*, the systems consisting of a small radio transmitter concealed on a subject's vehicle with its location monitored using a direction finding radio receiver located in the officer's vehicle. Such systems typically have a maximum range of two to five miles. Some transmitters emit a continuous signal while others emit a pulsating signal, and some are battery powered while *parasitic transmitters* receive their power from the subject vehicle electrical system and transmit indefinitely without battery replacement being necessary. Although such systems are a great aid, their capability is not comparable with today's much more sophisticated *Global Positioning Systems* (GPS). GPS makes it possible to obtain instant data via an internet connection on a vehicle's precise location anywhere in the world, and provide real-time monitoring of the vehicle's direction of travel and speed.

Surveillance of Terrorist Organizations

When a drug investigation uncovers evidence suggesting that an illicit drug operation has ties to a terrorist organization, the focus of the investigation must change accordingly. Whether the emphasis will shift from drugs to the terrorist organization itself, or both investigated simultaneously, will depend on circumstances. Either way, physical and technical surveillance are essential, although not used to the exclusion of other investigative methods.

When physical surveillance focuses on a terrorist subject or group, the surveillance techniques and methods will be the same as with most surveillance operations. The objective of the surveillance will continue to be gathering evidence and intelligence. Physical surveillance is necessary at locations that terrorists may attack, with likely targets including, but not limited to, water treatment plants, nuclear power plants, dams, government facilities, and radio towers. Certain companies, organizations, and industries are vulnerable to terrorist attack, and a quality threat assessment will determine the likelihood of an attack and their vulnerability.

Surveillance of terrorist suspects will usually include physical surveillance, but also technical surveillance. Technical surveillance is the electronic interception of conventional telephone conversations, cellular phone conversations, pager messages, facsimile (fax) messages, e-mail correspondence, and the monitoring of clandestine listening devices (bugs) and video cameras surreptitiously concealed in areas of interest. All are excellent means of gathering intelligence regarding terrorist activities and associates. Such methods minimize the amount of physical surveillance that must be done and therefore minimize the likelihood of the investigation being compromised by detection.

Electronic surveillance will usually provide officers with information such as the identity of terrorist group participants, and what the terrorists are doing or planning to do, i.e., where, when, and why something is to occur. A subsequent physical surveillance will often corroborate technical surveillance information. During physical surveillance, photography is often used to documented activity.

Unlike many conspiracy investigations where officers permit non-violent crimes to occur to strengthen a conspiracy charge, surveillance of terrorist subjects or organizations features the purpose of preventing an attack, as well as identifying members and associates of the organization to further investigative efforts. The officer may conduct surveillance to obtain enough evidence for a conspiracy charge, just short of permitting the crime to occur.

When terrorist subjects are the target of a drug investigation, the investigation will largely be the same as any drug investigation, although the investigation must switch from a passive to aggressive posture when explosives and/or other weapons intended for mass destruction exist. In such instances, the response is to make arrests and seize the weapons.

In this new climate of heightened security awareness in America and overseas as a result of the September 11, 2001, terrorist attacks on the World Trade Center and Pentagon, officers must be vigilant in their efforts to identify terrorist groups and cells and provide the people they have sworn to protect with a sense of safety and security. Officers must be alert when conducting investigations that have the potential of leading to terrorist organizations and act on information as it emerges. No one, with any degree of certainty, could have predicted the attacks that occurred on American soil on September 11, 2001, or the extent of the damage that resulted. Refer to Chapter 2, subheading "Illicit drugs and Terrorism–A Contemporary Problem."

VISUAL AIDS

Binoculars

Introduction

The distances characteristic of stationary surveillance generally prevent making meaningful observations with the unaided eye. Hence, optical aids such as binoculars are essential; they permit making observations from a distance that precludes detection by the subject.

Binoculars are unsurpassed as a visual aid for surveillance because, aside from ultra-high-powered instruments, they are compact, easy to use, available in a variety of sizes and magnifications so that there is a binocular that will accommodate virtually all surveillance needs, they permit making observations using both eyes, and even the better quality binoculars are reasonably economical. It is not surprising that binoculars are the most frequently used visual aid for physical surveillance (See Table I, Binocular Performance Characteristics).

Table I
BINOCULAR PERFORMANCE CHARACTERISTICS*

Binocular Size	*Relative Brightness*	*Exit Pupil Diameter*	*Twilight Factor*
2.5x17.5 (Binocular & Monocular)	**49.00**	**7.00mm**	**6.61**
2.5x23 (Opera Glass)	**84.64**	**9.20mm**	**7.58**
2.5x25 (Opera Glass)	**100.00**	**10.00mm**	**7.91**
3x22 (Opera Glass)	**53.73**	**7.33mm**	**8.12**
3x23 (Opera Glass)	**58.83**	**7.67mm**	**8.31**
3x25 (Opera Glass)	**69.39**	**8.33mm**	**8.66**
4x30	**56.25**	**7.50mm**	**10.95**
4x36	**81.00**	**9.00mm**	**12.00**
5x25	25.00	5.00mm	11.18
6x18	9.00	3.00mm	10.39
6x20	11.09	3.33mm	10.95
6x25	17.39	4.17mm	12.25
6x30	25.00	5.00mm	13.42
7x21	9.00	3.00mm	12.12
7x35 (best for general purpose day use)	25.00	5.00mm	15.65
7x50 (best general purpose binocular)	**51.00**	**7.14mm**	**18.71**
8x20	6.25	2.50mm	12.65
8x21 (very popular size)	6.92	2.63mm	12.96
8x24	9.00	3.00mm	13.86
8x25	9.80	3.13mm	14.14
8x30	14.06	3.75mm	15.49
8x40	25.00	5.00mm	17.89
8x42	27.56	5.25mm	18.33
8x56	**49.00**	**7.00mm**	**21.17**
9x35	15.13	3.89mm	17.75
9x63	**49.00**	**7.00mm**	**23.81**
9x65	**52.13**	**7.22mm**	**24.19**
10x20	4.00	2.00mm	14.14
10x25	6.25	2.50mm	15.81
10x40	16.00	4.00mm	20.00
10x50	25.00	5.00mm	22.36

Table I (cont.)

Binocular Size	*Relative Brightness*	*Exit Pupil Diameter*	*Twilight Factor*
10x70	**49.00**	**7.00mm**	**26.46**
11x70	40.45	6.36mm	27.75
11x80	**52.85**	**7.27mm**	**29.66**
12x63	27.56	5.25mm	27.50
14x100	**50.98**	**7.14mm**	**37.42**
15x60	16.00	4.00mm	30.00
15x63	17.64	4.20mm	30.74
15x70	21.81	4.67mm	32.40
15x80	28.41	5.33mm	34.64
15x110 (Soviet - border-guard)	**53.73**	**7.33mm**	**38.73**
16x80	25.00	5.00mm	35.78
20x50	6.25	2.50mm	31.62
20x60	9.00	3.00mm	34.64
20x80	16.00	4.00mm	40.00
20x110	30.25	5.50mm	46.90
20x140	**49.00**	**7.00mm**	**52.92**
25x100	16.00	4.00mm	50.00
25x150	**36.00**	**6.00mm**	**61.24**
26x70	7.24	2.69mm	42.66
30x80	7.13	2.67mm	48.99
30x90	9.00	3.00mm	51.96
30x120	16.00	4.00mm	60.00
30x180	**36.00**	**6.00mm**	**73.48**
40x150	14.06	3.75mm	77.46

***Exit Pupil Diameter:** Dividing the diameter of the objective lens by the magnifying power of the instrument determines Exit Pupil Diameter. **Relative Brightness:** Dividing the diameter of the objective lens by the magnifying power and squaring the quotient determines Relative Brightness. **Twilight Factor:** Multiplying the diameter of the objective lens by the magnifying power and finding the square root of the product determines Twilight Factor. *Those binoculars that are most conspicuously appropriate for low-light-level work, by virtue of exit pupil diameter and relative brightness have been set in bold print for the convenience of the reader.*

When planning the purchase of a binocular one should recognize that aside from quality, binoculars differ primarily in:

- Magnification
- Field of view
- Light-gathering capability

Generally, if a binocular excels for one application, it will suffer for others. For example, binoculars that feature extraordinary light-gathering capability and high magnification have large objective lenses and are, therefore, comparatively large and heavy and offer a narrow field of view. Conversely, if a binocular is compact and lightweight, it will feature small diameter objective lenses and will not perform well under low light conditions, although its compactness will be an asset during daytime surveillance.

Selecting a Binocular

The most desirable binocular features will depend upon the intended use of the instrument. To be considered are such things as the distance from which viewing will be done and the lighting conditions. Other considerations include whether the instrument is for stationary surveillance (stakeout) or moving surveillance, and whether moving surveillance is by foot or vehicle. Such considerations will influence whether one should select high magnification large aperture binoculars, or compact binoculars.

When selecting a binocular, the degree of magnification must be consistent with the anticipated subject-observer distances. For daytime use, light gathering ability of the instrument is not important. For night use, however, it is essential that the binocular feature an exit pupil diameter no less than 7mm. *The quickest and easiest way to determine if a binocular is suitable for night work is to divide the size of the objective lens by the magnifying power. If the quotient is 7mm or more, the binocular will perform well at night.* A quality binocular suited for night use provides impressive results. For example, a 7x50 binocular, which is ideal for night use, gathers approximately fifty times more light than does the unaided human eye.

The following are the recommended exit pupil diameters for various binocular applications.

- Daytime use: 2-4mm exit pupil diameter.
- Low light use: 5-6mm exit pupil diameter.
- Night use: 7mm or larger exit pupil diameter.

Types of Prisms

Binoculars employ a prism system that causes the light passing through them to travel a distance greater than the physical length of the instrument. Prisms accomplish that by causing the light to reverse direction of travel a number of times rather than traveling through the instrument in a straight path. The result is a high degree of magnification in a comparatively small size instrument. Moreover, because a lens projects an inverted image, prisms reverse the image so the viewer sees it as being upright and correct left-to-right. That is why the prisms are sometimes called *erecting prisms.*

Binoculars will feature either *Porro prisms* or *Roof prisms* (see Figure 10-1). Porro prism binoculars are recognizable by eyepiece lenses (oculars) that are not in line with the objective lenses, but offset. Roof prism binoculars are unique in appearance because of the "H" shape that results from the objective and eyepiece lenses being in-line. Although one prism type is not necessarily superior to the other, each offering advantages while suffering limitations, Roof prism binoculars are the more compact of the two types. However, most binoculars suitable for low-light use feature Porro prisms because the separation of the axes of the lenses permits the use of larger diameter objective lenses. Porro prism binoculars also offer enhanced stereoscopic perception, and often a wider field of view.

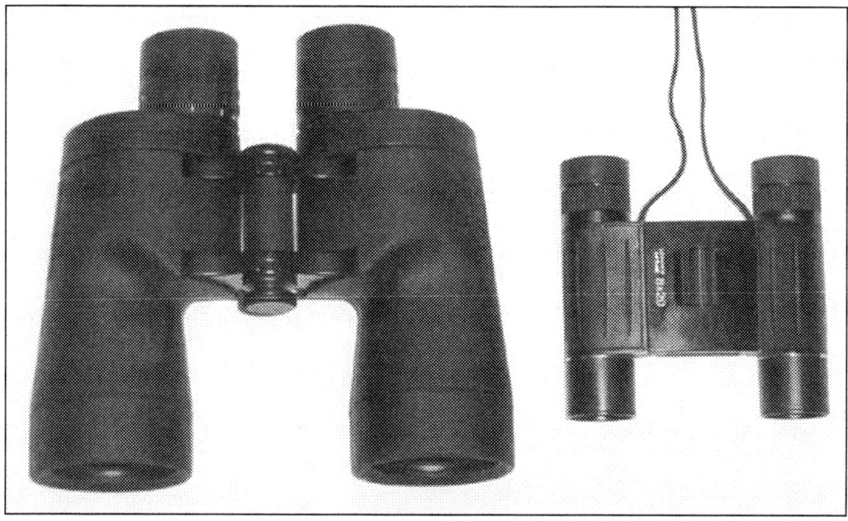

Figure 10-1. Porro prisms vs. Roof prisms. The Nikon 7x50 binocular on the left features Porro prisms. Note that the oculars (eyepiece lenses) and objective lenses are not in line; they are offset. The Bausch & Lomb 8x20 binocular on the right features Roof prisms. Note that the oculars and objective lenses are in line resulting in the "H" shape characteristic of Roof prism binoculars.

The two main types of glass used for binocular prisms are designated as BAK-4 (*barium crown*), and BK-7 (*borosilicate*). BAK-4 is the higher quality prism glass and virtually eliminates internal light loss making a sharp well-defined image possible. Low cost binoculars feature BK-7 prism glass and do not afford comparable image quality, although they are acceptable for most surveillance applications.

Coating of Optical Surfaces

The magnifying power of a binocular relative to the size of the objective lenses determines its light gathering capability. However, just as those factors are important, proper coating of the optical surfaces is also important to minimize internal light loss. There are between ten and sixteen optical surfaces in a binocular, depending on the design of the binocular, and if they do not feature quality antireflection coating, up to 50 percent of the light entering the objective lens can be lost by the time it exits the eyepiece lens (ocular).

Uncoated optics exhibit a hazy appearance characterized by reduced image contrast and washed-out detail. An unfortunate optical phenomenon is the fact that under normal circumstances, there is a 5%+ loss every time light passes through an air-to-glass surface. Accepting, as stated, that binoculars typically feature ten to sixteen optical surfaces, the cumulative light loss can be considerable.

Proper coating of optical surfaces can reduce light loss by half or more permitting the utilization of a full 75+ percent of the light entering the instrument. In fact, Nikon offers a binocular featuring BAK-4 prisms and *fully multi-coated* optical surfaces that results in a remarkable 95 percent light transmission (Nikon 7442 7x50 Sports and Marine Binocular). Properly coated, quality optics, do make a difference!

When using a binocular featuring fully multi-coated optics one will not only benefit from a bright crisp image, it will also be observed that when bright lights are in the field-of-view there is much less internal light flare to corrupt the image.

Binocular Suitability for Low Light Use–Final Comment

When selecting a binocular for night use, make sure it features an exit pupil diameter no less than 7mm–if the exit pupil diameter is less than 7mm, it is not suited for night use! That statement is true, but there are exceptions because many areas of the urban environment feature a level of *artificial illumination* sufficient to use a binocular, monocular, or telescope not normally suited for night use. Indeed, many areas of the nighttime urban environment feature a high level of artificial illumination.

Viewing the pump island area of a Chevron gasoline service station/market, from a distance of one-quarter mile late at night using the SkyHawk® 25/40x100 binocular, subject identification is excellent with vehicle license plate numbers easily read at both 25x and 40x magnification. From a distance of 1/2 mile, 25x magnification is insufficient and one must use the 40x oculars (eyepiece lenses) which results in excellent subject identification but vehicle license plate numbers discernable only some of the time. Whether license plate numbers are discernable from one-half mile depends on the contrast between the number and the background color of the plate, and the extent to which light is shining on the plate. Moreover, some plates are slightly recessed which sometimes diminishes readability. If the vehicle lights are on, and therefore the license plate is illuminated, the numbers are discernable.

Shopping centers feature large illuminated parking lots. The typical shopping center parking lot features sufficient artificial illumination at night to permit use of the SkyHawk® 25/40x100 binocular featuring a 4mm and 2.5mm exit pupil depending on the magnification selected. From a distance of one-quarter mile, subject identification is excellent with vehicle license plate numbers easily read at magnification settings 25x and 40x.

In the final analysis, although a 7mm exit pupil is necessary for night use, there are many areas in the urban environment featuring artificial illumination sufficient to use an optical instrument featuring a much smaller exit pupil as illustrated by the above examples. Keep that in mind when studying Table I, Binocular Performance Characteristics, because it lists several ultra-high-power binoculars featuring a 6mm exit pupil; they are excellent for the illuminated nighttime environments described above.

Image-Stabilized Binoculars

For daytime surveillance, image-stabilized binoculars are highly recommended because they reduce the effects of hand tremor, and they eliminate image movement when used from a moving automobile, watercraft, or aircraft. In fact, when hand-held, the image is as stable as if the binocular were tripod mounted.

Image-stabilized binoculars are generally in the high magnification category, with typical sizes including 8x25, 10x30, 12x36, 14x40, 15x45, 15x50, 16x40, 16x50, 18x50, and 20x60.

Some image-stabilized binoculars require batteries, while others do not. The 10x30 *Canon Image Stabilizer* binocular, illustrated in Figure 10-2, requires battery replacement every week during heavy surveillance use.

Ultra-High-Power Binoculars

Ultra high-power binoculars are useful for both urban and rural surveillance, but especially so for the later because of the great distances under which rural observations are typically made.

High magnification makes it possible to make quality observations from distances that preclude detection. Although remaining discreet when using

Figure 10-2. 10x30 Canon Image Stabilizer binocular.

ultra-high-power binoculars is not always easy, and people in the immediate vicinity will sometimes become aware of one's presence, the subject, being so far away, remains unaware.

In Figures 10-3 and 10-4 is pictured the SkyHawk® 25/40x100 ultra-high-powered binocular featuring 100mm objectives, the objectives being the large lenses at the front of the binocular. This binocular features double oculars (eyepiece lenses) on a rotating turret that provide a magnification choice of 25x and 40x.

This binocular is large, and heavy. The binocular weighs 26 pounds, and the hardwood tripod (not illustrated) weighs 16 pounds. Moreover, because of the high degree of magnification this binocular provides, small vibrations cause severe image deterioration. Hence, ensuring stability of the binocular during use is essential.

This binocular features BAK-4 (Barium Crown Glass) Porro prisms, BAK-4 being the preferred glass for binocular prisms, and the optical system is *fully multi-coated*, which is the highest grade of optical coating. Unfortunately, this binocular is not O-ring sealed and nitrogen-purged to make it water-resistant. The binocular must remain dry during inclement weather use.

With this binocular, under normal atmospheric conditions, one can read vehicle license plate numbers, using the 40x oculars, at three-quarter mile.

Figure 10-3. SkyHawk® 25/40x100 ultra-high-powered binocular mounted to a mini-tripod. This binocular features 100mm objectives, and offers a choice of 25x and 40x magnification via double oculars (eyepiece lenses) on a rotating turret.

Figure 10-4. SkyHawk® 25/40x100 ultra-high-powered binocular mounted to a mini-tripod that is setting on a platform over the passenger seat of the vehicle. Each individual must decide how creative he or she wishes to be when devising a method for using these large and heavy binoculars from within a vehicle.

That three-quarter mile distance will increase or decrease depending on atmospheric conditions; heat waves, for example, are a relentless limiting factor. Using the 25x oculars, which provide a 4mm exit pupil diameter, vehicle license plate numbers are discernable at one-quarter mile well into dusk without the benefit of artificial illumination. With this binocular, and appropriate atmospheric conditions, if one knows the subject and his or her vehicle, it is possible to watch for their arrival or departure from a distance as great as four miles using the 40x oculars.

The photographs appearing in Figures 10-10B and 10-12 are the result of a 2000mm photographic telephoto lens. A 2000mm lens provides an image forty times larger than the image produced by the camera's 50mm normal lens that approximates our normal vision. The photographs taken using a

2000mm telephoto lens are reasonably comparable to observations made using the 40x oculars (eyepiece lenses) of the SkyHawk binocular, although the view through the binocular is sharper and clearer than can actually be recorded on film when using a 2000mm telephoto lens. Nevertheless, image size is comparable.

Information about this binocular is available at www.SkyHawkoptics.com.

ATMOSPHERIC CONDITIONS. Because atmospheric conditions become such an important limiting factor when working with high-magnification binoculars, telescopes, and extreme telephoto lenses (surveillance photography), understanding a few important points is helpful.

Air turbulence and light scatter is a problem that has always plagued those who work with high magnification. When looking through a high-magnification binocular, spotting scope, or telephoto lens of 1000mm or more, it is apparent that air is visible and moves. The problems created by air turbulence and light scatter increases as magnification increases.

As the sun heats the earth's surface, the air near the ground expands, gets lighter, and then rises. As the heated air rises, cooler air from adjoining areas replaces the rising lighter air. As a result, the density of the air is not uniform, thus causing light rays traveling from the subject to the optical instrument to refract or bend causing a distorted image, an image that seems to dance in extreme cases.

Air turbulence is not as great in the early morning hours before the sun has heated the earth's surface, so if possible, make observations and take photographs at that time. Unfortunately, the luxury of making such a choice usually does not exist because observations and photographing must occur when the activity of interest occurs.

If there is more than one suitable vantage point from which to choose, there are some factors to consider. First, if observations can be made from a higher elevation such as on a hill or upper story of a building, looking somewhat down on the subject, much of the air turbulence that is almost always present close to the ground, even on cool days, can be avoided. If the subject's location is elevated, the benefit is the same. Second, the amount of air turbulence over a field or body of water will be notably less than over a surface such as a parking lot or roadway. Refer to and compare Figures 10-11 and 10-12 relative to distortion caused by heat waves. Observations and/or photographs are possible from greater distances in the winter than during summer because heat waves are not as extreme.

When using high magnification, whether a binocular, telescope, or telephoto camera lens, side lighting a bit from the front is preferable to direct front or back lighting. That is because light scatter tends to be severe with back lighting, and front lighting tends to reduce contrast.

Movement and vibration of the optical instrument are problems that become apparent when working with high magnification. The best optics will not provide a quality image if the instrument is not stable. The ideal situation, when working with high magnification, is to use a quality tripod. However, during surveillance, that is not always possible and one must improvise. One may improvise by bracing the optical instrument against or on a solid object or, if working from a vehicle, rest the instrument on a partially rolled-down window. Belt-pods are sometimes useful, as are monopods and gunstock mounts. One may also use a window-mount with lighter-weight instruments. A window-mount is a device featuring an articulating head similar to that of a tripod, and clamps to a partially rolled down vehicle window (see Figure 10-5). The point is, stability of the optical instrument is essential, but how that is accomplished is not important.

Figure 10-5. Window-mounts offer a convenient way to secure lighter weight although high magnification instruments when making observations from a stationary vehicle. Mounting a binocular and telescope (prismatic spotting scope) together permits use of the binocular for general observations of the subject area and then use the telescope for detailed observations.

Low Magnification Binoculars

There are occasions when a low magnification optical device is necessary, such as when an officer, during stationary surveillance, leaves the vehicle and moves closer to the subject's location by foot. Moving closer by foot often results in being too close to use, for example, a 7x50 binocular, yet too far from the subject to make meaningful observations with the unaided eye.

During daylight hours, any low-powered optical device will work whether it is a binocular or monocular.

For close-range low-light observations, consider the *Bushnell 4x30 PowerView® LiteVision™ Binocular.* This compact binocular features 4x magnification, fully-coated optics, and an exit pupil diameter of 7.5mm, making it excellent for low light use. It performs surprisingly well considering its low cost. Focusing is quick and easy via the rocker bar that focuses both eyepieces simultaneously. This binocular is actually a field glass inasmuch as it features a *Galilean* optical system (no prisms). As an alternative, consider a 3-power opera glass; they are very compact and perform well under low light conditions.

What to Purchase

URBAN SURVEILLANCE. Although there are numerous binocular sizes and features from which to choose, if the urban officer obtains the 10x30, 12x36, or 15x50 *Canon Image Stabilizer* binocular for daytime use and a 10x70 or 11x80 binocular for night use, optical magnification needs for most surveillance will be satisfied. If the urban officer must settle for just one binocular, however, consider the *Nikon 7442 7x50 Sports and Marine Binocular* (without built-in compass). It features 95 percent light transmission and therefore performs exceptionally well at night. This binocular features long eye-relief for eyeglass wearers, individual eyepiece focusing, and it is O-ring sealed and nitrogen purged, making it waterproof.

RURAL SURVEILLANCE. The rural officer needs a high degree of magnification because of great observer-subject distances. Worth considering for daytime use is the 18x50 *Canon Image Stabilizer* binocular, or the Zeiss 20x60 image stabilized binocular (expensive but *very* high quality). As an alternative to a high magnification binocular, the rural officer may consider a prismatic spotting scope with either fixed or variable magnification. Prismatic spotting scopes are discussed in the next section, Prismatic Telescopes.

Ideally suited for night use in the rural environment is a 14x100, 15x110, or 20x140 binocular. Nikon offers a 20x120 binocular that features a 6mm exit pupil (Note: High magnification large aperture binoculars are not only large and heavy, they are *very* expensive!). As an alternative, for night use, the rural officer may consider a 10x70 or 11x80 binocular because, at night, the officer often can move closer to the subject using the cover of darkness. When the officer moves comparatively close to the subject using the cover of darkness, however, he or she usually must retreat as dawn approaches. Having retreated at the approach of dawn, as it gets light, switch to one of the abovementioned binoculars or a spotting scope suited for daylight use.

Prismatic Telescopes (Spotting Scopes)

Prismatic telescopes, most commonly referred to as *spotting scopes*, are useful for physical surveillance in rural areas. Enforcement officers with agencies such as the Department of Game and Fish often use spotting scopes because of their compact size, light weight, and high magnification–they are easy to carry when moving about by foot (see Figure 10-6). Keep in mind that the larger the diameter of the objective lens, relative to magnification, the greater the exit pupil diameter and, therefore, the better the instrument will perform under poor lighting conditions. Additionally, a large diameter exit pupil during daylight hours is good because it makes it easier to find and hold the sight picture.

Figure 10-6. Spotting scope resting in the crotch of a tree branch provides reasonable stability.

The following spotting scopes are worth investigating although this list is not exhaustive – there are many good products not reflected here.

Nikon	**Carl Zeiss, Inc.**	**Bausch & Lomb**
Sky & Earth 15-45x60	Diascope 65 T* FL 15-45x65	Elite 15-45x60
Spotter XL 16-47x60	Diascope 85 T* FL 20-60x85	Elite 20-60x80
Sky & Earth 20x60	20x60 image-stabilized	

Fieldscope III Series 20x60
Fieldscope 78 ED Series 25x78
Fieldscope 82mm ED Body 25x82

Leupold

Golden Ring 10-20x40 (Lens/mirror system. 7 inches long)
Golden Ring 12-40x60 (Lens/mirror system. 12 inches long. Used by the U. S. Army)
Wind River 15-45x60 (Traditional prismatic type spotting scope)

Redfield

30x60 catadioptric scope (Lens/mirror system. 7 inches long)

Monocular (Mini-telescope)

Often neglected for physical surveillance is the monocular, a very compact mini-telescope that can be carried and used inconspicuously–good for foot surveillance. Although the monocular will perform well during daylight hours, most do not perform well under low light conditions because most feature an exit pupil diameter that is less than 7.00mm. Keep in mind, however, that many areas of the urban environment feature a high level of artificial illumination at night–many optical aids not intended for night use will work in such areas. See Figures 10-7, 10-8, and 10-9.

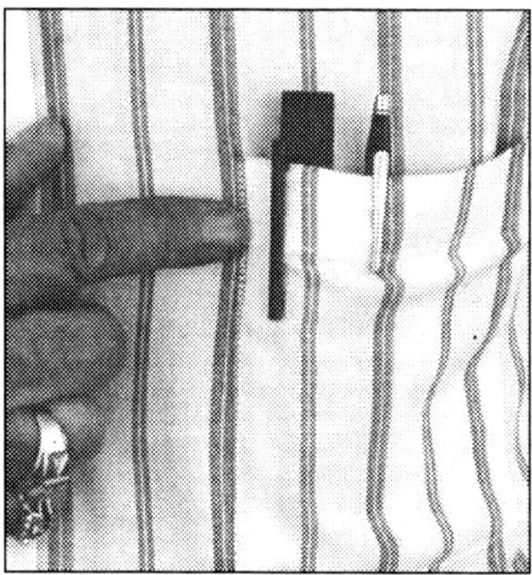

Figure 10-7. Zeiss MiniQuick 5x10 monocular is easily carried inconspicuously in a shirt pocket.

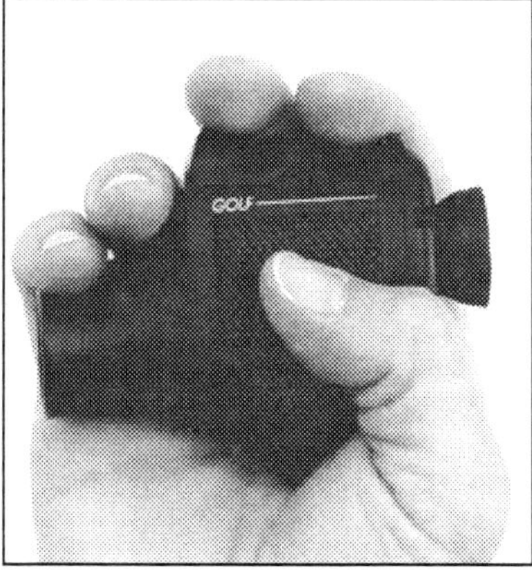

Figure 10-8. Golf Brand Bynolyt 5x20 Monocular. The "rocker bar" on top is used for focusing. Fine focus achieved by rotating the ocular (eyepiece).

Figure 10-9. Golf Brand Bynolyt 5x20 Monocular in use–it is inconspicuous.

Night Viewing Devices

Electronic light intensifiers, referred to as *Night Viewing Devices* (NVDs), operate by amplifying the existing level of illumination by several thousand times. The actual gain realized with NVDs will vary depending upon the make of the instrument, but a gain of 15,000 to 65,000 times is typical.

Most manufacturers of NVDs offer adapters to couple them with a digital single-lens-reflex camera (SLR), 35mm SLR camera, or video camcorder. Some models accept a variety of telephoto lenses, and for some, an adapter will permit using the lens system of a 35mm SLR.

The officer who is unfamiliar with NVDs, but contemplating the purchase of such equipment, should obtain promotional literature from the various companies offering such products, and speak with people who have field experience with them.

SURVEILLANCE PHOTOGRAPHY

Introduction

Because of the importance of photography during many surveillance operations, to document subject activity, officers must be reasonably proficient photographers. Those who desire more information on this exciting topic are encouraged to refer to the book *Applied Police and Fire Photography*, used as a text on the community college and university level, featuring 376 pages and 248 illustrations.[10]

To be an effective surveillance photographer, one must be a skilled surveillant, and be very proficient with the camera used. In that respect, when acquiring a camera with which one is unfamiliar, time must be devoted to reading the owner's manual and experimenting with the camera until comfortable with its operating features. Most cameras are not difficult to use once becoming familiar with them and the trend has been to make cameras increasingly user friendly. Hence, today it is possible to realize quality results with a photographic knowledge base much less than was required not too many years ago.

Before making a camera selection, one must carefully consider its intended use. That is important because there are many types of cameras from which to choose with each offering various features. Furthermore, when considering a camera, it is important to consider accessories because one is not just purchasing a camera, but buying into a system. This is an important consideration because, although a camera may offer desirable features, it may lack essential accessories that will limit its usefulness.

Telephoto Lens Capabilities

Extreme Telephoto Lenses

Figures 10-10A-B, 10-11, and 10-12 illustrate the capabilities of extreme telephoto lenses–the distances from which one can obtain useful photographs. Strong magnification enables the officer to make quality observations, and take photographs, from distances that preclude detection because distance provides good cover.

---

*Siljander, R., & Fredrickson, D. (1997). Applied police and fire photography (2nd edition). Springfield, IL: Charles C. Thomas.

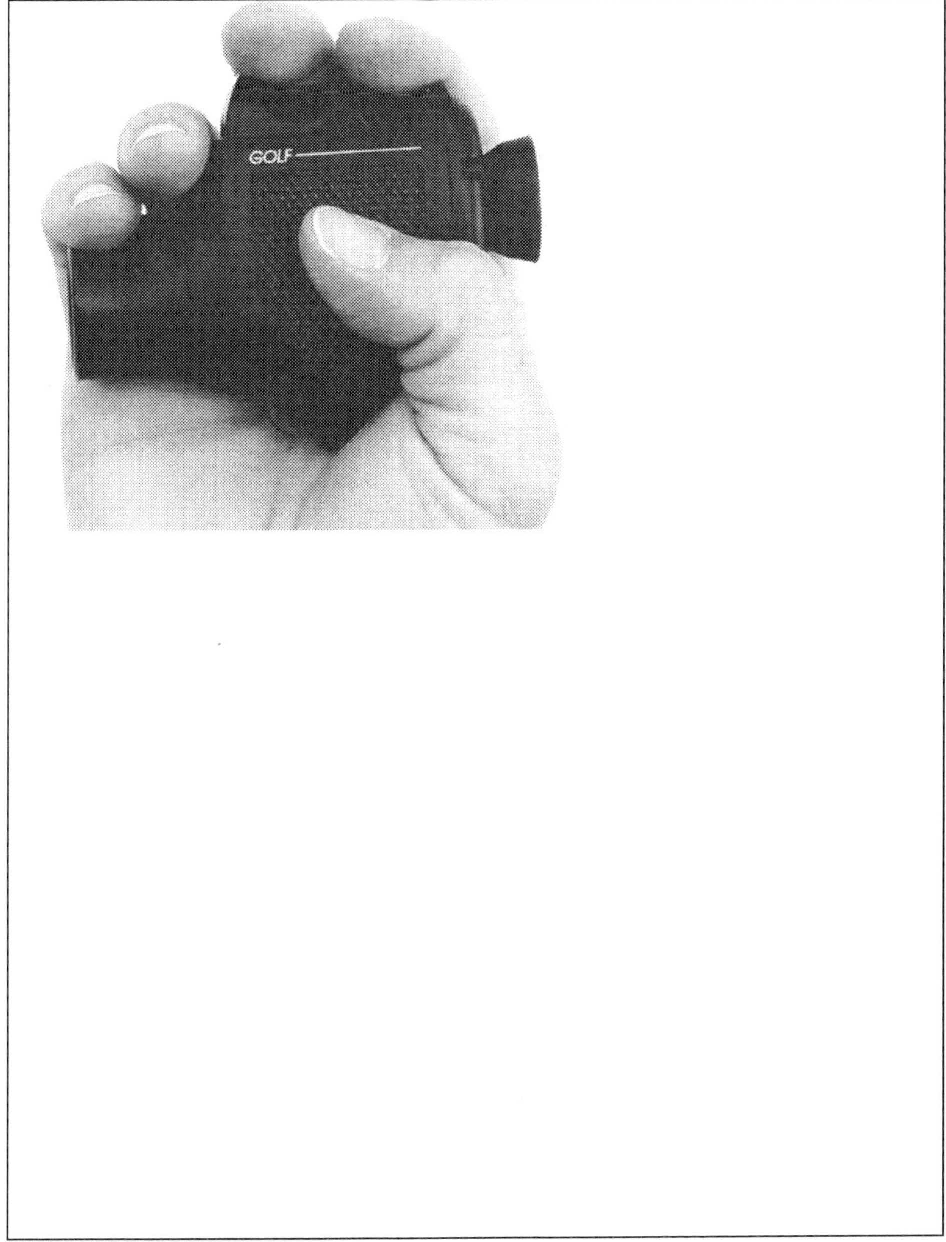

Figure 10-10A-B. Comparison photos of a subject taken from a distance of 400 feet using first a 50mm normal lens on a 35mm SLR camera to obtain an overview showing the general location (arrow shows subject location), and then a 2,000mm extreme telephoto lens to obtain subject identification. The camera and subject position is the same in both photographs. The 2,000mm lens offers a 40 times magnification over that of the 50mm normal lens.

Figure 10-11. Subject photographed from one-quarter mile using a Vivitar 800mm f/8 lens with a 3x teleconverter providing an effective focal length of 2,400mm; magnification is 48 times greater than the normal 50mm lens provides. Note the distortion caused by heat waves.

Figure 10-12. This photograph, taken from just over one-half mile (across a lake) using a 2000mm extreme telephoto lens coupled with a 35mm SLR camera body, illustrates the detail that is possible in the absence of heat waves. The water separating the camera and subject location minimized heat wave distortion. Note that detail is sufficient to count the 8x16 inch HCB blocks on the house on the left. Compare this illustration with Figure 10-11 relative to heat wave distortion.

In Figure 10-13 is illustrated a 2000mm Celestron 8® astronomical telescope coupled with a 35mm SLR camera body. This f/10 lens is ideal for long-range surveillance photography inasmuch as it is reasonably fast and compact. By *fast* is meant that the maximum aperture of the lens is large in relation to the focal length, thus allowing more light to pass to the film making it useful for available light photography (photography without a flash). This lens is very lightweight and compact considering its extreme focal length. The lens measures 17 inches in length, and weighs only 12.5 pounds.

Figure 10-13. Celestron 8® astronomical telescope coupled with a 35mm *single lens reflex* (SLR) Nikkormat® camera body. This 2000mm f/10 lens provides a magnification 40x greater than the normal (50mm) lens of a 35mm SLR and therefore it is ideal for long-range surveillance photography.

Digital SLR cameras are available, and image stabilized telephoto lenses are available, both useful for many surveillance applications (see Figures 10-14 and 10-15).

Figure 10-14. Canon EF 100-400mm f/4.5-5.6 image stabilized zoom lens with the Canon EOS 10D digital camera body. This is the lens/body assembly used to take the picture appearing in Figure 10-15.

Figure 10-15. Subject photographed from two-tenths mile using the camera/lens assembly appearing in Figure 10-14, the lens set at 400mm for this picture. Officer took this picture while standing and *handholding* the lens/body assembly–no tripod or other camera supports, the image stabilizing feature of the lens making that possible. This distance is the maximum from which doing a stakeout and photographing is usually necessary in the urban environment.

Video Cameras

Video Cameras can document crucial evidence during surveillance operations, or document crime scenes such as clandestine drug laboratories. Video cameras are comparatively easy to operate, very inexpensive to operate, activity can be record for extended periods without a tape change being necessary, and they provide instant results.

For surveillance applications, maximum focal length of the lens is important, as is the maximum aperture of the lens. Most video cameras feature a variable focal length (zoom) lens that goes from mild wide-angle to moderate telephoto, and teleconverters are usually available to increase the magnification of the lens. For many surveillance applications, the standard lens is sufficient.

For surveillance applications, the camera's low light capability is also important. The technical data of a video camera will usually specify recommended illumination and minimum illumination. For example, the Canon ZR45 Digital Camcorder has a recommended illumination level of at least 100 lux, but a minimum illumination level of 0.5 lux. *Lux* is a standard scale for the measurement of light that has largely replaced *candlepower* as a measure of illumination although illumination, expressed in foot-candles (fc) persists.

Although the technical specifications of a particular camera lets one know the minimum illumination level necessary for the camera to operate efficiently, it is necessary to know what that means in terms of the nighttime environment so that an appropriate camera selection can be made. Will a minimum illumination requirement of 10 lux be adequate, or does one need a camera that will work with only 3 lux, or perhaps 1 lux? Table II reflects typical nighttime illumination levels.

Table II

NIGHTTIME ILLUMINATION LEVELS	
Bright sunlight 50,000 – 100,000 lux	Gasoline service station pump island area 215 – 323 lux
Overcast day 2,000 – 10,000 lux	Well-lit street scene (down town) 10 – 20 lux
Dull day 1,000 lux	Urban roadways 3.2 – 17.2 lux
Typical office 200 – 300 lux	Suburban street 5 lux
Merchandise areas – indoor 320 – 1,000 lux	Rural road less than 1 lux
Public area in buildings 300 lux	Moonlight 0.4 lux
Shopping centers & commercial parking lots 8.6 – 38.7 lux	Starlight .002 lux

Many video cameras feature image stabilization, an extremely useful feature for surveillance applications. Sony, Canon, and Panasonic offer Mini DV (digital video) camcorders featuring image stabilization. If one is not familiar with these remarkably compact cameras, they are worth investigating. In Figure 10-16 is illustrated the Panasonic PV-GS70 Ultra-Compact Digital Palmcorder© MultiCam Camcorder. In Figure 10-17 is illustrated a shirt/blouse button that is actually a pinhole camera lens disguised to look like a button. The lens is connected to a mini DV camcorder concealed on the undercover officer's body, illustrated in Figure 10-18.

Figure 10-16. Panasonic PV-GS70 Ultra-Compact Digital Palmcorder© MultiCam Camcorder with 2.5 Inch Digital Color swivel LCD Monitor. This pocket-sized miniDV features a 2.45–24.5 f/1.8 10x zoom lens, 700x digital zoom, digital image stabilizer, and a USB port. Minimum illumination requirement is 12 lux. The camera accepts an auxiliary lens such as that illustrated in Figure 10-17. The digital zoom of camcorders offer little value to the surveillance photographer because image quality deteriorates rapidly as magnification is electronically increased.

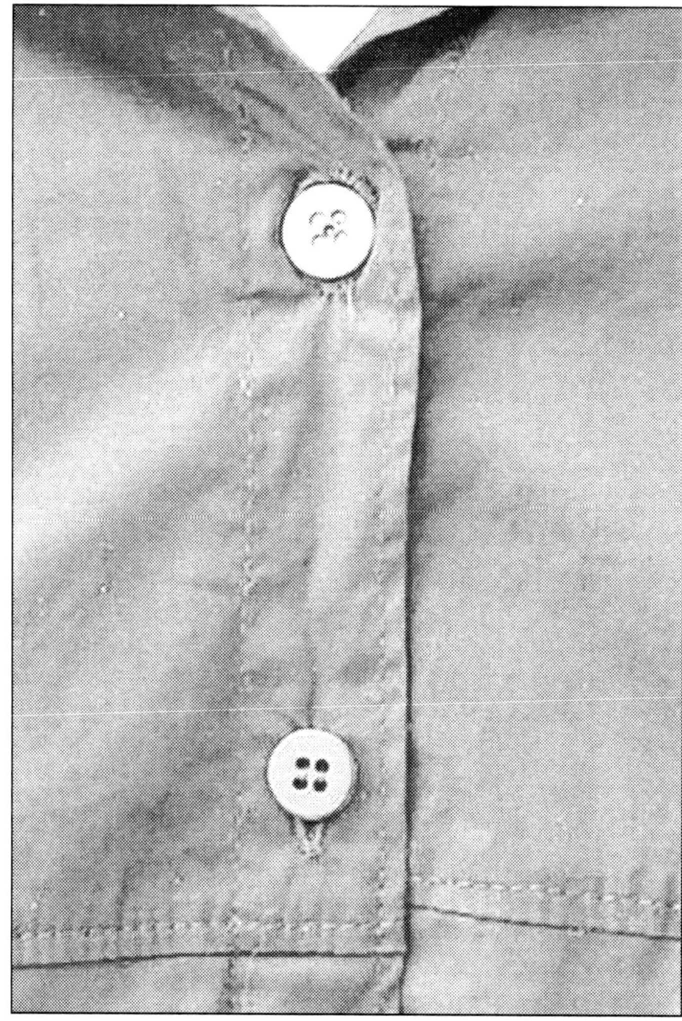

Figure 10-17 The top button of the shirt/blouse is actually a pinhole camera lens disguised to look like a button. The lens is connected to a mini DV camcorder concealed on the undercover officer's body.

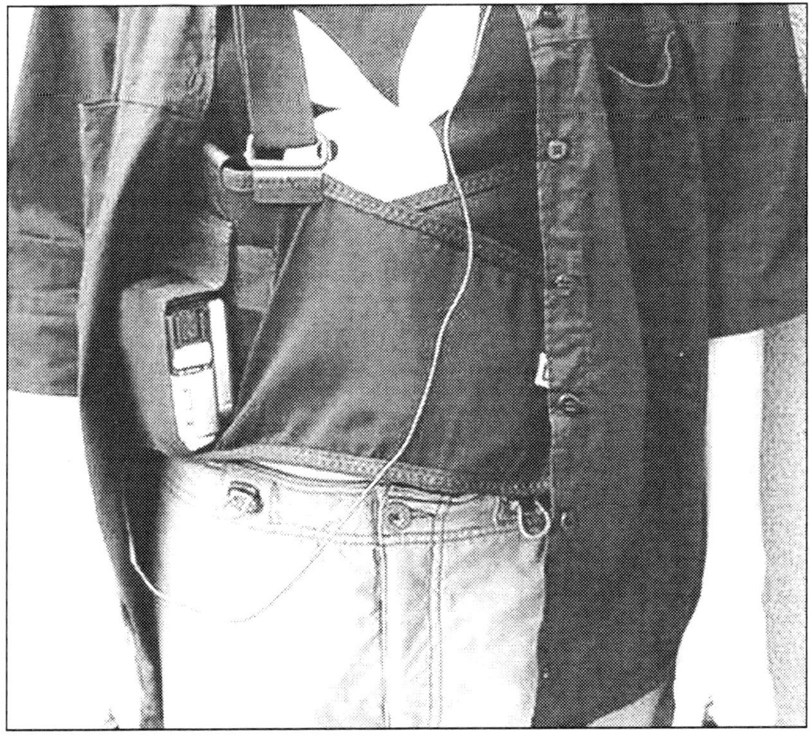

Figure 10-18. Mini DV recorder concealed on the undercover officer's body. The camera lens is disguised as a shirt/blouse button and connected with this recorder via the wire clearly visible in this photograph.

Chapter 11

SEARCH WARRANTS AND RAID PLANNING

SEARCH WARRANT PLANNING

Police officers utilizing search warrants in drug investigations should be thoroughly familiar with their agency's policies covering search warrants, search and seizure laws, as well as the appropriate state statutes covering search warrants. They should also remain current of all new court decisions pertaining to search and seizure. Often, prosecuting agencies or one's legal department can provide updates on recent court decisions as well as specifics on rulings that involve drug investigation.

A search warrant is an order in writing signed by a judge or magistrate authorizing a peace officer to search for certain property or persons in a certain place. The affidavit must set forth facts establishing probable cause to believe evidence of criminal activity will be located at the time and place the warrant is to be served.

Officers must serve search warrants between the hours of 6:30 a.m. to 10:00 p.m., although a judge will authorize a nighttime search warrant when shown appropriate cause. Appropriate cause includes circumstances such as:

- The suspect may have a limited supply of drugs in possession and heavy dealing may eliminate his or her supply.
- The officer receives supporting probable cause for a warrant after 10:00 p.m. or shortly before, and an exigent circumstance exists.
- The suspect is home only during nighttime hours, or the suspect conceals drugs during daytime hours and deals only at night.
- The suspect comes and goes at varied, unpredictable times, requiring extensive surveillance coupled with the ability to serve the warrant at any hour when the suspect is present.

Once an affidavit and search warrant are prepared, officers present them to a judge for review and signing. Officers must swear to and affirm the truthfulness of everything contained therein to the best of their knowledge. It has happened that a judge signed an affidavit and search warrant without swearing in the officer. It is required that an officer's testimony supplied in an affidavit be under oath. Additionally, most states require an audible recording of verbal testimony supporting the affidavit.

Telephonic and faxed search warrants can expedite the process of obtaining a search warrant, but that must be done in a manner that complies with the legal requirements of search warrant issuance.

KNOCK AND ANNOUNCE

The Fourth Amendment to the United States Constitution governs search warrant service requirements. It requires officers to knock, announce their authority and purpose, and wait prior to making entry. Although the affidavit supporting a search warrant is sufficient for a search, if officers fail to announce their presence and purpose prior to entry, the evidence will likely be suppressed. Officers are required to wait a reasonable amount of time prior to making forced entry. During the execution of a search warrant, however, officers are justified in making immediate entry to prevent the destruction of evidence if that is apparent by suspects heard scurrying about inside, toilets flushing, etc. The courts have not set a standard (benchmark) as to how many seconds establishes a "reasonable amount of time," but will instead look at each case based on the circumstances surrounding the entry.

After knocking on a door, officers need not state authority and purpose until necessary. Many times a suspect will open the door not realizing police are outside–announcing authority and purpose may prevent that. Officers may employ a ruse to induce the suspect to open the door, but officers must remember to announce authority and purpose prior to making entry, e.g., "police officers, we're here to execute a search warrant."

NO-KNOCK WARRANTS

These search warrants are issued in situations where it is established that a knock and announce may create a dangerous situation for officers executing the search warrant. Officers should refer to their agency's policies regarding serving these types of search warrants.

SEARCH WARRANT ENTRY

Upon initial entry, all occupants should be located as quickly as possible and secured with the use of plastic flex-cuffs or standard metal handcuffs.

Police frisk all occupants for weapons except in extenuating circumstances such as children, elderly persons, or innocent family members or relatives. If there is any doubt as to a person's involvement, police must search him or her. Same sex officers should search subjects.

Persons on the premises may be subject to a search of their person if it is reasonably likely they posses property or items listed in the search warrant. This only applies to persons located on the premises at the time of the warrant, and not persons arriving at the location during the search, although police may frisk new arrivals for weapons. Persons arriving after the search warrant has been executed can only be searched if independent probable cause is first developed. Prior to searching persons located on the premises for drugs or other evidence, officers should establish if persons are drug addicts (track marks, admissions, etc.), as this will strengthen the legality of the search. Other circumstances, such as burning marijuana in the air, also strengthen legality of the search; identify such factors prior to searching.

Search the premises only after photographing the entire residence. The task of searching may be divided among officers who will select rooms, locate items of evidence, and subsequently inform a designated "finder" of the items of evidence. The "finder" is an officer assigned with the duties of locating and documenting items of evidence, seizing them, and impounding them according to established policies. Although the "finder" may not actually personally find the items, they will most likely be the officer called to testify should the case go to trial. It is best if the "finder" is familiar with the case because they will know what items to seize, items relevant to the investigation.

After the search, leave the residence in a reasonable condition, although a thorough search will often result in some disarray. Clothing removed from drawers or closets should be left stacked on the bed, for example.

SEARCH WARRANT EXECUTION

By

SERGEANT MIKE TORRES, POLICE DEPARTMENT, PHOENIX, ARIZONA

Introduction

Many agencies utilize full-time SWAT (Special Weapons and Tactics) teams to execute search warrants, conduct surveillance, and apprehend dangerous suspects. The Phoenix Police Department, for example, utilizes one (or more) of four full-time SWAT teams to execute high-risk search warrants. "High-risk" entries are those where the suspect(s) are known to be armed, have a criminal history of high violence, and the location to be searched has a known history for violence. High-risk entries are not discussed in this chapter because they are reserved for teams that train and practice on a regular basis (10-20 percent of their on-duty time).

The focus of this chapter is raid preparation for officers where the abovementioned situations do not exist. If one's agency does have a SWAT team or a dedicated tactical search warrant entry team and the aforementioned conditions exist, it is recommend that officers conduct surveillance for the purpose of taking off (apprehending) the primary suspect prior to executing the search warrant. For example, officers can follow the suspect and a "street jump" (apprehension) initiated when it is most advantageous for officers to do so, thus minimizing danger to officers and the surrounding community. Officers serve the search warrant once the suspect is in custody. This technique minimizes risk and liability to officers and their agency, and minimizes risk to the community.

A tactical search warrant entry is a raid by law enforcement on the curtilage or property of another, where the owner or occupant is summarily deprived control of the property. It is analogous to a military led invasion where forces take control of a country through speed, surprise, and violence of action with control maintained through military occupation. The execution of a search warrant is no different since officers are executing a "legal invasion" into someone's property and attempts to obtain control of the property with speed, surprise, and the threat of violent action. Officers maintain control by "occupying" the property until the search portion of the investigation is complete. The primary difference between a military operation as described and a civilian law enforcement operation is that the military operation is offensive while the law enforcement operation is defensive.

Officers must remember that search warrant entries are inherently dangerous. They are dangerous because, in the United States, laws favor a person protecting his or her "castle," and persons often go to great lengths to protect it. Most states do not authorize "no knock" search warrants. "No knock warrants" are search warrants authorized by a magistrate in special circumstances; law enforcement officers are not required to "knock and announce" their intention to serve a search warrant. Therefore, because most states do not authorize such search warrants, officers suffer compromise at the door during the "knock and announce." If persons inside a residence are intent on harming officers, the requirement that officers announce themselves before entry provides the subject an advantage. Incidentally, if one's state allows "no knock" search warrants, a tactical team should execute the entry and subsequent clearing of the interior areas. Using a tactical team in this way is important because "no knock" warrants are usually limited to cases where a propensity for violence exists and a "knock and announce" will place officers at increased risk of injury or death, or a "knock and announce" will result in the destruction of evidence.

Several things are prerequisite to the success of a raid operation. It is important to document everything done in preparation for a search warrant execution, and compliance with state and local laws is essential. If documentation is weak, and laws violated, the officers and the agency they represent are vulnerable to subsequent legal maneuvering and challenges by the defense. Simply stated, taking shortcuts can contaminate a criminal investigation and compromise its outcome.

Planning also becomes a critical issue should the operation become the focus of a civil lawsuit, or if the defense challenges certain aspects of the operation during criminal court proceedings. A checklist to ensure thoroughness and legal compliance is useful–most police departments in the United States use some form of pre-search warrant entry checklist. The completed checklist is subsequently archived for future use should the need arise.

Planning

Lack of planning will compromise officers by increasing the likelihood of the operation suffering a disastrous outcome. Officers should anticipate, plan well, and document well, because those things may be the subject of future critique. Raid operations will look more professional, and injuries minimized, if quality operational plans are developed and officers receive adequate training. Remember, however, although planning is essential, one can "what if" a situation to the point that planning actually encumbers the operation, and therefore becomes counterproductive.

Search warrant operations result in an "adrenaline rush" and it is important to keep that in mind during planning. Physiological things occur to the human body when adrenaline kicks in, with one well-documented physiological occurrence being short-term memory loss. For that reason, supervisors planning search warrant operations should not overburden entry officers with more than two assignments. For example, the officer assigned to breach a door should execute that function only, i.e., do not assign him or her also as the primary entry officer. Those two assignments by themselves are major adrenaline producers. Instead, the breaching officer should continue to be the breaching officer throughout the operation, but can become a prisoner handler when breaching is no longer necessary. In the final analysis, why overburden individual officers? Logic and experience suggests that it is better for each officer to do one thing efficiently than several things poorly. Plan assignments accordingly or the ultimate price will be paid–compromised officer safety!

When planning the execution of a search warrant, carefully consider the objectives of the warrant. Is the primary objective of the warrant to round up individuals, look for evidence, or a combination of both? There are also options that exist in lieu of procuring a search warrant such as surveillance that ends with a street-jump (apprehension), a ruse to get the individual out of a building, or the issuance of an arrest warrant if time permits. Keep in mind, however, that doing these things in conjunction with the search warrant operation remains an option.

Once clarifying the objectives of the warrant, scrutinize the location specified in the warrant, physically and informationally. When scrutinizing the location at which officers will execute the warrant, gather information to help execute the warrant safely and successfully.

When doing a preliminary survey, i.e., visually scrutinizing the location specified in the warrant, evaluate the size of the structure and attempt to determine the number of rooms. The rule-of-thumb is that safely taking control of a normal size room generally requires two officers. Assigning an appropriate number of personnel, i.e., two officers per room, ensures speed and surprise and that translates into safety and efficiency. According to this rule-of-thumb, sixteen entry officers are required for an eight-room structure (two officers per room). Assigning two officers per room makes it possible to enter and control all rooms simultaneously, and that ensures speed, surprise, and safety. However, assigning two officers per room may not always be possible because of human resource limitations. In the real world, tactical teams often must sacrifice speed and surprise in favor of smaller entry teams. Substituted for person power are safety equipment, training, and tactics.

Scrutinizing the location reveals what the structure is constructed of, where utilities can be shut-off, presence of children and elderly people, the location's proximity to schools, access gates, as well as access to the rear yard and rear doors. Scrutinizing the property also enables officers to identify other concerns such as dogs and holes, and the existence of multiple living quarters that may contain other tenants. When other structures exist on the property, they often require additional officers. The surrounding neighborhood also begs scrutiny because there may be nearby "friendlies" or sympathizers that present a danger to the operation.

When scrutinizing the location, identify a primary and secondary breaching point, and note the direction of door swing–in or out. Identifying breaching points makes it possible to select appropriate entry tools and devise an appropriate tactical plan.

The preliminary survey enables planners to identify the most appropriate route for the entry team to take to the target location, and identify a safe staging area for the team. The staging area is where the entry team meets a final time to ensure everyone is ready for the execution of the search warrant, and receive any updated information.

When aircraft is available, take aerial photos of the location prior to execution of the search warrant. Aerial photographs are useful for planning purposes, and they facilitate pointing out critical areas of concern during briefing of the operation team members.

Prior to executing a search warrant, research both the location and the subject for intelligence information that may exist. A criminal history check may provide insight into what may be expected. If one or more search warrants were previously executed at the location, determine if the paperwork surrounding them provides information that will enhance the efficiency of the current operation. When possible, obtain the floor plan of a similar structure to use for planning purposes–many tract homes feature a limited number of identical floor plans. Scrutinize what informants reveal about the location. If the subject has a phone, having the number is useful should phone contact become necessary. Determine what types of weapons the subject may have, or that may be inside the structure. Consider the types of illicit drugs likely to be found and expected quantities–a large amount of drugs may increase the danger level. If the suspect uses illicit drugs, determine the types of drugs he or she use. Making that determination is important because some types of drugs, such as methamphetamine, can make users more violent. These are all concerns to address when preparing for the execution of a search warrant.

The planning process should include a timeline because a timeline often facilitates identifying the best day and time for execution of the search warrant. For example, a daytime operation is usually best if children live on site because children are likely to be in school, whereas other circumstances favor a nighttime operation.

Once the preliminary survey of the location is complete, determine the number of personnel needed to execute the search warrant as quickly, safely, and thoroughly as possible. The selection of officers will depend on factors unique to each situation. Some of the factors to consider include, but are not limited to, the following:

- Size of the structure (total rooms) determines the number of entry officers needed.
- Are there other structures that need to be covered?
- Anticipated number of subjects determines necessary number of prisoner handlers.
- Will canine officers be necessary?
- Are there potentially vicious dogs on site? If so, decide how to deal with them.

- If the suspect has "friendlies" living in the area, assign cover officers to deal with them.
- Is there a need for air support?
- Assign uniformed officers for traffic control and other necessary functions.
- If there is the possibility of finding a working drug lab, personnel must use SCBAs (Self-Contained Breathing Apparatus). Proper training in the use of SCBAs is important.
- When necessary, have fire department personnel and equipment staged nearby.
- Have paramedics staged nearby.
- If necessary, assign specially trained shotgun or carbine officers.
- Determine the necessary number of "breachers."
- Have breaching personnel available for alternate breaching points.

It is important to address these types of issues during planning to facilitate selecting the appropriate number of personnel, and selecting personnel with specialized skills when necessary.

During planning, identify a location at which to brief all personnel on the operational goals of the search warrant. The briefing is to include all intelligence pertaining to the subjects and the location. During the briefing, clarify communication guidelines and specify the radio frequencies to use. Although a briefing just prior to execution of the search warrant is important, it is common to also hold a briefing a day prior to the scheduled search warrant execution.

Efficient planning ensures that officers have time to gather necessary tools, and efficient planning ensures pre-warrant surveillance. Clarify the radio channel surveillance personnel must use to ensure that important information reaches appropriate raid personnel in a timely manner.

At the briefing location, all officers involved in the operation must be present and physically see each other so they are aware of everyone involved. This is especially important when undercover officers are involved in the operation–undercover officers often look more like a suspect than a police officer and that can be dangerous. Recent tragedies have resulted when officers failed to recognize undercover officers as fellow officers during the heat of battle. Remember what adrenaline does to the human body!

To avoid confusion, the briefing should allow officers to ask questions and contribute ideas that will enhance operational efficiency. During the briefing, clarify what each officer must do, and then solicit a "brief-back." A "brief-back" is when officers involved in the operation recite back what they understand their assignments to be. During the briefing, depending of course on circumstances, use visual aids such as photographs, videos, and chalkboards or dry erase boards for diagrams.

When assigning specific responsibilities, it is important to match the skills of individual officers with their assignment. For example, when a door requires breaching and the ram weighs 50 lbs., assign that responsibility to an officer with appropriate strength and stamina.

Tactics That Enhance Officer Safety

There are various philosophies regarding tactical search warrant entries. The DEA, for example, uses the "snake" method, while other agencies often use different styles of entry. Specific tactics vary throughout the country, even though they bear similarities in many instances because humankind tends to find similar solutions to similar problems. Tactics will vary based on regional circumstances, training, equipment, department philosophies, and local laws. Some tactics are basic for officer safety when dealing with building entries into a hostile environment regardless of style. Some suggestions for entry tactics include, but are not limited to, the following:

- Always provide a cover officer for the breacher. Moreover, a bullet resistant shield at the door will further enhance the breacher's safety.
- If possible, the entry team should stack (position themselves) opposite the hinge side of a door. This allows the first officer in the stack to visually clear a major portion of the room from the outside when the door opens.
- Always identify alternate breaching points.
- Never bypass an unchecked room. This is a common error made by police and usually done in situations when officers feel the need to get to an interior location quickly, such as the bathroom, to prevent the destruction of evidence such as by flushing drugs down the toilet. In doing so, the officers bypass unchecked portions of the interior. When evidence is subject to destruction, consider deploying a two-person "rake and break" team." For example, if the suspect may flush evidence down a toilet, the "rake and break team" is deployed to the bathroom window. Once the "'knock and announce" has been implemented, one of the "rake and break" officers uses a tool to break out the bathroom window and rake the edges of the window clean creating a port into the room from the outside. The second officer will provide cover to the "rake and break" officer and move up to control the bathroom from the outside once window porting is complete. Windows are cheap to replace. Besides firearms, the "rake and break" team is armed with less lethal weapons for the purposes of controlling the bathroom from the outside to prevent flushing drugs down the toilet should a suspect attempt it. Naturally, members of the entry team must be aware of this tactic to prevent confusion, an issue covered during briefing.

- At least two officers should make simultaneous entry into every room of the interior. Assigning two officers to work as a team is a fundamental officer-safety rule. When entering a room, the pair of officers should immediately go to opposite sides of the room. "Sneak and peek" and "cutting the pie" techniques can be used by officers prior to entering rooms. This allows clearing a major portion of the room visually from the outside before entering thus enhancing officer safety.
- The entry team should proceed quickly, but not move too fast to react to circumstances in the environment. Every officer will move at a speed with which he or she is comfortable, and therefore speed will differ from one officer to the next. Unless the entry team has practiced together a great deal, the entry team should move at a walking speed when securing the interior. As a rule of thumb, moving faster than walking speed can compromise the search for suspects. Experience has shown that an eight-person entry team can clear a 1400 square foot building (size of an average 3-bedroom/2-bath home) in about one to two minutes when the team moves at a walking speed, thus not compromising officer safety.
- Always have a cover officer covering the forward movement of an entry team, whether this is a sole assignment or if the responsibility is traded off as the team moves deeper into the interior.
- Always have a cover officer covering the rear of the entry team. A suspect can surprise entry team officers from behind, or may have been in hiding and therefore overlooked during the search of a room.
- Use mirrors initially to look into areas such as attics and crawl spaces. Eventually an officer must physically clear these types of areas, but the danger is minimized when using mirrors on poles.
- After securing the interior of the premises, conduct a second search.
- A contingency plan should be in place in the event entry officers sustain injury, or a hostage/barricade situation occurs. Who will do rescue, what is the safest cover position to retreat to, etc.?
- Assign an officer (usually a supervisor) to act as a control officer to direct the movement of the entry team. This person should have no responsibility but to supervise the entry.
- Provide for "outer security" officers during the search warrant execution. Never use search team officers for search team security unless it is probable that all elements of danger have passed. Uniformed officers can provide cover while the search warrant entry team conducts a search of the interior of the structure.
- When finding a suspicious object at the search warrant location, officers should back away and summon appropriate personnel such as explosive experts.

Use common sense, do not take shortcuts, and do not compromise officer safety!

Chapter 12

REPORT WRITING AND COURTROOM TESTIMONY

INTRODUCTION

Written reports and oral testimony are the two methods by which the officer makes known his or her investigative findings. Hence, one cannot overstate the importance of properly written reports, and the importance of properly testifying in court.

Usually, when an investigation is complete, that is the end of the officer's involvement in the matter until, of course, the officer is required to testify in court relative to information developed during the investigation. Once subpoenaed to testify, the officer is appearing in court as a witness–it is no longer his or her case, but that of the prosecutor.

REPORT WRITING

Introduction

All investigations require one or more written reports that accurately reflect information that was developed. Reports must be clear and concise and conform to the format that is required by the law enforcement agency in question. A well-written report serves four primary purposes:

- The officer's supervisor can critique investigation progress and thoroughness by examining the report.
- Any officer can resume where the original officer left off simply by examining the report. In addition, in many cases, the original officer, the one who wrote the report, will refer to it when the investigation continues later. The report will provide a quick review of previous accomplishments.
- The officer will use the report to refresh his or her memory prior to testifying in court, testimony sometimes being required long after the investigation is complete.

- The report will be the basis of factual information for the prosecution when the case is submitted for prosecution.

For a report to be of value, it must be factual and complete. For example, the report must identify all sources of information checked and all people interviewed or interrogated, even if nothing of value resulted. If not reported, people reading the report will not know the status of the investigation and may conclude that it was incomplete. Similarly, if another officer at some point resumes the investigation, valuable time may be wasted rechecking previously checked sources that provided nothing of value.

Reports must be timely. Reports written while information is still fresh in the officer's memory are generally better than those that are later prepared by working from field notes and faded memory. What constitutes timeliness will vary depending on circumstances such as whether an investigation will require one report at its conclusion, or interim reports. A brief investigation may require nothing more than a report written at its conclusion, while a lengthy on-going investigation involving several officers almost certainly will require interim reports.

All reports should feature a heading that reflects the date, name of the investigating agency, name of the officer, name of the subject or subjects, case number, type of investigation, and the time the investigation began and was concluded if that is relevant such as with a physical surveillance.

General Investigation Reports

The format of investigation reports will vary depending upon the type of investigation and the requirements of the investigating agency. General investigations featuring witness interviews and suspect interrogations are generally narrative. When sources of information such as public and private records are checked, the report will list each source followed by a brief but accurate statement of findings. Surveillance, however, will always require a time caption report wherein a brief but suitably complete description of what occurred follows each time entry.

When describing people and vehicles in an investigative report, it is helpful to use a standardized format. For example, when describing a person, describe him or her in the following sequence:

- Race
- Sex (gender)
- Age
- Height

- Weight
- Build
- Complexion
- Hair
- Eyes
- Peculiarities
- Dress

Example: Hispanic, female, 32 years old, 5 feet 2 inches, 105 pounds, slender build, olive complexion, black hair, brown eyes, walks with a very erect posture, moves gracefully, wearing a knee length flower pattern dress, earrings, wrist bracelets, finger rings, and black high-heeled shoes.

When describing a vehicle, describe it in the following sequence:

- Year
- Color (top over bottom)
- Make
- Model
- State of registration
- Registration number (license plate)

Example: 1999, white over blue, Lincoln Continental, two-door sedan, Arizona registration number ABC-123.

Sample Investigation Report

The following is a sample investigation report. All names, addresses, vehicle license plate numbers, and case numbers are fictitious, although the case is factual.

Example Report: Drug Investigation (stakeout)

Metropolis Police Department Drug Enforcement Bureau

Surveillance Report

Detectives: David Roberts and Wilfred Lee

Location and/or suspect investigated: 15000 N. Black Canyon Highway/ the Late Stay Hotel, room #202

Type of investigation:	Manufacturing Methamphetamine
Date investigated:	October 20, 200X
Vehicle Information:	200X black/white Pontiac Firebird (AZ Plate GEB392)
Subject Information:	Billy Waters. Male, white, DOB 02/14/72, 6', 150 lbs., skinny, acne, shaved head, hazel eyes. SS# 123-45-6789

Summary of Surveillance:

On October 20, 200X, Detectives Roberts and Lee of the Metropolis Police Department's Drug Enforcement Bureau conducted surveillance at the Late Stay Hotel located at 15000 N. Black Canyon Highway, room #202. While conducting surveillance of the room, Detectives observed a white male, later identified as Billy Waters, leave the hotel room carrying a plastic tote crate. He placed the crate in his vehicle and drove from the property. Subsequently he threw a bag of trash from his vehicle into a dumpster behind a grocery store. The bag, retrieved by Detectives, contained waste chemicals and equipment used in the manufacture of Methamphetamine. Officers of the Metropolis Police Department subsequently arrested Billy Waters. The tote crate contained a Methamphetamine laboratory.

October 20, 200X.

8:35 a.m. Detectives Roberts and Lee assumed a stakeout position at the Late Stay Hotel, room #202, located at 15000 N. Black Canyon Highway, Phoenix, Arizona.

9:53 a.m. A 200X Black Pontiac Firebird with white stripes entered the parking lot and parked near room #202. A white male, approximately 30 years old, six feet tall, 150 lbs., skinny, acne, shaved head, wearing a black t-shirt, blue jeans, and brown shoes exited the vehicle, looked around the parking lot nervously, and proceeded to room #202 using a key to gain entry. The individual was later identified as Billy Waters, DOB 02/14/72.

10:10 a.m. A white female, early 20s, 5'6", 105 lbs., skinny, pale complexion, long blond hair, white spaghetti-strap top and blue denim shorts rode up on a bicycle and leaned it against the wall next to room #202. She knocked on the door and Billy Waters looked through the curtains, nodded his head and then opened the door allowing her to enter.

10:16 a.m. The above described female exited room #202, mounted her bicycle, and proceeded west through the parking lot leaving the premises–Detectives did not follow her.

11:20 a.m. Billy Waters emerged from room #202 carrying a blue plastic tote crate and proceeded to the 200X black Pontiac Firebird, opened the back hatch of the vehicle long enough to place the crate inside, all the while looking around nervously. Waters then reentered room #202 but reappeared seconds later carrying a white plastic trash bag which he tossed into the backseat of the Firebird, and then reentered room #202.

11:34 a.m. Billy Waters emerged from room #202, got into the Firebird and drove slowly around the parking lot and, while so doing, appeared to be looking into vehicles. He then left the premises via the west entrance/exit and proceeded south on 26th Avenue. Suddenly, Waters turned west on Acoma Street and accelerated rapidly into the neighborhood. Instead of following Waters, detectives set up surveillance of the exits leading from the neighborhood with the intention of resuming surveillance when Waters reappeared.

11:37 a.m. The black Firebird exits the neighborhood on 24th Avenue, and Detectives are able to confirm that it is still Billy Waters driving. Waters is followed south on 24th Avenue and then west on Hearn Road to 19th Avenue where he turns into the parking lot of Frankie's Deli.

11:45 a.m. Billy Waters parks the black Firebird next to a dumpster behind Frankie's Deli, exits the vehicle and, while looking around nervously, tosses a white plastic trash bag into the dumpster. Waters then gets into the Firebird and drives around the front of the Deli and turns north on 19th Avenue.

11:49 a.m. Detective Anthony Green retrieves the trash bag from the dumpster and discovers that it contains stained tubing, empty bottles, and boxes of chemicals utilized in the manufacture of Methamphetamine. Also in the bag are documents bearing the name "Billy Waters."

11:58 a.m. Officers Hoffman and Smith, who are operating a marked patrol vehicle, stop Billy Waters while driving the black Pontiac Firebird.

12:05 p.m. Billy Waters is arrested after which a search of the Pontiac Firebird reveals a Methamphetamine lab contained in the plastic tote crate.

COURTROOM TESTIMONY

The officer must approach every case with the realization that eventual criminal prosecution and civil litigation is possible, and conduct the investigation accordingly. When a case results in criminal prosecution, the officer almost certainly will be required to testify. The officer may also be required to testify when a criminal case later becomes the subject of a civil lawsuit, such as when a crime victim sues the perpetrator. Because officers must frequently testify at a criminal trial, and sometimes at a civil hearing, it is important to have an understanding of courtroom procedures and protocol, and display professional conduct when appearing as a witness.

Many people fear testifying in court because they do not understand courtroom procedures and protocol, and they fear the cross-examiner will challenge their credibility as a person and/or witness, harass them, and distort the meaning of things they say, and those things do occur. Common tactics attorneys use against a witness include badgering, displaying a condescending attitude, bombarding the person with rapid-fire questions, asking repetitious questions, asking suggestive questions, and, of course, they will reverse or otherwise distort a witness's words or the meaning of what they say. Although such fears are intimidating to those without courtroom experience, there are ways to defend against such tactics. For one thing, realize that the cross-examiner is only doing his or her job, and no matter how aggressive or obnoxious he or she becomes it is not personal. So, while it is understandable why many people are anxious when anticipating having to endure such tactics, and become flustered when subjected to such strategies, consider what one officer said. "I love it when an attorney gets aggressive and starts playing Perry Mason. I do not become distressed by them because I know what they are trying to do and can frustrate them by remaining calm and polite instead of responding as they expect. I view it as a challenge and am disappointed when such tactics are not attempted. It's fun watching them back-peddle after realizing the obnoxious approach failed. I've often wondered if while back-peddling they worry that my staying calm in the face of their obnoxiousness made them look bad to the jury and if their repugnant conduct may have prejudiced how the jury will decide. I know that happens because I've had jurors take the initiative to tell me so after a trial was over."

In the United States, when someone is charged with a crime, the state has the responsibility of proving guilt *beyond a reasonable doubt.* Meantime, the person's defense attorney is responsible for ensuring that the state fulfills its obligation. It is the defense attorney's job to scrutinize all evidence and testimony to ensure that it is admissible and not subject to exclusion because of some legal defect. Opinions differ and everyone has his or her own opinion as to what constitutes a defense attorney working within the system to ensure that the state adequately proves the defendant's guilt, versus trying to set a criminal free by "getting him or her off on a technicality," so to speak. To be sure, the United States Judicial system is not perfect, and that can be distressing, but it is better to let a criminal go free than to convict and incarcerate an innocent person.

For those without experience testifying in court, practicing the following recommendations will make the task of testifying easier. The reader who does not have experience testifying in court should spend some time carefully contemplating the following list to get the information firmly imprinted in his or her mind. When reading this list, keep in mind this quote by an unknown person: "If you study to remember, you will forget, but, if you study to understand, you will remember." Hence, instead of trying to memorize the contents of this list, contemplate the purpose of the various points. In addition to reviewing this list, those without courtroom experience will benefit by attending one or more civil hearings and criminal trials as an observer.

When reading the following list, it will become apparent that most of the issues relate to the following few points:

- Be prepared. Review investigative reports before testifying.
- Present proper grooming and attire.
- Maintain composure, even when cross-examination becomes aggressive.
- Speak loudly and with
  - –Clarity (clearness)
  - –Objectivity (impartiality)
  - –Brevity (briefness).
- Judges and juries, when observing a person testify, form opinions about that person's credibility. If the person appears professional, unbiased, and neutral, believability exists.
- Proper dress and grooming are important for the same reason that professional demeanor is important, although demeanor is the more important of the two. If the first impression is that the person dresses poorly, but his or her demeanor when questioned is proper, the judge and jury will likely view him or her as a credible witness. Conversely, if the person is dressed and groomed very well, creating a good first impression, but his or her demeanor on the stand is deplorable the favorable first impression will quickly fade.

- Be respectful at all times, displaying calm, confidence, neutrality, and professionalism. Address the judge as "Your Honor," with others addressed as "Sir" and "Ma'am." If you address a woman as "Madam," she may resent it.
- Be direct and brief when answering questions; if an attorney wants elaboration, he or she will request it. Remember, each attorney has a purpose for each question, and the phrasing of each question is carefully considered. If a witness begins offering elaboration, he or she creates greater opportunity for the cross-examiner to challenge his or her testimony.
- Speak loudly and clearly when answering questions on the witness stand–it is essential that everyone hear the testimony.
- Do not begin answering a question before it is complete, and understood. If one begins to answer incorrectly and then corrects him or herself, it may appear he or she is unsure of the information, and it provides the cross-examiner an opportunity to challenge one's credibility as a witness.
- When testifying, provide time for an objection following each question. When the judge sustains an objection do not answer the question, but answering the question is required when the objection is overruled.
- Never lie in an effort to ensure a conviction. It would seem that this point needs no mention, but it is too important to neglect. Lying is perjury, which is a felony in most jurisdictions, and getting caught lying will result in loss of credibility with all testimony likely disregarded as a result. In addition, if an officer has lost credibility with the courts he or she is at a severe disadvantage when submitting cases, and will forever be the subject to having his or her cases dismissed. In many jurisdictions, lying in reports or on the witness stand is grounds for termination of employment.
- Do not display animosity towards the cross-examiner, for he or she is just doing their job and has no personal animosity towards you. It is natural to view cross-examination with some degree of apprehension, for a legal scholar will be challenging one's testimony and personal credibility. In spite of this, if one sticks to the facts, remains calm and polite, and projects neutrality, there is little that the cross-examiner can do to compromise one's testimony and credibility. If, while being cross-examined, an inconsistency in one's testimony is illuminated, admit to it and explain it if permitted. If a discrepancy occurs and one readily admits to it, credibility as an impartial witness will probably survive in the eyes of the judge and jury.
- When testifying, avoid technical terminology and "jargon" that is characteristic of the law enforcement profession; speak in terms lay people

understand. If one uses technical terms and jargon that others do not understand, testimony will be less effective, and members of the jury may resent it as an insult to their intelligence or as a poor-taste attempt to impress them. "Jargon is the specialized, technical language used by those in the same profession to communicate rapidly" (Betz, Michael J., 1999). Hence, using jargon when speaking with other investigators expedites communication, but jargon impedes communication when speaking with people outside the profession–they will not understand it.

- At the time of trial, when appearing as a witness, do not discuss the case with anyone other than authorized personnel. Most likely the defense has "invoked the rule," which requires that witnesses not discuss the case, and so doing can result in a mistrial.

REFERENCES

Aguilar v. Texas, 378 U.S. 108 (1964).

ATF News. Department of the Treasury, Bureau of Alcohol, Tobacco and Firearms. (1999). *Operation lightening strike.* Retrieved September 11, 2003, from http://www.atf.treas.gov/press/field/fy99/lightning_strike.htm

Betz, Michael J. (1999). *Writing at work: A text for insurance personnel* (2nd ed.). Malvern, PA: Insurance Institute of America.

Caruso, D. (2003, September 14). *New terror laws used vs. common criminals.* Associated Press. Retrieved September 14 2003, from http://story.news.yahoo.com/news?tmpl=story&u=/ap/anti_terror_laws.

Davis v. Alaska, 415 U.S. 308 (1974).

DeMay, D., & Flowers, R., Jr. (1999). *Don't hire a crook.* Tempe, AZ: Facts on Demand Press. From HireRight. Retrieved November 24, 2003, from http://www.hireright.com/.

Goldstein, A. (2001). *Addiction: From biology to drug policy* (2nd ed.). Stanford, CA: Oxford University Press.

Illinois v. Gates, 462 U.S. 213 (1983).

Jacobson v. United States, 503 U.S. 540 (1992).

Liska, K. (1990). *Drugs and the human body: With implications for society* (3rd ed.). New York: Macmillan.

Marijuana. The Columbia Encyclopedia (6th ed.). New York: Columbia University Press, 2003. Retrieved September 10, 2003, from www.bartleby.com/65/ Reprinted with permission.

Marnell, T. (2003). *Drug identification bible.* Grand Junction, CO: Amera-Chem, Inc.

Olmstead v. United States, 277 U.S. 438 (1928).

Phoenix Police Department. (1999). *Drug Enforcement Bureau manual: Informant policy and procedures.* Phoenix, AZ.

Rankin, T. J. (n.d.). *Seizure and forfeiture of property pursuant to Arizona's asset forfeiture laws.* Tucson, AZ.

Remsberg, C. (1995). *Tactics for criminal patrol.* Northbrook, IL: Caliber Press.

Roviaro v. United States, 353 U.S. 53 (1957).

Smith v. Maryland, 442 U.S. 735 (1979).

Spinelli v. United States, 393 U.S. 410 (1969).

Substance Abuse and Mental Health Services Administration. (2003). *Highlights.* Retrieved January 10, 2004, from http://www.samhsa.gov/oas/2k3/school/school.cfm.

Substance Abuse and Mental Health Services Administration (2003). *Highlights of reports on parental, peer & school influences.* Retrieved January 7, 2004, from http://www.samhsa.gov/oas/parents.cfm.

Substance Abuse and Mental Health Services Administration. (2000). *Inhalant use among youths.* Retrieved September 23, 2003, from http://ncadi.samhsa.gov/govstudy/shortreports/inhalNS/

Substance Abuse and Mental Health Services Administration, Division of Workplace Programs, Workplace Resource Center–Prevention Research. (n.d.). *Substance abuse and violence in the workplace.* Retrieved September 20, 2003, from http://workplace.samhsa.gov/WPResearch/WPViolence/WPSecurity.html

Three terror suspects agree to extradition to U.S. (2003, January 6). The Associated Press, USA Today. Retrieved September 10, 2003, from http://www.usatoday.com/news/world/2003-01-06-terror-extradition_x.htm

The Prohibition Era. (2003). The Columbia Encyclopedia (6th ed.). New York: Columbia University Press. Retrieved October 2, 2003, from www.bartleby.com/65/ Reprinted with permission.

The Syndicate. (2003). The Columbia Encyclopedia (6th ed.). New York: Columbia University Press. Retrieved October 2, 2003, from www.bartleby.com/65/ Reprinted with permission.

United States v. New York Tel. Co., 434 U.S. 159 (1977).

United States Department of Justice, Bureau of Justice Statistics. (2003). *Public opinion about drugs.* Retrieved September 20, 2003, from http://www.ojp.usdoj.gov/bjs/dcf/poad.htm.

United States Department of Justice. (2003). *Children at clandestine methamphetamine labs: Helping meth's youngest victims.* OVC Bulletin, June 2003, Office for Victim of Crimes. Retrieved January 8, 2004, from http://www.ojp.gov/ovc/publications/bulletins/children/197590.pdf.

United States Department of Justice. (2002). *Children at risk.* Information Bulletin, July 2002, National Drug Information Center (NDIC).

United States Department of Justice, National Drug Intelligence Center. (2003, January 23). *National Drug Intelligence Center assessment cites New York City as major drug transshipment area.* Retrieved September 20, 2003, from: http://www.usdoj.gov/ndic/pubs/prs/03ny-dta/pr-nydta.htm.

United States Drug Enforcement Administration. (2003). *Controlled Substances Act.* Retrieved September 11, 2003, from http://www.usdoj.gov/dea/agency/csa.htm

United States Drug Enforcement Administration. (2003). *Drug trafficking in the United States.* Retrieved September 20, 2003, from http://www.usdoj.gov/dea/concern/drug_trafficking.html.

Various Items of Personal Property v. United States, 282 U. S. 577 (1931).

INDEX

D

S

T